ROMMEL'S ARMY IN AFRICA

ROMMEL'S ARMY IN AFRICA

Dal McGuirk

GUILD PUBLISHING LONDON

This edition published 1987 by
Book Club Associates
by arrangement with
Century Hutchinson Ltd
Brookmount House, 62–65 Chandos Place,
Covent Garden, London WC2N 4NW

First published 1987

Copyright © Dal McGuirk 1987

Set in 11/12 pt Ehrhardt Roman

Printed and bound in Great Britain by
Butler & Tanner Ltd, Frome and London

Front jacket *shows the 1943 pocket diary issued to all German troops in Africa; a flattened section of brass shell case showing the DAK symbol (colour photograph 127); and a well used field cap carrying the pink soutache (with typical grease stains on the peak or visor) of a Panzer crewman in 1941.*

Back jacket *shows pages from a Paratrooper's paybook showing his awards and decorations; two examples of the Afrikakorps ring, in original style with gold inlay for the central motif (on the left) and all in silver with crudely etched detail; field caps (left to right) – other ranks field cap with the copper-brown soutache of the Reconnaissance units (colour photograph 48); other ranks field cap with the gold-yellow soutache of the first Reconnaissance units to reach Libya in 1941 (colour photograph 52); other ranks field cap with the light green soutache as used by the Rifle Regiments and members of the MG Battalions in 1941 (colour photograph 46); a cap as used by the Motorcycle Battalion in 1941 with the uncommon grass-green soutache (colour photograph 46).*

Endpapers: *Map included as a supplement to the Panzerarmee Afrika Kalender 1943, showing the North African coast from Tripoli to Palestine.*

Contents

Introduction

MY INTENTION in writing this book has been to try to add something new to what has already been written on the subject of the German Army in North Africa in World War II, based on *Afrikakorps* (DAK) memorabilia I have collected over a number of years. Wherever possible, my conclusions have been checked with primary sources.

In reading published works on the subject of the war in North Africa, one cannot help but be struck by the way in which most authors keep repeating a lot of what has already been written. The same events, the same stories – albeit with different emphases on some particular areas – are covered time after time. It is not easy for a reader to break significantly new ground when the subject has already been treated so similarly by so many previous writers.

This book represents my own view of the *Afrikakorps*. It is certainly not meant to be a definitive or total view. Indeed, in many ways, because of the nature and extent of the resources used as background reference, it is a narrow view, as it is impossible to collect source material to order. One has to accept whatever is available, which in turn is determined by whatever is accessible and by the preferences for souvenir material shown by the ex-servicemen who collected it in the first place. At the end of the war there was far more material of the kind I have been collecting. However, since then much of it has been lost forever, and soon there will be very little still accessible. I was fortunate to have been collecting at a time when there was still a wide range of souvenir items available, especially documents and photos. Without these there would not have been the means of finding a focus for this work.

As far as the uniforms are concerned, there has been now for many years a thriving industry in manufacturing and selling modern reproductions to satisfy the collector market. For collectors, especially younger ones just beginning, it is becoming increasingly difficult to tell the real from what has been faked. The uniform illustrations in this book are all of original items.

I have attempted to present the information in this book in much the same way as an archaeologist might draw conclusions about a place after a site has been excavated, and all the reclaimed artefacts have been assembled and studied to give a picture of what may have happened there long ago. But I did not have to go to the deserts of North Africa to dig in the sand for these items. Much of what is described and illustrated here was found in the homes of Australian and New Zealand returned servicemen – in old suitcases long stored in a corner of a garage, canvas army bags kept in cupboards and drawers, with other mementoes on shelves, in dens or workrooms; or photos and papers stored with relics of family history in photo albums and in cardboard boxes tied with string or ribbon.

My own interest in collecting *Afrikakorps* souvenirs was stimulated by a desire to find a three-dimensional substance for the black and white photos in war histories and wartime magazines I had pored over as a young Grade 8 student in Queensland. In my imagination this provided a step through time and space. I found my interest spread to the identity of the soldiers to whom these relics must have once belonged. And the interest in the individual soldiers gradually broadened to encompass the Army with which these material objects had once been associated.

Many of the photos reproduced here have come from institutions that hold collections of film taken by official (and therefore professional) photographers. These photos, naturally enough, are the ones that reproduce best. Not used for illustrations in the book are many more photos which would not have reproduced clearly enough. These are ones taken by ordinary German soldiers using simple cameras (not all German soldiers were lucky enough to afford a Leica). Most of these are inexpertly composed, or are out of focus, or show the effects of bright sunlight – either overexposed or catching reflected glare. Yet it is in these photos, in the total impression of the whole collection, that one gets an intimate feel for the men who took them, and for the men who were photographed. They show a level of simple humanity that is common to all men in any army – their sense of humour, a pride in their units and in themselves, boredom with a dull routine in an unfamiliar location, boisterous high spirits in a game or a swim at the beach, an acceptance of tedious routines in army life, the total mental and emotional immersion in a letter, or the curiosity of every tourist shown in the large number of repetitious photos of Arab village scenes and camels at waterholes and palm trees in oases, and Mosques. They show the jaunty angle of a cap and a large grin meant to reassure a mother – or father or wife or sweetheart – that all is well and carefree in the desert; and little mannerisms that are timeless in a facial expression that evokes a chord of empathy and some memory of a personality you know well yourself, for all are common human traits. If one were to remove the uniforms in the photos, the soldiers become ordinary men.

Another kind of photo not included in the illustrations are those that show corpses, often terribly mutilated in death. These are powerful statements about the real tragedy of war. But this book is about a war, and about one group of people who fought it. It is about their uniforms and their life in an army that fought a war. It is not meant to be a statement in favour of war, rather just a statement about something that was part of a war. I hope that readers of this book find something of interest in it that will communicate some part of the essence of the German Army that fought in Africa from 1941 to 1943. It was not a 'Nazi' Army of the ilk portrayed in war films and still written about in popular novels. Its members were soldiers, under military discipline and fighting in a war that they believed was

necessary to protect the interests of their nation. In this sense they were patriotic in the same way that all soldiers of the period were. For information they were dependent on a heavily censored news system which was cleverly monitored by a powerful propaganda organ. (Allied wartime propaganda and censorship was no less powerful or slanted than that which the Germans were subjected to.)

On the battlefield they fought fairly and with chivalry, and many Allied soldiers taken prisoner in North Africa owe their lives to the compassion and sense of shared humanity shown by individual German soldiers. The war in North Africa is held to have been a 'civilized' war as far as wars go. No war can ever be civilized, it is a highly organized form of mass brutality and systematic killing. That the fighting was not more barbarous than it was, much credit must go to the example set by Rommel and followed by the disciplined troops under his command. This book is one small slice of life in that army commanded in Africa by Erwin Rommel, a collection of surviving fragments, and observations.

Rommel inspects an artillery emplacement on the Egyptian border in mid-1941. (ECPA)

Dal McGuirk
Auckland, March 1986

Foreword

WHEN I WAS captured by a sergeant in a New Zealand night attack on 14/15 July 1942 at Ruweisat Ridge in the centre of the Alamein position, I did not expect that I would later meet up with and make friends with my adversaries. The New Zealand platoon sergeant was a fine soldier and a sensitive human being – he brewed a cup of tea that revived me, and I still consider that cup of tea the best and most welcome drink I have had in my life. (Sadly I learnt later that this sergeant was killed in a subsequent engagement.)

About thirty years later, after nearly five years as a 'Guest of His Majesty' in Canada behind barbed wire and working on farms in Ontario and Quebec, and in due time having rejoined the new German Army and having been posted to London as Military Attaché, I had the honour of meeting one of the bravest of my former adversaries, Captain Charles Upham VC and Bar. At a reception for VC and GC winners at New Zealand House we had an amicable talk lasting into the early hours, including the episode at Ruweisat Ridge.

Over the years I have met many of my former adversaries – British, Australians, New Zealanders, South Africans – who have travelled to Germany to attend our *Afrikakorps* reunions to shake hands with their old former foes. It has always given me a deep pleasure to be able to return a little of that hospitality extended to me during that night when I hovered between life and death.

Six years ago I read in our *Afrikakorps* Association's journal, *Die Oase*, a letter from Dal McGuirk asking for contact with former members of Rommel's Army in North Africa. I wrote back without hesitation offering to help him further his research, and soon this co-operation was to become a deep friendship. I became impressed by his wide knowledge of our uniforms, our equipment and our military organization. His expertise in this field far surpassed my own about our forces. His research into material for this book has been meticulous and thorough, and I would like to express my deepest admiration for his work. He has taken a unique and imaginative approach in writing his book, basing his information on a large collection of artefacts, papers and photos originally picked up as souvenirs from the battlefields of North Africa. In his writing he has shown an identification with a former adversary of his nation, and his view shows a sympathetic look at things from our side.

I hope that this book will be enjoyed by a wide public, especially younger readers with an interest in how it was in a war that took place well over forty years ago, and veterans who still wish to learn a little more about conditions in the North African campaigns.

Finally, I wish to salute the brave members of both sides, and the memories of our fallen comrades, who had to fight each other in this war. May we never have to fight again.

Karl-Heinz Böttger
Oberst a.D.
(Former Vice-President, *Verband Deutsches Afrikakorps*)

Hamburg, April 1986

Thanks

THIS BOOK could not have been written without the help and encouragement of many people, given over a long period of time.

The book had its beginnings with my fascination as a young teenager with the war souvenirs brought back by returned servicemen from the fighting in North Africa. To all the Australian and New Zealand servicemen who parted with their hard-won war mementoes in order that I could indulge in my quixotic interest, I owe a special vote of thanks. (Unlike their American counterparts, who had official sanction and special postal facilities provided for souvenir collecting, Australian and New Zealand troops were actively discouraged from keeping any enemy material.)

The Association of Former Members of the *Afrikakorps* in West Germany generously gave its assistance and enabled me to contact a number of veterans from Rommel's Army in Africa. These men corresponded with me over the years it took to write this book, and I was humbled by their patient co-operation and willingness to try to answer every question put to them. In the course of writing this book I have made many friendships; the relationships built up with these men of the *Afrikakorps* are special and I am deeply grateful for the way they enriched with their friendship not only the contents of the book but my life as well. *Ich möchte Ihnen meinen besonderen Dank ausdrücken – 'Ein herzlich Danke schön!'*

For photos reproduced from official collections I am indebted to the staffs of the following institutions for their assistance and advice: The Alexander Turnbull Library in Wellington, which houses the War History Photo Collection of the New Zealand National Archives; The Australian War Memorial in Canberra; The Photographs Department of The Imperial War Museum in London; and the French Army Photographic Archives in Paris. (ECPA).

For copies of wartime papers relating to the *Afrikakorps* I am grateful to the staffs of the Auckland War Memorial Museum and Institute, the War History section of the New Zealand National Archives in Wellington, and the Military Archives Department of the West German Archives in Freiburg. Dr Faad Kamel, Secretary-General of the Matrouh Governate in Egypt and Curator of the Rommel Historical Museum, kindly made available information relating to material in his possession.

For assistance in Auckland I must express my appreciation to the Regional office of the NZ Returned Services Association, who helped to publicize my appeals for material, and to the members of the 21 Infantry Battalion Association, especially to past presidents Ted Manning and the late Wally von Schramm, and the Association's secretary and newsletter editor, Tony Ivicevich. The impressive collection of artefacts and documents maintained by the 21 Infantry Battalion Association was always open to my research needs, with warm hospitality and many a cup of tea or a glass of cold beer offered in their clubrooms.

In gathering my collection I also had the assistance of the journal of the NZ Returned Services Association, *Review*, and the friendly help of fellow collectors and militaria dealers in many countries – New Zealand, Australia, the United Kingdom, South Africa, the United States of America, the Federal Republic of Germany, France and Japan. I am indebted to René Pellegrin for permission to quote information from his privately published manuscript entitled *La Phalange Africaine – La L.V.F. en Tunisie 1942–43* (Paris, 1973), dealing with the French and Arab volunteer force which fought under the German Army in Tunisia.

For help in translating German documents – many handwritten in faint lead pencil – I owe special thanks to Dr Karl Toepfer Oberfeldvet.d.R., Hans Schilling, Heinz Puschmann and Renate Tschöcke. Karl, Hans and Heinz also gave me the benefit of the memories of their time serving in the *Wehrmacht* to fill out many of the parts of the book. Renate tutored me in the peculiar idiom of German military grammar, and I was much helped by her warm humour and friendship.

The following very kindly allowed me to photograph items from their collections in order to extend the range of material featured in the colour illustrations: Peter Cue, Paul Williams, Charles J. Hinz, Greg Carter, John Morris, David Hunter, Rod Bellars, Paul Farmer, John Collins.

Rex Trye gave me friendly advice for the section dealing with the Italians from his vast store of knowledge of the Italian Army in World War II and opened his collection from North Africa to me. Geoff and David Oldham passed on their wide experience and expert knowledge in the field of collecting war souvenirs whenever I needed it, and David, with his ready familiarity of German fighting vehicles, helped me analyse photos.

In the long and hard job of photographing material from my collection for use as illustrations I was grateful for the help given by John Nicholson.

The pencil sketches featured in the book were drawn in North Africa during 1941 and 1942 by Wilhelm Wessel, the official *Afrikakorps* war artist, and are reproduced from his wartime book on the African campaign, *Mit Rommel in der wüste* (with Rommel in the Desert).

For typing up the manuscript I have to give warm thanks to my sister Jennifer Ball and to Mrs Jenny Kitchener. They kindly endured the many revisions and coped with my indifferent typing and the unfamiliar German words scattered through the text. For proofreading the text I offer a big 'thanks' to my wife and to my father. My friend Greg Carter went out of his way to help locate much of the material included in the illustrations and offered encouragement and support whenever I needed it.

There are four more people who deserve special mention and thanks, because without their love, help and encouragement this book would not have been written: Karl-Heinz Böttger, who wrote enough letters to fill a book and who tirelessly worked with his comrades in the *Verband Deutsches Afrikakorps* in West Germany to answer an endless stream of questions and requests for help, and graciously consented to write a foreword; Charles Hinz, who shared his immense knowledge of the *Afrikakorps* with me and led me to understand much of what this book has to say on the subject, and gave in friendship more than I could ever repay; Peter Cue, my old school mate, who shared my youthful collecting and later sacrificed much time and energy in finding significant parts of my collection while the book was in the making and never asked for anything in return; and my wife Christine, who endured experiences undreamt of when we were married, and gave up much so that the book might come about.

My publishing agent, Ray Richards, guided me with understanding, encouragement, and gentle advice along the road from when this book was an idea to where it stands now.

Finally, my thanks to Harley Wilson and Barbara Ross of GM Studios in Onehunga, who copied many of the black and white photographs reproduced in these pages.

To everyone who gave their assistance in making this book possible, I can only say from my heart 'THANK YOU' – this book belongs to you too.

In alphabetical order: Greg Allan; Stanley Baldwin; Brian Ball; Jennifer Ball; David Balmer; Gary Beadle; Rod Bellars; Roger Bender; Andrew Biwandi; Robert Borchardt, Major a.D.; Karl-Heinz Böttger, Oberst a.D.; Graeme Brailsford; Herbert Brandhoff; Colin Brown; Chris Bruner; Gregory N. Carter; Terry Chase; John Collins; Peter Cue; Alan Culhane; Steve de Jong; Michael Dunne; Dr Hans Düsel; Jürgen Eichler; Paul Farmer; Malcolm Fisher; Dr Roger Fletcher; Kerry Foster; Noel Gardiner; Paul Heiniger; Dieter Hellriegel; Wolfgang Hermann; Charles J. Hinz; Peter Huckstepp; David Hunter; David Irving; Tony Ivicevich; Dr Eric Johansson; Pierre A. Kaat; Dr Faad Kamel; John Keener; Akira Komiya; Werner Kost, Major a.D.; Ronald Kwan; Dick and Patsy LaFayette; Albert Lawson; Antoine Lebel; James S. Lucas; Bob Lyons; Frank McGuirk, QX2812 Australian 9th Division; Ron Manion; Ted Manning; John Morris; John Nicholson; Geoffrey P. Oldham; David Oldham; René Pellegrin; George A. Petersen; Heinz Puschmann; the late Peter Read; Ray Richards; Herb Rickards; Manfred Rommel; Fürst Salm zu Horstmar, Major a.D.; Hans Schilling; Paul Erich Schläfer; Robert Sevier; Mick Shepherd; Dr Karl T. Toepfer, Oberfeldvet.d.R.; Rex Trye; Renate Tschöcke; Gerry van Wyk; the late Wally von Schramm; Lt Col. T. C. Wallace, QSM, ED, JP; Joe Wallace; Leo Walsh; Kurt Watermann; David Weatherley; the late Siegfried Westphal, General der Kavallerie a.D.; Garry Willett; Paul Williams; Ron Wolin; Ray Zyla.

The Luftwaffe *Field Marshal, Albert Kesselring, Rommel's immediate superior in the Mediterranean, with General Gause during the final El Alamein battle in October 1942. (ECPA)*

Rommel

Erwin Johannes Eugen Rommel was born in Heidenheim, in the southern German state of Swabia, on 15 November 1891, the son of a mathematics master at a secondary school.

In 1910, against his father's wishes, Erwin Rommel joined the Army. He had a distinguished career in World War I, winning the highest German award for bravery, the *Pour le Mérite*, for action against the Italians in the offensive to the Piave River in late 1917. In this battle Rommel showed some of the qualities which were to become his hallmark as a military commander in World War II, the swift advance with maximum firepower at the point of attack designed to throw the enemy off balance and then to keep up the pressure at any cost. In World War II he was to do this with tanks and mobile anti-tank guns, but in World War I it was the massed firepower of artillery that broke the enemy's front.

After returning to El Alamein in October 1942 Rommel found time to award the German Cross to Colonel Bayerlein, the Afrikakorps' *Chief of Staff. (ECPA)*

Rommel's official portrait in the uniform of a Field Marshal holding the ornate baton that went with the rank. This photo was taken in Berlin after Rommel returned to Germany in September 1942 on sick leave. (Author's collection)

On 12 February 1941, Rommel, then a Major General, flew into Tripoli to take command of the German troops being rushed across the Mediterranean to bolster up the shaky Italian position in Libya. As later events were to show, the right man had arrived at the right time and place.

The choice of leader for the soon to be named *Afrikakorps* was Adolf Hitler's, and it was another of his characteristic intuitive decisions. But Hitler had known Rommel well since 1937, when Rommel had published *Infanterie Greift an* (The Infantry Attacks), a manual for infantry training which was based on his own experiences in World War I and filled out with the lecture notes he used while an instructor at the War Academy at Potsdam in 1935. The book was a big success and it

was acknowledged to be an excellent work, communicating clearly Rommel's ideas of bold and aggressive attack as the right tactics for infantry fighting. Hitler read it and was impressed, so much so that he now took an active interest in the career of the ambitious and forceful *Oberst* (Colonel) Rommel. When Hitler marched into the Sudetenland in September 1938, and occupied the rump of Czechoslovakia in March 1939, Rommel was selected on both occasions to command the special army escort detailed to accompany the Führer. This was a sign of Hitler's favour, and when Germany invaded Poland at the end of August 1939, Rommel again accompanied Hitler, this time as the commander of the Führer's Headquarters (*Führerhauptquartier*).

It was during this period that Rommel was able to observe at close quarters the conflict between Hitler and the more conservative Generals who dominated the General Staff, and Rommel found himself mentally siding with Hitler. Rommel also saw, through the perspective of the Führer's headquarters, the dazzling success of the Panzer divisions in the offensive against Poland. At the end of the Polish campaign Rommel took advantage of Hitler's high regard to ask for the command of a Panzer division, which were to be increased in number from five to ten. Hitler was happy to grant Rommel his request, though the decision was strongly opposed by the personnel department of the army, who would normally have proposed such an appointment. They looked to Rommel's World War I record and suggested an Alpine division as being more suitable. But Hitler overruled the Generals and in February 1940 Rommel was given command of the 7th Panzer Division, then being put together at Bad Godesberg. He already held the rank of Major General, to which he had been promoted on his appointment to command the *Führerhauptquartier* in August 1939.

Rommel was now in his element and threw all his energies into the training of his Panzer Division. He worked hard to improve the effective co-operation of all the component parts of the division, ordering long route marches to toughen them and insisting his troops were confident in the use of the radio as a means of producing coherent and rapid advance through enemy territory. His discipline was strict and he brooked no lapses in performance. The hard training and Rommel's driving personality paid off, and in the invasion of France, which commenced on 10 May 1940, Rommel's Panzer Division came out with the most spectacular record of any of the Panzer formations, earning the title of the 'Ghost' or 'Spook' Division. Hitler was very pleased with Rommel's success, and showed his delight by decorating Rommel on 27 May with the first Knights Cross awarded to a divisional commander in the campaign. Further evidence of Hitler's favour came on 2 June, when the Führer invited Rommel to a special conference held at Charleville to consider the options to complete the defeat of France. He was the only divisional commander Hitler bothered to invite to this meeting.

Rommel crowned the exploits of his division in the decisive first stage of the campaign by being the first German divisional commander to reach the Channel coast, at Saint-Valery, where he accepted the surrender of the 51st Highland Division and the remnants of the French 9th Corps. In this dash to the Channel coast his men covered from 40 to 50 miles in a day, a very fast speed at that time for a Panzer division. In the last act of the French collapse Rommel drove his division at even greater speed to end up at Cherbourg, where he took the surrender of the large French garrison.

The French campaign established Rommel as one of the foremost exponents of the military art of armoured *Blitzkrieg*, and the German news agencies showered praise and glory on him. Rommel showed he was not averse to this publicity, accepting it as the price to be paid for fame. Not everyone was dazzled by Rommel though, and there were many voices in the High Command of the Army who were critical of his methods: his disregard for the security of his flanks, his failure to provide adequate logistical support for his spearheads, his tendency to act on impulse rather than considered judgement, his egotism and unwillingness to acknowledge the contribution of others. Lastly, there was jealousy of his special relationship with Hitler. Many of these same criticisms would surface again later, but Rommel knew well that ultimately the success or failure of his actions were what counted.

Of all the factors that contributed to the Rommel legend, none is more important than the special position Rommel held in Hitler's estimation. During the early stages of the war it was a relationship based on mutual

Rommel in discussion with officers of Sonderverband 288 *in March 1942 south of Derna. The Knights Cross bearer to Rommel's left is* Hauptmann *Robert Borchardt, then commander of the* PzAbwAbt *in SV288. (Werner Kost)*

Men of Rommel's Begleitkommando *(Escort Group) in November 1941 near Wadi Matratin. (Dieter Hellriegel)*

admiration, and in many ways the two men had a lot in common. Both had come from lower middle class backgrounds, and both had experienced the snobbery of the aristocratic ruling class, which was firmly established in the higher echelons of the German Army. The two men shared a belief in naked willpower as a means of achieving success. For Rommel on the battlefield this was a matter of overlooking apparent reality and applying the will to win. In a battle he knew it was easy to feel too strongly one's own losses, the attrition of men and material, and to overlook the real possibility that the enemy must be just as exhausted and weakened by the fighting. In such a situation the victory went to the commander with the strongest nerve and the ability to inspire his troops to hold on and to keep the pressure on against the enemy. This doctrine was preached by Hitler to his generals right up to the last days of his life, though Rommel was to change his views after his crushing defeat at El Alamein in late 1942.

Both men had a sure sense of the place of psychological pressure in warfare, an awareness that in some situations bluff and deception could be just as powerful weapons as the hard steel of guns and bullets, and that it was the enemy's perception of strength that determined his reaction more than its true state. Rommel's plans were never directed solely against the enemy troops in front of him; he always had in mind the possible interpretation the opposing commander would give to his moves. And in this respect Rommel relied on what his sixth sense picked up while directing a

battle from the front units, or by overflying a battlefield in his command spotter aircraft.

On the morning of 6 February 1941, Rommel was called to the Reich Chancellery in Berlin to receive his new appointment from Hitler: 'Commander-in-Chief, German Troops in Libya.' His promotion to *Generalleutnant* (Lt General) was promulgated the next day. The decision to send Rommel to Libya was Hitler's, and in 1942 he told an Italian diplomat that he picked Rommel 'because he knows how to inspire his troops'. As the unfolding campaign was to show, Hitler's choice was a wise one, though it was to have consequences unseen at the time and Rommel's successes were to prove a serious drain on Germany's resources by the end of the African campaign.

No other German theatre of war during World War II was as remote from the day-to-day influence of Berlin as was Libya. Rommel had already demonstrated his ability to act independently in action, twisting orders to suit his own interests if it meant he could bring a victory to a speedier end, trusting in his success to turn aside any negative criticism. Hitler must have realized that Rommel would be inclined to act according to how he found conditions in North Africa, and not be bound by the strict control that the High Command liked to exercise over its field commanders. Going on past record, Hitler must also have realized that Rommel would, if necessary, appeal to him directly if there was any serious conflict with the directives laid down in Rommel's orders. For Rommel, the important thing was that he knew he enjoyed Hitler's confidence.

Rommel had a special channel of communication to Hitler which he used more and more as the tide of war turned against him: *Leutnant* Alfred Berndt, a member of Dr Josef Goebbels' Propaganda Ministry. Berndt was appointed to Rommel's staff as an overseer of propaganda but acted more as a means of obtaining immediate access to Hitler through the offices of Goebbels, who also liked to see himself as Rommel's patron. In June 1943, after the general surrender of German and Italian forces in Tunisia, it was Berndt who broadcast through the German radio networks an apologia for the *Afrikakorps*. This address was syndicated by the German Press Agency for release throughout the neutral world as an official account of the *Afrikakorps*.

From the very beginning, Rommel showed that he was not going to accept tamely directions from the Italians, or to take as gospel truth their appreciation of the current situation and likely developments. His memories of events at Caporetto in northern Italy in 1917 must have weighed heavily in his assessment of Italian capabilities in February 1941, when he made the first of many low-level flights over the front-line area, only hours after landing in Libya.

One hallmark of Rommel's generalship in North Africa was his ability to improvise quickly, and he enjoyed involving himself personally in the mechanical details of constructing whatever was needed to impress or to deceive the enemy. For example, it was Rommel's idea, in March 1941, to make the British think his armoured strength was stronger than it really was by constructing the shapes of tanks on some small Volkswagen utility cars, using a wooden frame with sections of canvas painted in gunmetal grey stretched over them.

Rommel's first advance, from El Agheila up to the Egyptian border, displayed all the driving force he had shown as commander of the 7th Panzer Division in France during the previous summer, and more, as now he was operating in unfamiliar terrain and conditions. But he put himself in the vanguard of his advance, everywhere exhorting his unit commanders to faster speed and greater effort. When a tank column was stranded in the desert with not enough fuel to proceed, Rommel impatiently ordered that all fuel was to be emptied from the transport vehicles and poured into the tanks. If there was still not enough, then the tanks themselves were to be divided and one half was to give its fuel to the other half in order that the advance could be maintained.

It was at Tobruk in the second half of April and the first days of May 1941 that Rommel showed his limitations for the first time. He was later to be accused of callously shedding unnecessary lives in his obsession

A pleased Rommel watches a display of gun laying and firing by members of PzArtlRgt33 in July 1941. (P. E. Schläfer)

to capture Tobruk, though it is fair to say this criticism would not have been uttered if he had managed to take it. Rommel's shock tactics that had rolled the British back from Cyrenaica failed dismally when faced with the strong and well-entrenched Australian positions. Rommel undertook a series of attacks against Tobruk with insufficient knowledge of either the defences or the strength of the garrison, and he persisted in these attacks when other commanders might have thought it wise to call a halt to assess the situation. This is what most generals would have done, but Rommel was not like most generals, even those in the German Army.

The worst side of Rommel appeared after Tobruk when he blamed General Streich, the Commander of the 5th Light Division, and Colonel Olbrich, who commanded the 5th Panzer Regiment, for their failure to capture it. Rommel accused them of failing to carry out his orders, and of failing to show the necessary will to succeed in the attacks. Both men were obliged to return to Germany after Rommel requested that they be reassigned somewhere outside Africa.

It was in the fluid battles on the open desert that Rommel was master and no one on the Allied side, with the exception of the American General Patton, could match him at this sort of fighting. A former 8th Army intelligence officer, B. F. (Mick) Shepherd, had this to say about Rommel's ability to control a battle in the open desert, remarks which applied to the period from March 1941 until the middle of 1942, when Rommel was halted at El Alamein.

'It was clear that Rommel had a unique appreciation of the possibilities of the vastness of the desert – the fact that units must inevitably exist in isolated clumps and that this isolation from one another did not matter at all as long as the armour could be quickly concentrated; all that was important to Rommel was that he could attack (or withdraw) in a long, sweeping curve. It did not matter if no one was behind, or if his flanks seemed to be open at any one moment for the curve took care of that, allowing him to always turn, either to fight or to change the arc of withdrawal.

So long as Rommel had petrol and ammunition, he utilized the tremendous built-in defence permitted by unfettered mobility with its very low casualty rates. The British ideas in comparison seemed to be obsessed with anchoring flanks and advancing like a bulldozer blade – straight-line style.

'Rommel rested his security in using tanks offensively, not in dribs and drabs but together so that

Rommel listens to an account of the fighting by PzArtlRgt33 in the Sollum Battle of June 1941 from an NCO gunner. (P. E. Schläfer)

their power was irresistible. Rommel's tactics were to keep moving and keep hitting, knocking bits off everything he came up against – spreading alarm and general despondency among the survivors, who would be groping for coherence and still trusting in the "system" instead of relying on themselves. This was, of course, a deficiency in the British training at the time; the Germans were far better trained in the way they could re-form and quickly co-operate again. Rommel also realized that a unit which had fought a static defence against a mobile attack could become momentarily defenceless and somehow leaderless because it could seldom generate a purpose in itself – the normal reaction was to ask someone else what to do, for a short while at least. This is why Rommel would keep his pressure on. Tactics did not defeat Rommel in the end, it was the great superiority our side had in Sherman tanks, the new 6pdr and 17pdr anti-tank guns, and naval and air attacks on his supply lines.'

Regardless of the setbacks at Tobruk, Rommel had the success of the two engagements with Wavell on the Egyptian border in May and June 1941 to his credit and these two victories restored his image and confidence. The German propaganda machine worked well throughout this period to communicate the Rommel legend to the people of Germany and the occupied countries of Western and Central Europe. Rommel was easy material for the photographers, the press, and newsreel cameramen. Although the invasion of the Soviet Union in June 1941 overshadowed events in Africa, Rommel was an established hero and he continued to receive good attention in the German media.

Many stories circulated, some revealing a lot about the character of the person in the limelight – like the one printed in Germany in early 1942 concerning the infamous Italian tins of sausage meat. The story goes like this:

Food is one of the main interests for the soldiers of the *Afrikakorps*, as it is for soldiers of every army, and usually a subject of their day-to-day humour. This is particularly so in the desert because of the climate, the great distances, and the absence of any surrounding agriculture with which to augment and improve the military diet.

During the time when there is action, the food consists of tinned stuff only, and after a few days it loses its attraction. The tins of preserved meat which had the cryptic stamp 'AM' on the top were supplied by the Italian stores. Most soldiers knew that 'AM' stood for *Administrazione militare* – until one day when General Rommel was inspecting the positions around Halfaya Pass. A soldier of the *Afrikakorps* who had a specially active sense of humour was occupied fishing little pieces of meat out of a tin with the point of his bayonet, a difficult task as he also needed the bayonet to chase away the swarms of flies. Suddenly the General emerged from behind a large rock and the soldier did not immediately know who he was because Rommel stood with his back to the sun.

'Na,' said the General, 'how does the "Old Man" taste?' (The German for 'Old Man' is *Alter Mann*.)

The soldier recognized his commanding general as he spoke and without standing to attention he said smartly, 'Thank you, Herr General, but I thought I was eating an old mule, if you don't mind, Herr General!' (The German for 'old mule' is *Alter Maulesel*.)

This exchange caused much laughter and the story spread right across the African front. The question of whether the 'AM' stood for *Alter Mann* or *Alter Maulesel* was finally decided months later in General Rommel's favour and now wherever one goes on the African front you will hear it referred to as *Alter Mann*, just as it was coined by the General himself.

Another story printed in the same publication concerned an incident that took place in the autumn of 1941 in Libya:

General Rommel was sitting in a lightly constructed Italian colonial farmhouse having his portrait painted when an air-raid by the English started. A bomb came down about 40 metres across the road and another bomb landed just behind the house where the cliff fell away to the sea. The dust from the explosions was blowing in through the door and broken windows and the plaster was dropping from the ceiling. Rommel continued to sit quietly on his stool and showed no sign of moving into the shelter, the cellar under the farmhouse. The artist became very hesitant with his sketching because he could already hear another wave of bombers approaching and the increasing fire of the nearby Flak guns.

The General looked carefully at the artist for a few seconds and said quietly, 'Does this disturb you?'

'No, no, Herr General.'

'Then carry on, carry on,' said Rommel.

No portrait was ever finished faster.

Such stories were avidly picked up by the war correspondents and sent back to Germany. Another story

Rommel arriving at a gunnery display put on by PzArtlRgt33 in July 1941. (P. E. Schläfer)

related by Wilhelm Wessel, the official military war artist assigned to the *Afrikakorps*, was more typical of Rommel and is suitably terse and to the point. It concerned an incident where Rommel, in his usual style, was moving across the battlefield and quickly acquainting himself with what his units were doing.

Suddenly at a front-line divisional headquarters Rommel's car arrives and even before it had completely come to a stop the General was out and was addressing the divisional 1A. 'There is an English Armoured Brigade getting ready to attack you from the north, and in the south there is an English mixed force which is advancing. Take care that you are finished with the first before the second arrives!' Rommel quickly returned the officer's salute and took off in his car

Die Karawane

Herausgeber : P.K.

Sonntag, 13. Dezember 1942

Nummer 2.

1262 PANZER IN ZEHN TAGEN VERNICHTET

Gute Fortschritte im Osten - Panzererfolg in Tunis

UNSERE FRONT

Nach den ersten Angriffserfolgen

Eichenlaubtraeger General Fischer

Sieger von Tebourba, Sedan, Calais, der Beresina

Die Karawane front page 13 December 1942. (Antoine Lebel)

had established a bridgehead in Tunisia in November 1942, the Propaganda company attached to the 5th Panzer Army HQ were quick to get their own field newspaper into print. This was common practice in the German Army; a field newspaper being distributed within each command of Army size was an effective morale booster for the troops. The first field newspaper to appear on 12 December 1942 in Tunis, was *Die Karawane* (The Caravan), printed daily. This paper carried a selection of local military news and reports from other fronts.

When the retreat by Rommel's forces in 1943 brought them into the Tunisian area hitherto catered for by *Die Karawane* it was decided to combine the two field newspapers. Both, however, kept their separate identities, with *Die Karawane* continuing as a daily newspaper covering the military and other international news, while *Die Oase* became a medium for more popular reading matter designed specially for the German troops in Africa. In this new format, *Die Oase* remained a weekly publication and the daily issue of *Die Karawane* was now sub-titled *Nachrichtenblatt der Feldzeitung Die Oase* (News Bulletin of the Field Newspaper *The Oasis*).

As well as writing for *Die Oase*, the staff also gathered news from the African theatre to send back to Germany. The staff size increased steadily during 1941 and by the middle of 1942 it had grown to full company strength. The numbers were further increased in 1943 when the staff of *Die Karawane* was absorbed.

Throughout the African campaign the field newspapers were distributed by the Army Field Post units, which took the newspapers into every corner where German troops were stationed, along with their mail deliveries.

Newspapers in Africa

At the same time as the 5th Light Division was being loaded in Naples for the crossing to Tripoli, a detachment of ten men from an Army Propaganda unit in Berlin was preparing to follow them. These men, under the command of *Leutnant* Kölbel, were to start an Army field newspaper on African soil. The newspaper they began to print a few weeks later was called *Die Oase* (The Oasis), and it was to become a famous part of the history of the *Afrikakorps* right up to the end of the campaign in Tunisia just over two years later.

The first issues were printed in Tripoli, but after the Axis advance to the Egyptian border the typewriters and printing presses were moved into a permanent office in Benghazi. *Die Oase* came out weekly with news from Germany and the other fronts, and a selection of international reports and stories from the African theatre.

After newly arrived German units

In 1943 it became a problem printing the two parts of the African field newspaper, though *Die Karawane* continued to appear daily up to the end of April 1943. No supplies of newsprint and other printing material could be sent from Europe after February 1943 and *Die Oase* turned to local newspaper publishers for supplies. By these means the paper was able to continue, but distribution became more difficult. The last issue to be widely circulated was published on Sunday 25 April 1943, and the very last edition was printed on 6 May 1943, using the presses of a Tunis newspaper. Arab helpers were enlisted to carry bundles of *Die Oase* through the streets of Tunis, handing them to any German troops they saw. The journal published after the war in West Germany by the Association of former members of the *Afrikakorps* bears the same name – *Die Oase* – as their old field newspaper.

Another widely read journal in North Africa was *Adler von Hellas* (The Eagle from Hellas), a bi-weekly magazine distributed by the *Luftwaffe* throughout the Mediterranean. This 20-page picture magazine carried a variety of popular articles with some stories originating from the Mediterranean theatre, and a couple of pages of jokes, puzzles and crosswords. It was printed in Vienna and distributed to *Luftwaffe* units from Athens. In Africa many copies found their way into Army units where it was a welcome item of leisure-time reading.

In addition to the field newspaper and the magazine distributed by the *Luftwaffe*, the *Afrikakorps* were well served with current issues of German newspapers and magazines which were sent to Africa by the families of men serving there. In the sweep through Cyrenaica in late 1941 the 8th Army soldiers found papers much more recent than the ones they had themselves received from home. The selection picked up by British troops in December 1941 reflected the regional affinities still shown in the *Afrikakorps* at this time, with most coming from cities like Berlin, Stettin, Frankfurt an der Oder (21st Panzer Div), and Mannheim, Kaiserslautern and Karlsruhe (15th Panzer Div).

Very different from the above were the mimeographed sheets printed by divisional and regimental staffs for purely military matters. These newssheets, usually three or four sheets stapled together, were distributed on a near-daily basis down to company level. One printed on 27 May 1941, and circulated among units of the 5th Light Division, contained such diverse information as an increase in the allowance of razor soap, ammunition for use in the tropics would have the initials Tp stamped on cartridges, a short dissertation on how driving in the desert is not the same as driving in Europe, and an order that sole surviving sons of families (where other sons have been killed in action) would no longer be returned to Germany, but would be withdrawn from the front line and be posted to reserve units in Africa.

The other usual form of military 'newsletter' was the Battalion Order of the Day. One such battalion daily order, found at El Alamein by Australian troops, was from records of the 125th Infantry Regiment in the 164th Light Division. Dated 19 May 1942, it relates to a period this division spent on Crete as a 'fortress' garrison. The first item is a punishment pronouncement, and is reproduced here in full as it is a clear example of the type and strength of German military discipline:

'From the Battalion Commander:
I hereby sentence *Obergefreiter* Willi Seuberth of the 12th Company 125th Regiment to 21 days' close arrest, with secondary punishment of 28 days loss of daily leave entitlement as follows – three hours to be added to curfew time, because on 16 May 1942,

1. the order to report to the Medical Officer for a clinical examination was disobeyed,
2. he spent several hours beyond the curfew limit in the town,
3. during the investigation of this matter he lied in an uncouth and outrageous manner to his Company Commander, and
4. orders to immediately resume his routine duties were ignored.'

The punishment 21 days' close arrest – *21 Tagen geschärften Arrest* – was a standard military one, and entailed being confined with only a wooden bench to sleep on, one blanket issued regardless of season, and a diet of bread and water.

Other items on this battalion daily order included promotions, transfers of personnel within the battalion, and the appointment of four local barbers as 'Armed Forces Barbers' (*Wehrmachtfriseur*).

The field newspaper of the Afrikakorps, Die Oase, *being read by a* Hauptmann *in the summer of 1941. (ECPA)*

On 5 July 1941 in Bardia, Rommel presented Hauptmann *Walter Fromm with the Knights Cross for his success in knocking out a British tank attack with his 88mm guns. (Walter Fromm)*

again. When Rommel is moving around in his command vehicle in a battle, long discussions are not necessary – he knows his commanders and they understand him.

Rommel was very conscious of his image, both with the popular press and with the troops he commanded. In battle he made constant use of his *Kampfstaffel* (Combat Group), and the relatively high number of Knights Crosses awarded to such a small unit – it was fixed at four companies in strength – is an indication of how often Rommel was close to the centre of battle. As supplied by Dieter Hellriegel, they were awarded to: *Hauptmann* (Captain) Rudolf Kiehl, *Major* Medicus, and *Oberleutnant* (First Lieutenant) Harro Brenner. For a group that did not number above 500 personnel, three is an unusually high number of Knights Crosses. Hellriegel, who served in Rommel's 'Escort Group' (*Begleitkommando*), a select combat force drawn from the General's *Kampfstaffel*, related how Rommel would always fly up to the front in his Fieseler Storch, a light spotter aircraft, when he had any inspections to make. When he arrived as close as he could to the front he would change over to his car. In this way his soldiers always saw him arriving from the direction of the front, never from the rear. Not for Rommel was the image of

a commander who spent his time behind the lines with the possible associations of leisure and comfort while his troops had to endure the rigours of open desert living close to the danger of the front line.

Dieter Hellriegel, who witnessed Rommel's style of command at close hand, remembers, 'Rommel had the habit of speeding off at a moment's notice to some part of the battlefield with an uncanny sense of orientation. He arrived without warning standing up in his car yelling at everyone, "*Angreifen! Angreifen!*" (Attack! Attack!). Often this was what kept the battle going. Just his presence galvanized all ranks into renewed effort.'

Dieter Hellriegel also tells how Rommel made a point of asking soldiers he talked with how long they had been in Africa because there was hardly any leave and many only got home through sickness. Once Rommel said to Dieter Hellriegel, '*Warum bekommen Sie nicht die Scheisserei, dann kann ich Sie nach Hause schicken*' ('Why haven't you got dysentery yet, then I would be able to send you back home.')

Right through his time in Africa, and especially before the summer of 1942, Rommel possessed enormous energy, even more than a much younger and stronger person could have been expected to have. His hours were long and his work was demanding. As well as the purely military tasks he set himself, he had a heavy load of correspondence to handle as his popularity grew in Germany. This ranged from letters sent by his adoring public, to the many official letters he received from organizations wishing him success or inviting him to visit some function or city when next in Germany. Even if Rommel did not actually write the letters himself he took the time to sign them personally.

Though he was a hero to those at home, Rommel did make mistakes. For example, he made a serious miscalculation in the fighting during November and December 1941 which cost him victory in Operation Crusader. This was the famous 'dash to the wire' (see page 106), when he personally led the *Afrikakorps* (the two Panzer divisions) in a wild foray across the Egyptian frontier which aimed to unnerve the British command and to interrupt the flow of supplies to the 8th Army. He was out of touch for nearly two days with his own headquarters still south of Tobruk and he lost an opportunity to deal with a dispersed British tank force. But his quick recovery in January 1942 showed he had lost none of his dash and sense of how to push his opponent off balance. His crowning moment of glorious victory came on 21 June 1942, when the Tobruk commander surrendered his remaining force to him. On 22 June, Hitler made Rommel a Field Marshal, the highest rank attainable in the German Army. Shortly afterwards, Rommel met Field Marshal Kesselring who took the crossed baton devices from his own shoulder straps and presented them to Rommel. Rommel then removed the three small silver pips of a *Generaloberst* from each of his shoulder straps and gave them as a memento to General Nehring, who was standing nearby, before attaching the crossed batons.

His second major, and fatal error, was to immediately resume his advance beyond Tobruk in June 1942 before Malta could be attacked and occupied. Its capture would have ensured a regular flow of supplies for a further advance into Egypt. This course would have avoided the later costly defeat at El Alamein as the British would almost certainly have stood to defend Egypt inside the frontier in June/July 1942 which could have allowed Rommel's outflanking moves from the open desert to the South.

Despite his extraordinary energy, Rommel suffered from the same complaints that affected his troops, and he ate the same food. Before he left Germany, he had had bouts of rheumatism, but this did not worry him unduly in North Africa. When he finally agreed to take sick leave, from the El Alamein position in September 1942, he was the only German officer over 40 years of age to have lasted so long in Africa. At this time he was mentally and physically exhausted and his reserves were running so low, he was unable to get over a head cold.

The period Rommel spent at El Alamein, both before and after his sick leave, was responsible for a change in his health and resulted in a pessimistic outlook about the outcome of the war. Some historians believe that Rommel had lost his last chance of victory when he ordered a retreat from the advance made by the *Afrikakorps* against the Alam Halfa ridge. Whether or not he still had a last chance to advance to the Nile is a moot point, but the Rommel who had ordered attack after attack against the Tobruk perimeter fifteen months before was no longer in command. The bloody fighting, the loss of his two reliable sources of intelligence about the other side (see page 121), the failure of supplies to arrive, the distance that was growing between him and Hitler as the fighting in Russia took more and more of Germany's strength and Hitler's attention, the unhealthy conditions of the Alamein line, the growing realization of the consequences for Germany of American involvement in the war on the Allied side, the lack of tactical freedom imposed on him by the Alamein position, the accumulated fatigue of nearly eighteen months in North Africa spent in long hours of work and tension – all combined to breed a pessimism in

Rommel that was not to be overcome until after the surrender in Tunisia. At this later stage, back in favour with Hitler and with time to recuperate from the physical draining that occurred in Africa, he was something of his old self.

One episode that is a real and lasting testimony to the quality of the man is the long retreat from El Alamein to the Tunisian frontier. Rommel carefully husbanded his remaining forces, skilfully retreating step by step to avoid any further battle with the superior forces of the ponderous Montgomery. His main aim was to preserve his army. This he did, and his reputation was like a shield held up to the following 8th Army, for Montgomery dared not risk a fight in the open ground of the desert with even a weakened *Afrikakorps*.

There was a brief final moment of exhilarating victory for Rommel when he overwhelmed an American force at Kasserine Pass in Tunisia in February 1943. His desert veterans combined with some of the newly arrived units of the 5th Panzer Army (see page 47) and

An unhappy-looking Rommel is not satisfied by explanations about the siting of a gun position from 15PzDiv in March 1942. Karl-Heinz Böttger, the Asst. Divisional Commander's Adjutant, stands in the centre of this photo listening to Rommel dressing down the responsible officers. (Karl-Heinz Böttger)

On his return to the El Alamein fighting on 25 October 1942, a grim-faced Rommel discusses the position with Bayerlein and Kesselring. (ECPA)

the green American troops fell back in confusion. But his last major engagement in Africa, at Medinine against the 8th Army, must have left a bitter taste with Rommel, for his tanks advanced into a carefully laid trap prepared by the waiting British. His sixth sense and his feel for Montgomery's generalship, which he did not hold in any high regard, told Rommel that the British must have had prior knowledge of his plan of attack. He blamed the Italians for a reckless lapse of security, but the British knew everything about his movements through ULTRA, a British secret interception operation which cracked German signal codes enciphered through an elaborate transmission system known as Enigma.

Rommel's part in the North African war is something that will endure, and he will be remembered for his example of decency and respect towards his adversaries that did so much to make the fighting in North Africa relatively clean and allowed humane attitudes a place on the battlefields. And in a world that was increasingly racist, he will be respected for his refusal to practise racism even though the regime he fought for promoted and condoned it. Indeed, discrimination was found more among the Allied Armies than in Rommel's Army, where all enemy were treated alike regardless of colour.

Rommel will also be identified with such innovations as using the powerful 88mm anti-aircraft gun as an anti-tank weapon (although not the first to do so) and mounting aircraft engines on the back of lorries to stir up billowing clouds of dust to hide his moving supply and armoured columns from air attack. In short, the history of the *Afrikakorps* is indelibly linked with the name of Rommel (though he was only one of its commanders) and he will be remembered as a soldier's soldier.

On 9 March 1943, Rommel left Africa for the last time, flying from an airfield at Sfax in Tunisia to Italy. Before he left, he had taken the time to assemble the thirteen remaining members of the 2nd Company of his *Kampfstaffel*, old hands of his *Begleitkommando*, so that he could take them back to Germany with him and so save them from the inevitable collapse of the Axis front in Tunisia. To these men, among them Dieter Hellriegel, this gesture by their 'Chef' said more than any words could ever say about the commander they had served in Africa.

Rommel's uniforms

When Rommel first arrived in Africa, on 12 February 1941, he had had only six hectic days to prepare for his posting to Libya and he arrived wearing a quite unsuitable tailor-made woollen Continental uniform. However, before leaving Germany he had arranged for a number of special tropical uniforms to be made up for him and sent across to Libya when they were ready. These were made from olive tan cotton twill material and consisted of a tunic with pleated pockets top and bottom and straight pocket flaps, and breeches with red stripes running the length of the outer edges. These uniforms – which were completed by a general's *Schirmmütze*, the high peaked cap which had silvered metal insignia and gold cording to the crown and band edges, and by a pair of black high leather boots which were conventionally worn with breeches – received a lot of wear. This is apparent by their bleached appearance after the early summer of 1941 and the signs of wear on the gold-coloured General's breast eagle and collar tabs.

At times, as photos show, Rommel did wear combinations of the standard issue Army tropical clothing, such as the pith helmet or, on even rarer occasions, the cloth field cap, and in the hot summer months he was often seen wearing shorts together with low canvas and leather boots and knee-length socks.

For his tropical shirts, Rommel favoured the modified French Army variety (see page 142) with the button-down collar points which made it easier to wear his Knights Cross and *Pour le Mérite*. These medals were worn on ribbons around the neck and held by metal suspension loops which were held firmly in place by the closed collar of the French shirts. (Many other Knights Cross winners in Africa preferred the

French shirt for the same reason.)

Another article of clothing, much worn by Rommel during the winter of 1941–42, was a long dark olive leather overcoat, similar to the normal German military overcoat popular with officers. This coat was usually worn with a chequered scarf which Rommel wore around his neck and tucked into the exposed V of his open collar.

Rommel's best-known addition to his uniform was undoubtedly his goggles. In March 1941, Rommel was inspecting a captured British dump at Mechili when he noticed cartons of British anti-dust goggles. These were a simple design of thin Perspex and Rommel took a supply to wear over his *Schirmmütze*. For the remainder of the African campaign these goggles were an ever-present part of the Rommel image.

Rommel's *Schirmmütze* that had seen so much service did not return with Rommel after his brief spell of sick leave. In its place was a peaked cap something in the style of the 'Old Style Officer's Field Cap', a cap with no chinstrap and with embroidered insignia in place of the metal insignia of his old cap. This cap did not have such a pronounced peak to the crown and had a smaller circumference.

The other significant article of cloth-

Rommel addressing officers from MG Battalion 8 in April 1942 behind the Gazala line: a rare shot showing him wearing shorts and a pith helmet. (Author's collection)

ing which Rommel wore nearly continuously after El Alamein was an olive brown woollen overcoat with red velvet facing panels on the turn-back lapels of the collar. This was a standard feature of General rank overcoats, and an AFRIKAKORPS cufftitle was stitched in the normal position on the lower right sleeve. Rommel continued to wear this cufftitle in Tunisia until his departure in March 1943 contrary to the order that it was to be removed in anticipation of the AFRIKA campaign cufftitle.

Rommel often chose to wear long trousers with low leather or canvas and leather boots during this later period, probably because it was a more comfortable combination. The same style of British dust goggles were to be seen on the new peaked cap, but otherwise Rommel's appearance was quite different to the old Desert Fox. His face was drawn, and the new cap gave his features a wider appearance, as if his eyes and cheeks were slightly puffy.

Rommel with his Chief of Staff, General Gause, in Tunisia around the time of the occupation of the Mareth Line in February 1943. (ECPA)

A Sd.Kfz. 232 eight-wheeled armoured car from Rommel's Kampfstaffel at El Alamein. (Dieter Hellriegel)

A British Crusader Mk I tank with its turret removed to serve the Germans as a battlefield resupply vehicle. Its low profile together with its armour and speed made it an ideal means of transporting fuel and ammunition up to tanks during a battle. This particular tank was used by the Panzer Company in Rommel's Kampfstaffel at El Alamein in 1942. (Dieter Hellriegel)

By the end of 1942 Rommel, here with Bayerlein, was moving back across Tripolitania for the last time. (ECPA)

Lt Wolfgang Döring of Rommel's Begleitkommando (Escort Group) on the Via Balbia in September 1941. (Dieter Hellriegel)

The last of the American-built Stuart tanks from Rommel's Kampfstaffel photographed in Tunisia in March 1943. Twelve of these tanks, captured in June 1942, were used from the time of the early Alamein battles by the Panzer Company in Rommel's Kampfstaffel. (Dieter Hellriegel)

An envelope addressed by Rommel to his sister (left) (Author's collection)

The Men of Rommel's Army in North Africa

The Sollum Battle, June 1941 – Oberleutnant *Dröber and his NCO observing fall of artillery fire. The vehicle is a Sd.Kfz. 250/2. (P. E. Schläfer)*

WARTIME WRITERS who reported on the fighting in North Africa have commented on the large quantities of paper material that littered the battlefields after every major engagement. They described how for days after a battle pieces of paper were scattered around abandoned vehicles, foxholes and trenches, caught and held by clumps of camel thorn bush or blowing with the wind across the desert.

Some of this paper litter would have come adrift in the course of battle, but for the most part it was caused by opposing troops occupying a captured area, usually for only a short period of time. In their hurried search for any loot (food, usable weapons, souvenirs or anything of some practical value), everything was disturbed. Papers were important sources of intelligence information, as well as having souvenir value. Everything left behind by the retreating enemy was ransacked, even corpses – these were a prime source for documents. Photos of dead troops invariably show raised pocket flaps left by the searchers, and overcoats pulled up to the chest to obtain access to pockets on inner clothing. What was not considered worth keeping was thrown on the ground to join the other paper flotsam left by the passing battle.

A wide selection of German books and papers, that came originally from several of the battlefields in North Africa, was taken as souvenirs by Allied servicemen and they give interesting insights into the lives of the men who once owned them. Some items, like paybooks, were carried by all German soldiers. Other papers, more personal and individual in nature, reflect something of a soldier's private life. The official German Army papers and records on the other hand have more to say about the Army itself, its character and administration. While these official papers have much in common with similar German military bureaucratic records from other theatres of war, those souvenirs taken from the battlefields of North Africa do shed light on the special conditions there, and the following are examples of what was brought back by Allied troops.

Paybook (*Soldbuch*)

The paybook (*Soldbuch*) was the single most important document carried by a German soldier, and he was required to carry it on him at all times. However, in Africa this was not always obeyed, as photos show. The *Soldbuch* (size 10·5cm × 14·5cm) was too large to fit into the pockets of the standard German tropical shirt, nor would it fit in the pockets of the trousers or breeches without being crushed. Whenever a tunic was being worn the *Soldbuch* was evidently carried.

The paybook was issued to every soldier when posted to his initial depot unit. The book carried both the military service number and the number he was given in his unit – which was the actual paybook number that appeared along with his unit number and type on the metal identity disc ('dog tag') worn on a cord around his neck. These discs were worn at all times. Unit numbers in the paybook were generally of a low order as they were assigned on a company basis, not a regimental or divisional one, though high-ranking officers did have a divisional or regimental identification as they had no company attachment – General Walter Neumann-Silkow had the number '1' in his paybook, as divisional commander of the 15th Panzer Division.

The information contained in the paybook covered a variety of aspects of military interest: a physical description acting as a means of checking identity; name and rank and an ink signature; blood group; a full list of all units served in, including training units and replacement groups in the event of the current field unit having to be re-formed; family details with home address; a comprehensive record of all clothing and equipment issued; type of weapons issued with serial numbers; inoculations and hospitalization; eyesight test results; pay rates with any special theatre of operations bonus; details of promotions and decorations awarded; the issue of body and razor soap; and a list of leave passes for any period over five days. There was a special rate of pay for service in Africa, and so the paybook had an entry on the page detailing pay scales noting the date of arrival in Africa. The standard form was an entry, written or ink-stamped, reading '*Inhaber hat am 14.3.41 afrikanischen Boden betreten*' (Holder arrived in Africa on 14.3.41).

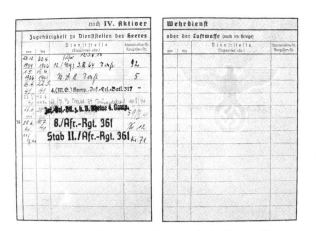

Page twelve of the Wehrpass *showing the holder's military service record. (Author's collection)*

Rommel standing on the dockside watching a PzII being unloaded from a German merchant ship, Tripoli, 14 February 1941. (Imperial War Museum)

Important details of service, and current unit, were listed on page four of the paybook and troops were given very strict orders that this page had to be removed and destroyed before surrendering.

The paybook used by German troops in Africa did not carry a photo of the holder, unlike the one carried on service in Europe from the mid-war period when the addition of photos was a response to the increasing level of partisan/guerrilla activity and the consequent need for a more positive means of identification than that provided by the physical description. These circumstances did not arise in the African theatre, even in 1943 when the photo system was introduced.

The Army paybook and those used by the *Luftwaffe* were similar in overall design and content, but Army ones had a tan-coloured cardboard cover bearing an Army eagle and swastika, while the *Luftwaffe* version had a blue-coloured cardboard cover with a *Luftwaffe* eagle and swastika. The *Luftwaffe* paybooks also had an added page headed 'Ten Commandments for the Conduct of War by German Soldiers', which was pasted over the inside cover. Special instructions on subjects

such as hygiene in Africa were issued separately for inclusion in a folding pocket inside the rear cover. The paybook carried by a soldier in the field often held personal papers like family photos, letters, copies of award citations, and paper money, all of which were kept in the pocket inside the rear cover. These books had constant use and handling and it is common to see copies that had been repaired and had the spine binding reinforced.

The primary function of the paybook was to record a soldier's pay and it listed the pay scales under four categories:

1. *Wehrsold* (Army pay)
2. *Frontzulage* (Active Service Allowance)
3. *Afrikazulage* (Africa Allowance)
4. *Kriegsbesoldung* (War emoluments) or
   Friedengebührnisse (Peace emoluments)

Studio portrait of a Hauptfeldwebel *from the* Pioniere *Battalion 15PzDiv, taken in Germany in April 1941. (Author's collection)*

Studio portrait taken in late 1941 of a young Grenadier in tropical uniform on the eve of departure for Africa. (Author's collection)

Oberst *Mildebrath, Commander of Panzer Regiment 5, at El Alamein in August 1942 on the occasion of his receiving the Knights Cross. (ECPA)*

An Obergefreiter *showing the Iron Cross II ribbon in his tunic button-hole, and the Silver Infantry Assault Badge on his breast pocket. (Charles Hinz)*

Old field Cap, New Iron Cross II, El Alamein 1942. (ECPA)

A Sonderführer *poses for a photograph after being awarded his Iron Cross I, El Alamein 1942. (ECPA)*

Unteroffizier *Kurt Gerhardt, of 1st Battalion of 104th Motorised Infantry Regiment, captured at Halfaya on 17 January 1942, after his battalion, had been cut off for six weeks. The privations suffered by this garrison are shown in the gaunt and tired face of Kurt Gerhardt. (Imperial War Museum)*

Oberleutnant *Behrens, PzDiv, El Alamein 1942, (ECPA)*

Grenadier *Günter Halm, the youngest Knights Cross winner in the German Army. This nineteen-year-old soldier in the 104PzGrenRgt of 21PzDiv, was the only surviving member of a 76.2 mm anti-tank gun crew who stopped a British tank advance on 22 July 1942. This photo was taken on 29 July 1942, after he had received his Knights Cross from Rommel. (ECPA)*

Oberst *Alfred Brüer, Commander of ArtlRgt155 in 21PzDiv at El Alamein 1942. (ECPA)*

Hauptmann *Werner Reissmann, who won his Knights Cross in action against New Zealanders at Ruweisat Ridge in July 1942. (ECPA)*

Oberleutnant *Albert Panzenhagen, Commander of InfRgt361 in 90th Light Division – El Alamein 1942. (ECPA)*

Men of the 5th Light Division crossing the Mediterranean, February 1941. All are wearing European theatre woollen uniforms and inflatable vests. (Author's collection)

Army pay was paid out on the 1st, 11th and 21st of every month, and officers and other ranks received their pay from the same pay clerk and the same channels. The rates in 1942 ranged from 96 *lire* for a private, to 258 *lire* for a lieutenant for the ten-day pay period (1 *Reichsmark* (RM) equalled 7.7 *lire*).

Active Service Allowance was set at 1RM per day for each soldier, irrespective of rank, and was paid with the Army pay.

Africa Allowance was calculated from the date of arrival in Africa, but was not included with the pay. Instead it was built up as a credit which the soldier could only cash in when he returned to Germany, at an Army pay office. The scale of payment was as follows: for privates 2RM per day; for NCOs, 3RM per day; for officers, 4RM per day.

War emoluments and Peace emoluments differed only slightly from each other: the former was drawn by officers and NCOs who were civilians in peacetime, the latter by regular Army officers and NCOs from the standing Army. In both cases a fixed amount was paid into the bank account of the individual soldier. A corporal, for instance, received between 70RM and 90RM per month, depending on housing rents in his home area – in wartime Germany housing rents were higher in country villages than in large urban areas.

German troops serving in Africa could amass large sums of money in Italian currency, though there was little that could be done with it, apart from that spent on leave with Italian and Arab traders, or in gambling. In fact, the greater part of the money paid out to troops

in Africa was remitted back to Germany. Once a month money could be handed to the pay clerk, who issued a stamped receipt and sent the money to a personal bank account in Germany where, once lodged, it could be withdrawn by the soldier's family.

Paybooks issued to troops who served in Africa are identifiable mostly by their combat unit, which should tally with any of the published orders of battle for forces in Africa at the time. (Paybooks known to have been taken as souvenirs in North Africa do not always agree with the published orders of battle, showing that these lists of units are not always complete.) Secondly, there was the special insert page for the issue of tropical uniform and field equipment for those troops who arrived after mid-1941. This page, long and folding, is not always present, as it was only glued along one edge and it often came adrift. Lastly, there are the entries for Africa theatre pay allowance and an entry for the award of the Italo-German Commemorative Medal which nearly always was shown on the page for medals and awards as *Italienisch-Deutsche Erinnerungsmedaille* (though this was sometimes entered as *Deutsch-Italienische Erinnerungsmedaille*, or just *Ital.Errinngs-Medaille*).

Two members of PzRgt5 in Naples, February 1941. (Author's collection)

Service record (*Wehrpass*)

The second military booklet used by all German soldiers was the Service Record (*Wehrpass*), but this was not issued or carried concurrently with the paybook. It was only used by the soldier when away from his active unit, such as on transfer to a new unit, or on a training course. At all other times it was held by the soldier's company HQ.

The information contained in the Service Record complemented the paybook, and contained, in addition to personal and family details, information of any training in the State Labour Service, a full record of all special military training, a listing of promotions and awards; units served in, any meritorious service in particular campaigns, and specialist weapons training and proficiency. An identical booklet was used by the Army and *Luftwaffe*. Its cover was a greenish stiff cardboard bearing the title below an eagle and swastika, and an ink stamp for *Heer* (Army) or *Luftwaffe*. Unlike the paybook, the *Wehrpass* normally carried a photo of the holder, stapled inside the front. Unless it was a reissued one, this photo showed the holder in civilian clothes – the photo taken at the time of induction into the service.

The numbers shown in the Service Record were the soldier's military service number, and the initial paybook number for the first unit posting. Examples of the *Wehrpass* taken as souvenirs by Allied servicemen in North Africa were usually ones removed from captured German company headquarters. It would have been rare for a soldier to have been carrying his *Wehrpass* at the front.

Africa theatre booklets

For each of three calendar years that the German Army was in North Africa, a special theatre of operations booklet was issued to all troops, Army and *Luftwaffe* (including aircraft squadron personnel). In 1941 it contained general information, in many ways like the tourist pamphlets that evidently provided the German Army Publications Branch with some of its Libyan information. The booklets issued in 1942 and 1943 were in the form of personal souvenir diaries but incorporated some description of local climate and geography from the earlier booklet.

The 1941 booklet, *Der Soldat in Libyen* (The Soldier in Libya), consisted of 70 pages covering: a potted history of Libya; its climate and topography, the Italian and Arab population; ten pages of tourist-type photos of desert, oases and cities, a chapter on hygiene and health for desert living, ten pages of Italian military rank diagrams with translations of terms, a colour foldout

Tank crewmen of PzRgt5 on board a ship crossing the Mediterranean, February 1941. (Author's collection)

section illustrating uniforms and rank insignia of British Empire and French Armies, and a photo identification for Italian, British and French armoured vehicles. This booklet, published in February by the German Supreme Command, was rushed into print as Rommel was arriving in Tripoli with the leading elements of the 5th Light Division (see page 42). It is interesting to note that action against the French Army in Tunisia must have been anticipated as a large part of the 'identification of enemy' pages dealt specifically with French units stationed in Tunisia. During Operation Crusader in November–December 1941 copies of this booklet were taken from German POWs by 8th Army troops, and judging by the large number it must have been popular with the members of the *Afrikakorps*.

A map of the eastern end of the Mediterranean (from Tunisia to the Nile Delta) was folded and glued inside the back cover, and many German troops traced on this map the course of their journey from Europe to North

Men of 1st Battalion, InfRgt104 (mot), assembled for the award of decorations, Halfaya, July 1941. (ECPA)

Africa – from Italy or Greece to Libya, and their subsequent movements on African soil.

The 1942 booklet, a diary, featured on the cover a representation of the *Afrikakorps* symbol, a swastika superimposed over a palm tree. It was titled *Panzergruppe Afrika Kalender 1942*, which was already out of date when the diary came into use as the German command was redesignated *Panzerarmee Afrika* in January 1942. The diary was published by the Ministry of Propaganda and the preamble contained a historical justification for the presence of German troops in Africa, based on past German colonization of the African continent. The former colonies – German East Africa, the Cameroons, German South West Africa and Togoland – were described in a chapter attacking the Treaty of Versailles which in 1919 took these territories away from Germany.

One chapter which must have appeared incongruous to its readers was entitled 'Hunting in Africa', and covered big game such as lions and leopards (with a pointed warning that these animals were dangerous), as well as buffalo, elephants, antelopes and gazelles. A series of sketches of footprints of wild animals completed this chapter.

The diary was sprinkled with reminders of important dates in the histories of Hitler's Reich and Italy's Fascist State. The end section contained a literal and phonetic glossary of 500 words and phrases in German, Italian, French, English, Egyptian-Arabic, Haussa and Swahili, followed by a list of do's and don'ts for basic health and hygiene in the desert. There was also the same map of the eastern Mediterranean, this time folded and loose, held by a glued paper loop attached to the inside back cover.

The 1943 booklet, the last one issued, was titled *Panzerarmee Afrika Kalender 1943* and again featured the *Afrikakorps* symbol on the front cover. The title, however, was out of date by February as the forces of the 1942 *Panzerarmee Afrika* were then renamed 1st Italian Army. This diary was also distributed among units of the newly built-up 5th Panzer Army in Tunisia and all *Luftwaffe* units in Africa.

Much of the text for the new diary was reprinted from the previous one, but the chapter on big game hunting in Africa was replaced by more appropriate information about animal and plant life which could be encountered in the desert. The glossary of words and phrases from different languages and the section on health and hygiene were included again, but new additions were a three-page section on Italian military ranks and an article on how to show proper respect to the Moslem faith written by Professor Dr E. Rodenwalt, an advisor to the Supreme Command (OKW).

The map of the North African coastline supplied with the 1943 diary differed from the one included with the earlier booklets. The 1943 version covered an area more to the east, leaving Tunisia out completely, and extending to a point beyond the Nile Delta to show Palestine and adjacent territory in Syria and Trans-jordan. In the light of developments in late 1942, the optimism of the publishers of the 1943 diary must have seemed ironic to the German troops receiving the diaries in Tunisia. However, when the diary was being prepared for printing in 1942 the Axis front-line was at El Alamein. It would therefore have seemed logical to anticipate a further advance to Cairo and beyond in 1943. The 1943 edition of the map was loose and stored inside a paper pocket glued behind the back cover.

These three booklets were popular souvenirs among Allied servicemen, especially the 1942 and 1943 diaries because of the representation on the covers of the *Afrikakorps* symbol. It was even common practice for Allied servicemen who had them to continue to use them as diaries. The same type of entries were carried on, in another language and written by former enemies in another army – routine matters of military duties, a record of letters received and letters written, distances covered in a day when on the move, brief comments on battles, any out-of-the-ordinary food eaten on that day, notes about maintenance of vehicles. The blank pages for notes were used for the names and home addresses of comrades or to keep scores in card games. For the ordinary soldiers of the opposing armies the daily existence of desert living and military routines were similar.

As well as these official issue diaries, German troops used a wide variety of small pocket-sized diaries. Many of these were distributed by the various political and para-military organizations that flourished in the Third Reich. They contained no information on Africa, but were well packed with pages of conversion charts for weights and measures, and a mini Guinness-like book of records on statistics for such things as steeple heights for European churches and economic and political indices. From this it can be inferred that the information was intended to satisfy arguments on which city had the largest railway station, or which country ate the most fish. All these unofficial diaries carried coloured illustrated tables showing the rank and insignia used by the multitude of uniformed organizations sanctioned by the Third Reich.

Personal papers

Among the souvenirs brought home from the battle-fields were personal papers that had belonged to members of Rommel's Army. It might seem strange that Allied soldiers would choose such items, but often these papers were the contents of a leather writing case, or a wallet – and it was these pieces which were the souvenirs. Such papers should have been handed to Intelligence staff but, rather than risk losing what was considered a valuable souvenir, some Allied troops kept the folders or wallets along with their contents.

These personal papers included letters from home, postcards, photos, diaries and mementoes of places visited, such as admission tickets and restaurant menus. By the time of the El Alamein battles in the summer and autumn of 1942, quite a number of German troops who had served on the Russian Front were fighting

Rommel stands to the right of the Company Commander, and Hauptmann Bach stands second from right at the rear on the same occasion as illustrated opposite. (ECPA)

A replacement draft en route to Africa, sightseeing on a lava flow outside Naples, July 1941. (Author's collection)

in Africa. From souvenirs collected at El Alamein by Australian and New Zealand troops it is evident that German troops had similar tastes in war souvenirs as their Allied counterparts. From abandoned German positions and vehicles came not only German papers, but also Russian letters, Russian photos and clippings from Russian newspapers which were presumably looted from Russian cities and villages and taken to Africa. These were popular souvenirs among Allied troops in 1942 for their curiosity value, and rarity.

Among the letters and postcards taken as souvenirs from captured German soldiers there are several common themes. One is an expression of sympathy by those at home for the privations endured by the men who had to live in the desert. Evidently the soldiers in their letters home made mention of some of the more unpleasant realities of desert life, and these comments were not deleted by the censors.

Much of the mail posted to Germany from soldiers serving in Africa did not arrive – presumably it went instead to the bottom of the Mediterranean Sea. This failure of a large part of the mail to arrive caused some anxiety among those waiting at home for letters in return. Again and again in letters sent to Africa, there are requests for reassurances that a friendship still exists, or in the case of girl-friends that a loving relationship continues since the last leave spent together. The reporting of the war in North Africa by the German press would not have included the news that a high proportion of the ships carrying supplies (and mail) to and from Africa had been sunk, so those waiting for mail would never have known why it failed to arrive. In a message on a postcard dated 10 February 1943 and addressed to a *Gefreiter* Gerhard Weiss, the point was clearly stated: 'Warm greetings from your girl-friend, Friedl. Why haven't you written to me? Are you cross with me? (signed) Friedl Burge.' Such disappointment was not restricted to the later period in Tunisia either. In a letter written in May 1942 there is the passage, 'you promised to write me a long letter, but I have not heard from you . . . you are still the one I love'.

Because of the rarity of home leave to Germany from Africa, the mention of other members of the family serving in the *Wehrmacht* getting leave must have caused some envy. The arrival home on leave of a family member or friend always provided a good deal of comment in letters and may have been one way of indirectly referring to the apparent failure of the *Afrikakorps* to grant the same to its soldiers. References to leave enjoyed by more fortunate members of the family were usually described in glowing terms of outings and meetings with old friends. Often a postcard or letter to a soldier in Africa from a wife and mother would have a postscript written in a childish hand to an absent father. In these cases the failure of mail to reach Germany must have been very painful, and it would have been impossible for a father to try to explain to a child why his letter hadn't arrived at home. Even if it could have been explained, a censor would not have allowed such a passage to remain in a letter.

German troops were prolific writers of letters, as can be seen by the entries in their diaries – the most common ones have to do with mail sent and received. Many soldiers numbered the letters they sent home, a logical way to keep track of the numbers of missing letters in a correspondence. Parcels were also received – and noted – by the troops: knitted socks, soap, foodstuffs such as cakes and biscuits, and toilet accessories were the most usual.

The diary entries reveal several similar observations about travel from Germany through Italy, or the Balkans and Crete, *en route* to Africa. Often the delays in getting transport to Africa were considerable, and the troops evidently had an enjoyable time doing the things a tourist would do in a foreign country. Whenever a unit was moved, it was normal to leave at 0400 and this was true for Germany as well as Italy or Greece and Crete, according to the number of diaries reporting movement times. One member of the 15th Panzer Division noted in his diary that it took three days to receive his full issue of tropical clothing and equipment while he was at a barracks in Kaiserslautern.

Another comment often seen in diaries is a disappointment at being separated in Africa from the comrades made in the draft sent as replacements for Africa. Usually these groups were put together in Germany and depending on how long they spent in transit — sometimes it was months before they finally reached North Africa — strong friendships were made which were forcibly broken when the individuals were sent to different units. (The German formations were reinforced on the 'trickle' system whereby a unit was sent a continuous stream of replacements in the field, rather than having a unit withdrawn from the line and brought back to strength with a large single intake. This system had the advantage of gradually building up a unit around a permanent core of men with battle experience.)

Surprisingly, some diaries were not written with much thought to security, and it was not difficult to work out to which unit such owners had belonged. The daily routines recorded in the diary entries had a lot to say about the organization of the German Army, and the morale of the average German soldier was evident in his comments about food and military life (it was invariably described in good humour, even when things were not going well).

Mail posted to a member of the German Army in North Africa was addressed showing the soldier's rank and name followed by a *Feldpost* number. This was the only information required for it to be forwarded inside the military postal system. For someone in the *Luftwaffe*, the *Feldpost* number was prefixed by the letter 'L' and included the city of Munich, which was a collecting point for *Luftwaffe* mail destined for Africa. The *Feldpostnummer* for both Army and *Luftwaffe* was an indication of the military postal unit responsible in the field for distribution of mail.

Vehicles of 2nd Battalion, PzArtlRgt33, after receiving their desert camouflage, Baumholder, April 1941. (P. E. Schläfer)

Photos taken to North Africa by the German troops in 1941 show interesting backgrounds which must have been common to much of the German Army in 1941 — service in the RAD (State Labour Service), membership of the Hitler Youth, small villages and tidy valleys, prewar civilian jobs, sporting events, Nazi Party parades, homes and families, sweethearts and friends left behind. Some photos showed battlefield scenes in Poland and France which indicated that some men were veterans of these earlier campaigns and members of the pre-war Army. Paybooks belonging to men who went to Africa also show a large proportion of young junior rank soldiers who had entered the Army after the outbreak of war.

Photos originally taken as souvenirs by Allied servicemen from captured German positions show the routes the Germans took to Africa in 1941 and 1942. The men of the 5th Light Division travelled by train through Italy to Naples and then by ship across the Mediterranean to Tripoli. Their photos feature snow-covered alps in Austria and northern Italy and fuzzy views of Italian railway stations and backyard views of Italian towns and cities. From the pictures it can be seen that the men travelled as far as Libya in their woollen Continental uniforms (it was still cold in Italy at this time in late winter). Photos taken aboard the merchant ships crossing the Mediterranean show many

During the closing stages of the Sollum Battle, tanks of 15 PzDiv. moving towards Halfaya. The dust clouds on the horizon show the fall of British artillery shells. (P. E. Schläfer)

of these ships had German *Kriegsmarine* (Naval) crews. Later in 1941, after Rommel's advance to the Egyptian frontier and the German capture of Yugoslavia and Greece, a common route to North Africa was by rail through the Balkans to Athens (and Crete), and a large number of these troops were flown across to airfields at Derna and Tobruk. The major route, for vehicles and equipment as well as personnel during 1941 and for most of 1942, was by sea to Tripoli, but as this way became more and more unsafe men were increasingly flown into Libya.

* * *

From mid-1941, German troops who arrived in North Africa through Tripoli were issued with a set of standing orders for the time they spent in this rear area well behind the front line. This printed sheet of orders is an interesting statement of German Army attitudes, and is reproduced here translated in full. Former German soldiers who served in Africa have been at pains to point out that such orders were not in force at the front, where military discipline was much more realistic and concerned with fighting preparedness and general well-being of the troops.

German soldiers in Africa

1. The German soldier is a representative of the German People and a fighter for the Greater German Reich in Africa, which is a friendly land. German soldier – behave yourself properly, salute smartly, and keep yourself clean and dressed according to regulations. Avoid excess alcohol!

2. The following are the only permitted uniform combinations:
   a. Long trousers, field tunic, lace-up shoes, field cap, shirt with tie, belt with bayonet or pistol.
   b. Breeches, field tunic, long lace boots, field cap, shirt with tie, belt with bayonet or pistol.
   c. Shorts with long socks, lace-up shoes, field cap, field tunic or shirt with tie and rank insignia, belt with bayonet or pistol.

3. Cameras may be carried, but only with a long suspension strap and must be worn over the left shoulder.

4. For members of the German Armed Forces (officers excepted), only the brothel at No. 4* Via Tassoni in Tripoli is available. The use of other brothels, including those licensed to serve the Italian Armed Forces, is strictly forbidden.

*The brothel at No. 4 Via Tassoni was a large multi-storied building near the waterfront. Photos taken by German soldiers who patronized this establishment show that from the roof-deck one got a good panoramic view of the harbour in Tripoli. The brothel was staffed by Italian women.

Attention is drawn to the penalty provisions of the German Race Acts.

5. It is prohibited to enter restaurants in the native quarter and to consume any drinks there.

6. After 1900 hours it is prohibited for members of the German Armed Forces to enter the native quarter.

7. The Mosques are sacred to the Arabs. It is prohibited to enter them.

8. The consumption of ice-cream, refrigerated drinks, cold milk, unboiled water, uncooked meat, unpeeled fruit and unclean or cold food of any kind is prohibited because of the (risk of) transmission of dysentery and typhus-causing organisms.

9. Do not buy anything from Jews. The non-Jewish shops are clearly marked.

10. The curfew for all members of the German Armed Forces is set at 2200 hours.

The Military Police have been ordered to enforce the observance of these orders, and they are ordered to arrest transgressors in the case of serious violations.

> The Commander of Rear Army Territory
> (signed) *Müller-Gebhard*
> Major General

The point in order number 4 regarding the penalties provided under the 'German Race Acts' refers to the 'Law for the Protection of German Blood and German Honour', promulgated on 15 September 1935 at the Nuremberg 'Reich Party Rally of Freedom', and the relevant section alluded to was that aimed at prohibiting extra-marital intercourse with females of Jewish origin. (Clauses affecting marriage between Germans and citizens of non-German states were not covered by this law in the case of soldiers as this was a German Army matter, not a civil government one.) The matter of patronizing Jewish merchants, and the possibility of sexual intercourse with Jewish females, received mention in the order by Müller-Gebhard because Italy had not enacted any restrictions against her Jewish citizens, and Libya was a territory under sovereign Italian control.

The presence of an openly integrated and free Jewish population in Libya evidently did not receive any attention from the German Army in North Africa, apart from the references in this order written by Müller-Gebhard. This single mention of the consequences of possible commercial or other contact between German troops and Jewish citizens is the only reference known of in German military documents dating from the period of the German presence in Libya. Enterprising Italian and Arab shopkeepers may have advertised their Gentile origins to entice German troops away from Jewish merchants, but photos taken by Italian and German troops of street scenes in Tripoli and Benghazi do not show any sign of such advertising. Tripoli and Benghazi were the only cities in Libya with large commercial districts. The Italian population were not disposed to persecute the Jewish population, though there was a long-standing state of uneasy separation between the Moslem Arabs and the Jews.

The German military presence in the Tripoli area was quite considerable during 1941 and 1942. The port of Tripoli remained the main entry point of heavy supplies right up to the last months of 1942, when Tunisia offered a shorter and safer means of shipping supplies through the deep-water ports of Bizerte and Tunis. Until the evacuation of Tripoli in early 1943 there were always large numbers of rear base support units stationed in and around the city. As well as the supply and transport units stationed in Tripoli, there was a large German Army base in the former Italian barracks known as 'Km 5', where drafts of reinforcements were collected before being sent to front-line units. These barracks, as the name suggests, were situated five kilometres outside Tripoli just off the road heading eastwards towards Cyrenaica.

Graffiti on a wall of a building in Bardia, summer 1941, relates the story of daily RAF visits and the ground orchestral arrangements provided by German Flak and British bombs. (Author's collection)

*   *   *

Much early wartime Allied reporting on the war in North Africa identified the *Afrikakorps* as an élite formation, a body of troops carefully selected, trained and acclimatized for fighting in the North African desert. This was not so, yet this impression created by Allied propaganda survived into many post-war accounts of the North African campaigns.

The small German force that went to Libya in early 1941 was typical of the German Army at that time. After its triumphs in Poland, Scandinavia and France, the German Army was riding on the crest of high morale and quick victories. It was a young force, professional and highly trained, with confidence in the revolutionary mobile tactics which had achieved victory at so little cost in Europe during 1939 and 1940. The same tactics of concentrated armoured thrusts, supported by a team of specialized service branches trained to fight together, were also to win victories in North Africa. This close co-operation between tanks, anti-tank guns, motorized infantry and artillery was not practised by the British Army at this time.

In many ways though the *Afrikakorps* did *become* an élite formation, but this was not a result of any deliberate process of pre-selection. The only policy of selection exercised by the German Army involved a quite cursory medical examination to establish a level of physical fitness suitable for the climatic extremes of the North African desert. The élite character of the *Afrikakorps* evolved later as a result of its successful adaptation to desert conditions, its cohesion and effectiveness as a fighting unit, the thoroughness of its training, the quality of the German soldier, and, most importantly, its leadership. Rommel was always a soldier's soldier, and his charisma, his driving personality and ability to inspire his troops to give their utmost were the most important factors in forging the outstanding fighting character of the *Afrikakorps*.

The 5th Light Division, the first part of what was to become the *Afrikakorps*, started to arrive in Libya on 14 February 1941. It was a diluted Panzer division built around the 5th Panzer Regiment, which had been detached from the 3rd Panzer Division. This Division had been raised before the war in and around Berlin so consequently most of the troops in it were either Berliners or Prussians from Brandenburg and western Silesia.

Medical examination for tropical service

Wartime British propaganda claimed that the men of the *Afrikakorps* were a unique breed of German soldier, specially selected and trained for service in North Africa. These claims were repeated after the war in many histories of the North African campaigns. This is patently untrue, in spite of there being a medical examination given to German troops before they were sent to Africa.

This medical examination was recorded on a standard form, *Wehrmachtärztliches Zeugnis über Tropendienstfähigkeit* (Armed Forces Medical Certificate of Fitness for Tropical Service) and was used for both Army and *Luftwaffe* personnel. It was not a rigorous test and could well have been used to certify fitness for service in Russia, or the Balkans, or for any other theatre of war.

The medical examination as covered by this form tested the following: height and weight, limbs, breathing passages, eyesight, nervous system (speech/ sensory perception/reflexes), lung capacity, heart and gluteal muscles, digestive system, teeth, quinine compatibility (through urine-testing – albumen and sediment rates), bladder and bowel functions, blood (blood count/haemoglobin/blood sedimentation/coagulation reaction).

As the form itself goes, this would have been an adequate medical examination if everything included in the headings had been tested. However, in practice, the testing of specimens was not done and barely one-third of the form was filled in and what *was* done was little more than a normal physical examination – height and weight, pulse and blood pressure, breathing, an inspection of the body externally, eyesight, and reflex tests.

Examples of this form dated in 1941 and 1942 show no difference in the extent and nature of the examination as far as it was recorded on the form.

For the members of the 5th Light Division hurriedly sent to Africa in February 1941, and for the 15th Panzer Division which soon followed them, no special medical testing was done and the only medical preparation carried out was inoculation against cholera and typhus (this was already standard practice as is indicated in the paybook).

Troops posted to Africa after the spring of 1941 were required to pass the Fitness for Tropical Service certificate, but the medical facilities needed to carry out the testing were apparently not always available or were dispensed with in favour of a straight physical test.

Ramcke Brigade paratrooper (see page 46) cleaning his weapon in a sangar made of rocks and sandbags at El Alamein, October 1942. The weapon is a Mauser Kar98k – note the rifle cleaning kit, canvas ammunition bandolier and paratroop helmet on edge of sangar. (Author's collection)

The second division of the *Afrikakorps* to arrive in Libya, starting in mid-April 1941, was the 15th Panzer Division. This Division was based on the 1941 strength with a reduced Panzer component i.e., from two Panzer regiments in 1940 to one in 1941. The Division had been formed in late 1940 by amalgamating the 33rd Infantry Division with the 8th Panzer Regiment. The 33rd Inf. Div. had been raised pre-war and so contained men mainly from west and south-west Germany, while the 8th Panzer Regiment (supplied by the 10th Panzer Division) had been raised in Stuttgart.

These two Panzer divisions (the 5th Light Division became the 21st Panzer Division in October 1941) were to form the tactical formation known as the *Afrikakorps*, though the full title of the Axis Army in North Africa (in 1942) was *Panzerarmee Afrika* and it included all the Italian divisions as well. From July 1941, all German Army troops serving in North Africa for more than two months were entitled to wear the AFRIKAKORPS cufftitle (see page 154).

The third German Division to see service in Africa was what was to be officially designated, in November 1941, the 90th Light Division (*90 leichte Afrika-Division*). This division was actually created in Libya and was first promulgated in August 1941 as *Afrika-Division z.b.V.* (*zur besonderen Verwendung* = for special purposes). It was made up of various non-motorized and unattached units already in Africa, various replacement drafts in Africa or *en route*, and two battalions withdrawn from the Eastern Front. This famous unit was in many ways the most colourful of the German divisions in Africa, drawing its personnel from all over Germany. Many of its number had previously served in the French Foreign Legion.

An artillery gunner captured by 9th Australian Division, El Alamein 1942 – both the man and his cap show wear and fatigue from desert fighting. (Australian War Memorial, Canberra)

The most exotic German formation to serve in North Africa was *Sonderverband 288* (Special Unit 288). In the early summer of 1941 it seemed to the OKW operations planning department that conditions were favourable for some sort of action against the oilfields of the Middle East. Arab sentiment was anti-British over the Palestine problem and Germany was well placed to tap this Arab nationalism because of her anti-Jewish policies. Not only was there a good possibility of exploiting such pro-German Arab figures as Rashid Ali in Iraq, who was willing to accept German help in rising against British control, but Syria too, with its anti-British and strongly pro-Vichy military commander General Henri Dentz, seemed favourably disposed to German infiltration.

On these assumptions planning proceeded to raise a special force which would operate against the oilfields of the Arabian Gulf behind Allied lines, rather like the British Long Range Desert Group, though on a more ambitious scale. Known as *Sonderverband 288*, or simply SV288, this special unit, which was assembled at the Höhenlohe Barracks in Potsdam in late July 1941, consisted of twelve independently structured companies as follows:

- Command staff with one staff company, and one Armoured Scout Car Company, one Reconnaissance section and a Company of Arab-speaking writers and printers (this staff component was equivalent to four companies)
- 1st Company: Specialist troops from *Abwehr Lehr-Regiment* z.b.V.800 (Brandenburgers)
- 2nd Company: *Gebirgsjäger* (from *Wehrkreis VII* – Mittenwald)
- 3rd Company: *Schützen* (motorized infantry – from *Wehrkreis XI* – Braunschweig)
- 4th Company: Machine Gunners (from *Wehrkreis IV* – Dresden)
- 5th Company: *Panzerjäger* (anti-tank, from *Wehrkreis VI* – Münster, with the Assault Gun Section from *Wehrkreis XIII* – Schweinfurt)
- 6th Company: Flak (anti-aircraft, from *Wehrkreis VI* – Münster)
- 7th Company: *Pioniere* (engineers, from *Wehrkreis XI* – Braunschweig)
- *Nachrichten* Company: (Signals, from *Wehrkreis IV* – Dresden)

Among the smaller specialist units under staff control – the staff officers were assigned from *Ersatz Abteilung 8* at Frankfurt an der Oder – was a group of twelve medical personnel, all experts in tropical diseases; a group of Arabists well versed in Arab culture, politics and religion who were attached to the printing unit (their function was to print and distribute posters in Arabic inciting opposition to the British); a group of oilfield engineers and analysts (*Öluntersuchungstrupp*); and a group of linguists. The first company, drafted from one of the crack *Abwehr* instruction units in the Brandenburg Division, were volunteers trained in demolition work and operating behind enemy lines.

In order to gather suitable men for this special unit a dragnet was quickly cast over the entire German Army. Its members as a consequence came from every corner of the Reich, though they tended to be better educated than the average soldier and were considered suited to out-of-the-ordinary operations by the *Abwehr* (Military counter-espionage and Security Service), who designed the unit's make-up.

The officers posted to SV288 were carefully hand-picked. For example, *Hauptmann* Robert Borchardt, who commanded the 5th *Panzerjäger* Company, had been trained in one of the few mechanized units in the *Weimar* (pre-Hitler) 100,000-man army and in 1935 with the rank of *Leutnant* he had been sent to China. He had been attached to Chiang Kai-chek's staff of military advisers specifically to train the first mechanized units of the Chinese Nationalist Army. After returning from China, Borchardt served in Spain collecting information on and evaluating the tactics of the Republican forces. It was this experience abroad – rare in those years – that influenced his selection for SV288. Only days before he was transferred to the special unit Borchardt won the Knights Cross in action near Uman in the Ukraine.

This then was the calibre of officers assigned to *Sonderverband 288*. Borchardt led one of the new (1942) battalions, and later commanded SV288 for a period in Egypt while its Commanding Officer, *Oberst* (Colonel) Menton, was ill.

Among the rank and file soldiers there were many who spoke Arabic – men who had served in the French Foreign Legion, some who had worked in the Middle East in commerce or on the oilfields, or merchant seamen who had a knowledge of Arab countries.

Although SV288 was the size of a regiment the normal organization into battalions was dispensed with and each of its twelve companies was intended to act independently of the others, to be totally self-sufficient for action behind enemy lines. If events called for a larger formation, two or more companies could be combined, depending on the specific action planned. Supply in the field was to have been provided by *Luftwaffe* aircraft operating under cover from Syria. It was also hoped that the Arab population could be called on to help provide food, and in this connection SV288 received visits from the Grand Mufti of Jerusalem – who was being used by the German propaganda machine to promote anti-Semitic and anti-British feeling in the Middle East – while they were in Greece awaiting deployment.

By the time SV288 was ready, in August 1941, events in the Middle East had changed. Rashid Ali's rising in Baghdad had been easily crushed by the British in May 1941, and in July control of Syria had passed to the Free French. Prospects for SV288 – to operate in the

New arrivals in Tunisia, possibly members of the 999th Light Division in the Arab Bazaar in Tunis, April 1943. Two of the men are wearing field caps with soutache, and the third a tunic with straight pocket flaps. (Author's collection)

Arabian peninsula, and to interrupt the flow of oil to Britain – looked decidedly poor. Instead, SV288 was flown across to Tripoli to reinforce the *Afrikakorps*, as by December 1941 Rommel had been forced to retreat to his original starting position at El Agheila.

In Africa it was found that the organization of SV288 into twelve independent companies was not suited to the new conditions it would have to fight under and it was therefore divided into three battalions, or battle groups, like a normal regiment. It was attached to the 90th Light Division in early 1942, and was finally renamed *Panzergrenadier Regiment Afrika* on 31 October

1942. In late February 1943 it was transferred to the 164th Light Division, which reinforced the *Afrikakorps* in the summer of 1942, where it remained until the end in May 1943.

SV288 distinguished itself in action, especially in the bitter fighting at Bir Hacheim against the Free French, in the later battles south of Tobruk in 1942, and as a rearguard for Rommel's long retreat from El Alamein to Tunisia.

The last unit sent to reinforce Rommel's Army in 1941 was Army Artillery Command 104, a force of siege artillery of regiment strength sent out specifically to assist in weakening the Tobruk fortress. The men of this unit were a composite group made up of troops drawn from various depots in Germany.

A Hauptfeldwebel (Regimental Sergeant Major) attached to the Freies Arabien *Legion, Tunisia, early 1943. The sleeve insignia is that worn by members of* Sonderverband 288. *(ECPA)*

No further formations were to arrive until July 1942 when Rommel's advance in the summer of 1942 had reached El Alamein. The first of these to land in Africa was the 164th Light Division which came by air from Crete where it had been garrisoned as 'Fortress Division Crete' (*Festungs-Division Kreta*). This division, which had been raised in late 1939, was based in Leipzig and its personnel were mainly from Saxony.

The second unit sent to reinforce Rommel at El Alamein was the Ramcke Paratroop Brigade, which had earlier been intended for employment in the projected airborne attack against Malta. This Brigade of paratroops, taking its name from its commander, Major-General Bernard Ramcke, began arriving in early August and went into the line as ordinary infantry. These men were an élite body of troops, rigorously selected and trained, and imbued with the spirit of Nationalist Socialist Germany.

After the opening stages of the final El Alamein battle in late October 1942, one further reinforcement was despatched to Rommel in Egypt. But it only began to arrive early in November and did not see action as a complete unit until the fighting in Tunisia in 1943. This unit was *Grenadier Regiment 47 (mot)*, detached from the *22 Luftlande Division*, which had been based in Oldenburg with personnel drawn from Lower Saxony, Oldenburg, Bremen and Hamburg, and had replaced the 164th Division in Crete as a garrison force. It did not appear on the order of battle of *Panzerarmee Afrika* until the end of November 1942, when its third battalion was recorded as being in Tripoli.

Also mentioned in this same order of battle for the first time was *Nebelwerfer Regiment 9*, a unit under *Panzerarmee* command which saw action in Tunisia with its multi-barrelled rocket launchers. The men of this regiment of three *Abteilungen* (battalions) had no regional affiliations with any one area of Germany.

As well as the men of the *Afrikakorps*, there were about 100 women in the nursing service of the German Armed Forces in Africa. About seventy served in the Army Nursing Branch, and thirty held positions in the medical services of the *Luftwaffe*, and all frequently came under fire – with some casualties.

The time of the Alamein battles marks the end of the original *Afrikakorps*, when it faced the British and Commonwealth Forces in Libya and Egypt. Just after the climax of the final El Alamein battle, as Rommel was pulling the still mobile parts of his army westwards towards the Libyan frontier, American and British Armies landed in Morocco and Algeria on 8 November. To provide a blocking force in Tunisia, and to create a

The Opel Admiral of Major General Bayer, Surgeon-General of the Afrikakorps, *with its driver Hans Schilling, Misurata, April 1942. (Hans Schilling)*

front behind Rommel, all available forces that could be scraped together were sent piecemeal to the Tunisian bridgehead during November and December 1942 and early 1943. These largely *ad hoc* formations were supplemented by regular divisions and those that did come under Rommel's command did not do so until much later in 1943. For the remainder of the campaign these forces were known collectively as 5th Panzer Army (originally named *Stab Nehring* and then *XC.Korps*).

The divisional and smaller units which made up this new command were (roughly in order of main arrival in Tunisia):

a) Division von Broich/von Manteuffel – an *ad hoc* collection of German paratroops and Army units which took its divisional title from the name of its commander at the time (e.g. Colonel von Broich, Major General von Manteuffel).

b) 10th Panzer Division – this was one of the original pre-war Panzer divisions which had already seen action in Poland, France and Russia and had supplied the 8th Panzer Regiment for the 15th Panzer Division. It was based around Stuttgart and its personnel were mainly from south-west Germany.

c) 334 Inf. Division – raised in the late autumn of 1942, it started to arrive in Tunisia in December 1942 Although nominally based at Grafenwöhr in northern Bavaria, it contained a cross-section of men drawn from south Germany and included one regiment (*Gebirgsjäger Rgt 756*) of Alpine troops raised around Salzburg

d) Division Hermann Göring – this redoubtable *Luftwaffe*-controlled division provided some of the first troops to arrive in Tunisia, though most of it did not arrive until early 1943. The division was roughly equivalent to the other Army Panzer divisions in Africa at this time. A part of it remained in Italy, and units drawn from other Army formations were used to build it up into a complete operational unit, its members coming from all parts of Germany.

A much publicized Panzer force which began to arrive in Tunisia in November 1942 was the Heavy Tank Battalion 501 with two companies of the new supertank, the PzVI Tiger. Later, part of another similar independent Panzer unit, Heavy Tank Battalion 504, arrived with more of the Tiger tanks.

After the battle, Paul Erich Schläfer asleep on his 10.5cm howitzer. (P. E. Schläfer)

The last substantial unit sent into Tunisia began to arrive during March and early April 1943 from depots in Holland and Belgium. This was the 999th Light Division (*999 leichte Afrika-Division*), made up mainly of rank and file German soldiers who had been court-martialled and had been given a chance to redeem themselves by service in this special division. It was not a penal unit, and the officers and NCOs were drawn from normal training schools and replacement drafts.

These then were the main units of the German Army which fought in Africa from February 1941 to May 1943. One further formation that needs to be mentioned was a small body of French and Arab nationalists. These men, numbering no more than a few thousand, fought alongside the Axis divisions in Tunisia in the last months of the campaign.

The idea of a French Army unit fighting side by side with Germans in North Africa was prompted by the landings in November 1942 of Allied troops on French territories there. Initially there was an enormous response from many Frenchmen volunteering to fight against the Allied Armies invading French territory, but the problem of transporting them from France to Tunisia was too great. By the middle of December the French Mission sent from Vichy to organize the African Phalanx in Tunisia – French and Arab volunteers who supported the Germans – were only able to enlist sympathizers living in Tunisia as Morocco and Algeria were already occupied by the Allies. On 1 January 1943 a recruiting station was opened in Tunis.

The total number of enlisted men was about 330, of whom 100 were Tunisian Arabs. Some came from former military units, now demobilized, while others belonged to various right-wing organizations. The unit was stationed just outside Tunis, at Bordj Cedria. After a short time the Germans decided to transfer the Arabs to another unit composed of Arab volunteers.

The remaining Frenchmen were organized into six platoons under the command of Captain Dupuis and they fought bravely under the 334th Infantry Division, notably at Medjez el Bab. The Phalangists were left to surrender on 7 May, and were given into the 'care' of the Gaullist Free French forces, who controlled Tunisia. Many received long prison sentences and some were executed. The members of the unit had their own distinctive insignia worn on the right pocket: a gold double-edged axe on a dark blue background.

The Arab volunteers – nearly 2,000 – were organized into three nominal battalions. The group was called collectively the Free Arabian Legion (*Freies Arabien*) and saw little fighting, ending up working as labour battalions preparing defensive positions around Tunis in the last weeks of the campaign. The legion was given Arabic-speaking NCOs and officers from the former *Sonderverband 288*, but there was not enough time or equipment to make the unit into a worthwhile fighting force before the end. Harsh French military justice was meted out to these Arab nationalists after the Axis surrender.

In addition to Army units in North Africa, there were many *Luftwaffe* Flak (anti-aircraft) formations which played a prominent role in the fighting. The use of anti-aircraft weapons against ground targets, especially tanks, had already proved successful in Europe. In the African desert they were to prove equally devastating against enemy tanks, right from the beginning of the campaign. Without their contribution, many an action could not have been won.

These *Luftwaffe* Flak units included *Flak Abteilungen* I/33, I/18, I/6, I/43, I/153 and II/25 (Abt./Rgt). The *Abteilungen* were later organized under regimental HQs and the two Flak regiments, 102 and 135, that fought in Libya and Egypt both had distinguished combat records fighting alongside their Army comrades.

Towards the final stages of the campaigns these original Flak formations, which also had to fulfil an anti-aircraft role around ports and army field operations in addition to their ground support tactical employment, were strengthened by many more units. Their organizational control was then vested in the HQ 19th Flak

Division supporting the *Panzerarmee Afrika*, and with HQ 20th Flak Division attached to the forces originally in Tunisia under 5th Panzer Army. The Flak divisions, each with a strength of around 10,000 men (including their own transport, signals and ancillary support units) were under *Luftwaffe* administrative control but tactical direction was exercised by the Army command.

Finally, there was the Italian Army in North Africa. This came out of the campaigns with a very poor fighting reputation. This judgement, written up mainly from the Allied side during the war, survived in a lot of post-war literature and is unfair to the individual Italian soldiers who in many cases fought bravely when given the chance to do so. However, the organization and equipment of the Italian Army was such that all too often Italian troops were not provided with either the means or the opportunity to fight on equal terms with their opponents, and the ordinary rank and file Italian soldier cannot be blamed for this failure.

The Italian Army in Libya before the war was large, well above 350,000 if the Libyan auxiliary units are included. It was superficially a powerful force, but this was true in size only. The strategy adopted by the Italian Supreme Command was essentially a defensive one, with a string of well-defended coastal points around the main towns in Cyrenaica and a number of fortified positions in the desert. This arrangement, especially the desert forts, proved adequate for handling the troublesome desert Senussi tribes, but did not anticipate the style and scope of fighting that occurred when Italy went to war with her British neighbour across the Egyptian frontier. Still, the main concern of the pre-war Italian Army seems to have been to project the image of a strong militaristic state in line with current Fascist ideology which promoted a strong brand of militaristic nationalism.

2nd Battalion, PzArtlRgt33 of 15PzDiv, parading after receiving their tropical uniform, Baumholder, April 1941. (P. E. Schläfer)

The total collapse of this façade in the wake of Wavell's offensives during November–December 1940 and January–February 1941 showed how rotten and archaic the state of the Italian Army was at this time. In the imagination of the British Army and the Allied press it was the Italian soldier who was perceived to be lacking in military skill and fighting spirit. Once this reputation for military ineptitude had gained ground after the crushing defeats from Sidi Barrani to Beda Fomm, it was perpetuated by the British as a propaganda tool. Man for man, the British Tommy was seen to be worth many of the unfortunate Italians. Actions taken by the British, and their Empire allies, to humiliate the Italians on the field of battle served to strengthen this impression of the Italian soldier as an inferior opponent – such as when the Australians in Tobruk sent a large number of captured Italians back to their own lines with the seats of their trousers cut out. Such

actions were also intended to fuel friction between the Italians and their German allies.

That the British believed their own propaganda is illustrated by the reluctance of British tank officers to admit to being decisively beaten by the Italian *Ariete* Armoured Division south of Sidi Rezegh in Operation Crusader, ascribing their battering instead to the German 15th Panzer Division.

Incredible as it may seem for an army intended to fight across the long stretches of the Libyan desert, only a small part of the Italian Army in Africa was motorized, and this illustrates further the defensive thinking of the Italians. But Italy's industrial resources were incapable of providing the range of military transport needed to motorize the units in Africa, and for the duration of the campaigns most of Italy's contribution consisted of unmotorized infantry formations.

The Italian armoured and artillery units were more formidable opponents, and recent books have accorded these units their full due and have acknowledged that they acquitted themselves as equals to their German and Allied counterparts. One reason for the higher performance of these units was the practice of selecting higher-calibre recruits. (Another branch to receive the better-quality recruit was the Engineering service.) This policy, however, worked to the detriment of the infantry

units, who were forced to accept what had been passed over by the more favoured specialized branches.

The equipment available to the Italian infantry and artillery was largely of World War I, or earlier, vintage. The tanks used in the armoured divisions were poorly designed, undergunned, underpowered and lacking strong defensive armourplate. The Italians were not alone in this area, but in spite of these major deficiencies the Italian crews engaged enemy tanks when ordered, even when the outcome was frighteningly predictable and the odds were stacked against them.

If the performance of the ordinary Italian soldier can be defended, it is difficult to justify the behaviour of the career Army officers. As a class, or as a caste, they perpetuated an élitist rank distinction between themselves and the men they commanded – an attitude that had by this time died out in nearly every other modern European army.

Generally speaking Italian officers looked to their own comfort first. This was most in evidence with food rations – the officers took first pick of everything and left the rest for the other ranks. Contrary to popular belief, this practice was not as per regulations but was a custom long accepted in the Italian Army and most officers were more than happy to see it continue. At least on a European battlefield there were always opportunities for the soldiers to scrounge extra food, but this was impossible in the African desert, so the rank and file were totally dependent on army-issue food with occasional supplementary offerings in parcels from home in Italy.

Even British Army officers, themselves inheritors of a strongly entrenched class system both inside and out of the Army, were aghast at the way many Italian Army officers maintained a relatively luxurious existence in the field at the expense of their men who had to accept a correspondingly low level of comfort and sustenance. British officers had their creature comforts well catered for in their clubs set up in the Nile Delta, but they did not transport the trappings of home comfort to the front as did many Italian officers in the early campaigns. To the Germans, who had only the one ration scale for both officers and ordinary ranks, the Italian officers who behaved as if they were a part of some medieval army were seen as selfish and out of touch with the men they were supposed to be leading.

Italian static positions were generally avoided by both German and Allied troops because the Italian trenches and dugouts were more likely to be infested with lice. This was also seen as a poor reflection on the quality of Italian troops, but many of the rank and file Italian

The end – members of InfRgt200 in the 90th Light Division going into captivity, snapped by a NZ Army photographer near Enfidaville, 12 May 1943. (NZ National Archives – Alexander Turnbull Library)

infantry were peasant recruits who had no real understanding of personal hygiene standards necessary for the desert conditions. The usual physical separation of officers and ordinary ranks in the Italian Army meant that there was no close supervision or instruction in these areas, and no ready example for the soldiers to model their habits on.

Unlike the Italian Air Force, which was much more modern in its approach to warfare and to relations between officers and lower ranks that reflected a strong Fascist influence, the Italian Army Officer Corps was strongly royalist in sympathy, and conservative in outlook. The reformist zeal which stemmed from the Fascist state and which influenced the Air Force was effectively blocked in the Army. It is therefore not surprising that the units that had the best fighting records and where morale was highest were those where the dead hand of old-fashioned conservatism was weakest. The infantry division that consistently performed with the highest distinction was the Young Fascist Motorized Division – which German historians have rated as being as good as any German division that fought in North Africa. Another excellent division was the Paratroop Division *Folgore*.

With the exception of what was transported by air by the *Luftwaffe*, it was primarily the responsibility of the Italians to supply Rommel in North Africa. Whenever supplies were critically low, and it seemed to Rommel that the British must be receiving information about the supply convoys, he blamed Italian treachery. This was unfair and wrong. The British did have full knowledge of the Italian convoys but this intelligence came from ULTRA, not from any Italian traitors.

Until he retreated into Tunisia, Rommel was always nominally under some level of Italian command and he was unable to interfere with the large volume of supplies sent to Libya to nourish not only the Italian formations but also the Italian colonial administration. They, and the remaining Italian civilian population, had to receive their share of the scarce shipping space too and this annoyed Rommel who accused the Italians of giving preference to their own needs above the needs of the front-line troops. But he was ignoring the realities of his situation – he was based in Libya on Italian territory defending Italian interests; indeed, until late 1942, his Army was largely Italian, there being two Italians for every German in the front line.

The Italian troops who fought under Rommel rightly regarded him as 'their' commander, just as the German troops did, and his mystique and charisma were felt throughout the Italian Army in a way that no Italian

Oberst *Menton, commander of* Sonderverband 288 *(on right), with* Hauptmann *Borchardt (one of the SV288 battalion commanders) in May 1942 shortly before the opening of the battle for the Gazala Line. (Robert Borchardt)*

commander was able to match. Rommel certainly had a great deal of sympathy for the Italian soldiers under his command, and his strongest criticism was always directed at the Italian officers when he felt that things had gone wrong.

Not all Italian equipment was sub-standard or obsolete. Australian troops respected and admired the Italian Breda machine gun, which, when captured, they used

Hauptmann *Robert Borchardt, battalion commander in* Sonderverband 288 *(standing at right), with an officer friend from 15PzDiv at El Alamein in July 1942. (Robert Borchardt)*

and attention on and off the battlefield.

During the period that the Germans and Italians fought together in Africa, many friendships developed between men of the two armies, though this happened more between officers than among the lower ranks because of the language difficulties. Contact at the personal level was not always easy and combat units were not mixed due to problems in communications as well as logistical and other organizational incompatibilities.

However, in order to stiffen some Italian units at Tobruk in 1941, and at El Alamein in 1942, Rommel used German troops in company or even battalion strength to reinforce them, but these were the only occasions when German and Italian soldiers fought in close proximity for any length of time.

That the German troops did make an effort to communicate with their Italian allies is shown by the large number of Italian language classes attended by German soldiers, and by the number of Italian-German grammar and phrase books found among the possessions of German POWs.

During almost three years' fighting in North Africa, the Italians lost a great many men killed, missing or prisoners. Most of these men fought and died bravely, and that they fought with so many antiquated and inferior weapons only adds to their stature as soldiers, and should not detract from it.

* * *

There was a great deal of cross-fertilization among all the German units that served in Africa. Regiments, battalions and companies were transferred from division to division to distribute evenly the available forces. In the course of every campaign, as a response to a particular situation, 'Battle Groups' were formed as independent fighting units. These Battle Groups could include units taken from different divisions and incorporated a cross-section of all arms of service found in a full division. They were named after their commanding officer and existed for as long as there was a need for them to operate as a tactical formation. The ordinary German soldier therefore identified with the *Afrikakorps* as a whole not just with his division or regiment.

A typical member of the *Afrikakorps* was Hans Schilling, who today lives with his New Zealand wife in Vancouver, British Columbia.

'When war broke out I was working in my home town Sömmerda in Thuringia making machine tools for the mass-production of bomb sights and so on. All my friends who were eighteen got into the Army and I was furious about this. I always excelled at sports and

themselves. Italian motor transport was generally good too – what there was of it. German troops made use of some items from Italian stores like shirts, tunics and boots. The distinctive Italian tropical tunic known as the *Sahariana*, with its wide scalloped breast pocket flaps, was used by German officers with the usual addition of a metal eagle and swastika badge pinned over the right top pocket. The Italian steel helmet was a modern design and served its purpose as well as its German equivalent.

As mentioned later, Italian medical units were professionally equal to the medical services in either the German or Allied armies. Italian field medical and surgical personnel treated many thousands of German and Allied soldiers, who owed their lives to this care thought I should be the first to get called up, but it didn't happen until early 1941. We did not live very far from Erfurt and I went into the 71st Infantry Regiment. My father had written to his old Colonel of this regiment and so that is why I went into this unit.

'At this stage I had no idea where I would end up. Poland and France were behind us and there was already some talk about going into Russia. We had five months' basic training and at the end of this period I had my final leave. The company commander had read out a notice calling for volunteers to go to North Africa and I had put myself forward. About twenty-five of us from my company decided "why not?" We knew nothing about North Africa, or the war there, but Africa sounded more interesting than anything else.

'We had heard of Rommel, but only in radio announcements. We did not get much time to read or to go to the movies during basic training and so I knew nothing about the *Afrikakorps* then. For me the primary interest was Africa. At this time I was what was known as an "officer aspirant". I had a private's rank but had been selected to attend an officer training course in Berlin. By deciding to go to Africa I lost the opportunity to become an officer in 1941.

'When I went home on that last leave in early June 1941 I told my family that my application to go to Africa had been accepted. My mother cried and went into the kitchen while my father, who was an old professional soldier from the First World War, just shook his head. He said, "Son, in the army you never volunteer for anything – you just go where you are told." Later, before I left, he said that I might have done the right thing. He was right; my old regiment was wiped out at Stalingrad the following year. Before leaving my mother warned me about eating too many dates. After I finished my leave I went back to the barracks in Erfurt and then started my journey to Africa. This was the last time I was to see my home for eight years.

'First we went to a barracks near Saarbrücken where we were issued with our tropical uniform. They measured us very carefully to see that everything fitted perfectly. Compared to the normal outfitting of uniform this was a different kettle of fish. Everything had to be just so; boots not too big or small, jacket and trousers fitting well – or you were given others to try on. There was no attempt made to brief us on what it was like in Africa – just something stuck on a notice board we were supposed to read about regulations for wearing the tropical uniform. We were told nothing about medical and hygiene problems, or about the climate.

Men of an Italian armoured unit sheltering from the sun under a tarpaulin canopy in the Alamein line in mid-1942. (Author's collection)

The High Command blueprint

Before arriving in North Africa, German troops usually had a highly romantic notion of where they were going, with images of oases and palm trees in abundance, exotic camel trails and mysterious sights. However, it was not only the ordinary German soldier who had this fantasy picture of North Africa, with oases and waterholes the prizes being fought over between the opposing Armies. In reality it was the vital coastal strip (with its one road) that was to be the bitterly contested feature, and oases had very little to do with supplying an army fighting in the desert.

A book published by the Army General Staff in Berlin in late 1940 seemed to encourage these fantasies. Titled *Militärgeographische Beschreibung von Nordost-Afrika* (Military-geographical Description of North-east Africa) it included a chapter which listed every known oasis with accompanying maps, and every known water well, with longitude and latitude and remarks on the quality of water, size and depth of the well.

Judging by this long chapter it is evident that the German Army was expected to be ranging out over the desert and replenishing its water from these wells. The many pages of very detailed topographical maps of the oases, with accompanying notes, reinforce the view that in 1940 at least the German General Staff shared the romantic ideas of its ordinary soldiers. The 140-page section of text is an academic exercise in language and treatment, and presumably the book was written in large part by archaeologists and others with an academic interest in North Africa.

Cover of the thick volume 'Military-geographical Description of North-east Africa', issued to German officers in 1941. (Author's collection)

Apart from the sections devoted to oases and waterholes, the book contains views on the demography, economy, ethnic and religious background of the area. There is a supplement of 140 pages of photos of everything from camels, Egyptian farming methods, Bedouin camps, a view from the top of the Cheops pyramid, featureless vistas of sand, desert forts, idyllic oasis scenes, leaving the impression similar to looking into someone's souvenir photograph album of a holiday spent in Libya and Egypt.

This then was the official German reference book on North Africa which was given to ranking officers in 1941 as they left Germany for the great unknown adventure in the desert. No acknowledgement is made in the book to any Italian source. However, it may be presumed that at least some Italian military sources were consulted for the parts of the book dealing with Libya. If they were, it says little for the realism displayed by the Italian Army about how a war should be fought in the desert.

'From Saarbrücken we went to another barracks at Grafenwöhr in Bavaria where drafts going to Africa were being collected. We only spent one or two days there before travelling by train down through Yugoslavia to Greece where we were housed in a big camp outside the harbour in Athens.

'The war in Russia had started by this time and we were just left sitting in Greece for months. There were a lot of us in transit waiting to get across to Libya. In the end it was early December 1941 when I flew across in a Ju52 via Crete to an airfield outside Tripoli.

'I had done my basic training in the infantry and so I expected we would all be sent to an infantry unit. But we were sent off to all sorts of units, and I ended up by going into the Service Corps 4B. which is medical staff. I had no idea at all of what was going on, and I was surprised to find myself attached to *Afrikakorps* Headquarters as the driver for Major-General Bayer, the Surgeon-General of the *Afrikakorps*. And this is where I found out what it was like to serve in Africa....

'It amazed me to see how people were walking around out of uniform and I thought they would not get away with that back in Germany. Everyone in Africa seemed

All troops qualified to drive a vehicle carried this licence, a simple folded single sheet in oilcloth giving name, rank, unit, age and birthplace, type of vehicle licensed to drive, and size limits. These licenses usually carried a photo of the holder. Illustrated is the cover of a military driver's licence belonging to a member of 21PzRgt5 in PzDiv. The licence was issued while he was serving in a replacement unit in Germany, before being posted to Africa. (Author's collection)

to have a different uniform, and they got away with it. There were a lot of fellows who had tried to make their uniforms look older and had bleached them to make them white. White field caps were the fashion and so I bleached mine until it was bone-white. I put lots of soap into it and let it dry out in the sun. It turned out though that this was a mistake because it got filthy very quickly and I had to clean it more often. The bleaching took away what we called the factory 'bullet proofing' in the material, and when this was lost there was no protection against dirt getting into the cloth.

'All that we arrived in Africa with was our tropical uniform and personal kit. Everything else was issued to us there. While I was the driver for Major-General Bayer I only had a rifle, a Kar98K, but I did not see any action during this period. One day though in the spring of 1942 there was a panic on somewhere, an attack was in progress and we had to go through a place manned by the *Feldgendarmerie* (Military Field Police). A great long line of trucks had pulled up and the General told me to drive on. So I pulled out of the line of traffic and took the Opel Admiral up to the front. A *Feldgendarme* ran out to me waving his little round indicator, yelling at me to stop, but I drove on and this man jumped on to the running board and held his pistol at my head. Heaven knows what he called me, but it was bad. The General then stood up in the back seat so the man could see his rank badges and he really dressed this man down. He was only a *Hauptfeldwebel* (senior NCO) and the General really let him have it: "Look up front, can't you see the sign on my car, look at me – if I tell my man to drive on, he drives on ..."

'But as far as discipline went, we were glad Rommel was very strict. It was the only way.

'Food was always a problem in the desert, and it was the same for everyone. I spent a lot of time with the *Afrikakorps* HQ and the officers ate the same food as we did. The generals might get an odd orange or banana but that was it. After Tobruk was captured in 1942 we all had a lot of bully beef. It was a pleasant change from the terrible old Italian tinned meat, called "AM", but we got sick of the bully beef too after a while. The other regular issue of Italian food we had was a type of big square thick biscuit. We called them "cement plates", and I felt sorry for the fellows who did not have good teeth because you had to grind it. The only vegetables we ever saw were the dehydrated stuff, we would throw them into boiling water and see them grow. I was always grateful for the German black bread *Dauerbrot* because it was good. The alternative was to eat Italian hard tack.

AM

The much-disliked tins of 'AM' even figured in a short story which had wide circulation among German troops in North Africa. A copy of this was found on the body of a German driver, two creased sheets of closely typed paper tucked inside his paybook. It was well worn around the edges and had been handled many times. Called 'Entry of the DAK into Berlin', it is not only a good example of soldierly humour but also a rare insight into the Germans' view of what post-war Europe would be like after a German victory.

'In United Europe there reigns a profound peace. All the barracks have been converted into youth hostels. Soldiers' boots crunch no more along the roads. The troops have all returned, even from Alaska and Tierra del Fuego. After unstinting activity our Führer, grizzled by the construction of his life's work but yet retaining his old vigour, and his esteemed *Reichsmarshall* Göring are enjoying their well-earned twilight years. Now they have the time to observe, from the window of the Reich Chancellery, their industrious and peaceful people. Suddenly a long procession turns the corner of the street, Unter den Linden. Men with long beards, humming songs from long ago, are enclosed by the respectfully distant crowd. In outward appearance they in no way resemble a European, or a citizen of one of the associated states. Bent and twisted, not only by the burden of the objects hanging from them, they push along before them all sorts of carts and ancient English scout cars loaded up with *Alter Mann* preserved meat. Their heads are covered with large cloths or by a tattered thing reminiscent of an old tropical sun helmet, while their bodies are wrapped in old sacks or coats of indiscernible colour. The Berliners, clothed in light white summer dress, begin to perspire profusely at this sight. Out of this strange procession there steps a man, probably the leader, who with a trembling hand pulls his coat tighter around his decrepit figure and turns to question the gaping crowd. Of the numerous incessantly recurring guttural noises, only the word 'track' is intelligible. A cheeky Berlin lad cannot restrain himself from asking, in Berlin dialect, 'What on earth is that?' The old man recoils in shock. Slowly, as if searching his memory for comprehension of the remarks thrown at him, he drops his lower jaw and from the toothless mouth can be heard *'Nikese kapire'*. A Berliner standing nearby lights a cigarette from a full 25 pack and a spark flashes in the old man's features. From his still gaping mouth issues the question, *'Nikese fumare?'*, as his claw-like fingers, with their bent nails, reach into the packet. Retreating in horror, the Berliner drops the packet out of sheer fright. Murmuring something like 'Gracia', the old man hungrily scoops up the cigarettes, a process in which even his naked and seemingly adept feet participate. Now the Berliners notice the other men gather up the cigarette butts lying about them and bury them in their utterly bottomless pockets. Nervously the ragtag figures shrink back from the cars roaring past them. While some of the fellows, using flint-stone and palm fibres, set alight the quickly distributed cigarette butts, the bulk of the procession reaches the Reich Chancellery. The Führer, who had witnessed this scene, does not know what to make of this pageant and turns to Hermann. 'On their shoulder straps, and on other parts of their uniforms they are wearing bits and pieces of the insignia of our glorious old army of 1939–45,' he says. 'But I cannot make out these cloths, sacks, coloured neckerchiefs and knives.' With his staff of interpreters Hermann goes down and speaks to a man in the procession. In response to the question, posed in all languages, 'Who are you and where do you come from?', only the Italian and Arabic translations appear to engender a spark of comprehension in the features of the person addressed. Again, however, the answer is only a *'Nikese kapire'*. A young girl seizes the old man's not very clean hand in order to have a closer look at a ring. At the touch of the soft feminine hand, the old man recoils in horror, as if he had come into contact with fire. Observing this, a Gestapo officer discovers on the ring, beside a palm tree and a swastika, the initials DAK. Now Hermann begins to see the light – *Deutsches Afrikakorps*. 'In the second year of the war we did send such an expedition to Africa,' he says. 'Could we have forgotten to bring the troops back? That is quite possible, as no leave transports from there reminded us of their existence.' All at once the ranks of the procession are filled with a murmur, 'Leave, Leave'. Yet belief in it seems to be completely shattered. At least this is the impression given by the gestures of resignation and the words *'Nikese niente mafish'*. Unfortunately the home address of the returnees could no longer be ascertained as their relatives had all long since died. On the evening of this day the following communiqué was issued by the Reich Chancellery:

'To the United Associated States of Europe and the German colonies of North and Equatorial Africa, and to the border states under national autonomy:

The glorious German *Afrikakorps* returned to the Reich capital this afternoon after an extended route march via Cairo, Jerusalem, Baghdad, Tiflis, Moscow and Warsaw. After years of heavy fighting, extreme deprivation and bitterly disappointing absence of leave, the *Afrikakorps* animated by an unshakeable will to victory, found its way home. On the occasion of the return of the DAK all

The staple and notorious meat diet – a can of Italian sausage meat with the exciting initials 'AM' stamped on to the top of the can, here being eaten by an NCO in one of the first detachments of the 5th Light Division to arrive in Tripoli in February 1941. (Author's collection)

Reich buildings will fly their flags for seven days.'

The men were given temporary quarters in the best hotels of the Unter den Linden. But as they were no longer accustomed to that sort of thing, they made absolutely no use of these facilities. Instead, and in very quick time, a section of the men dug anti-shellfire pits in the asphalt roadway and erected tent tarpaulins over them, while others of anxious mien distributed goods and chattels, among the latter being reccognizable some straw mats, herrings, spades, old petrol canisters, empty bottles and cans, empty sacks, erstwhile aeroplane engine cowls, old and defunct primus cookers minus their nozzles. Soon afterwards, at an open fireplace, the ancients prepared their meal, consisting of the contents of small cans indented with the initials A.M. On completion of the meal the men, each equipped with a spade and for a brief interval only, vanished one by one into nearby parks and gardens. To this day the Berliners have not comprehended the purpose of these excavatory excursions. For Berlin this situation could not be tolerated indefinitely. The bearded warriors, together with their traps and things, were sent into the scrub (*Schorfheide*) where the *Reichmarshall* allotted a settlement to the ancients now so estranged from the European way of life. By virtue of their advanced years, the old men proved incapable of re-learning the German language. Later, when all the Italian war surplus supplies of A.M. had been used up, the ancients died out because they could not be accustomed to other foodstuffs.'

A German interpreter (Sonderführer Dolmetscher) *stands arm in arm with an Italian lieutenant at El Alamein in the summer of 1942. A posed official photo but one that expresses the comradeship felt by many Germans and Italians for each other when there was a chance to develop a personal relationship.* (ECPA)

'Anything other than the Italian "AM" or corned beef was like paradise, although at first when we tasted corned beef we thought it was the ultimate in eating. And it was amazing the variety of meals you could make up with it. But the tops was the couple of occasions we had an issue of *Bierwurst*, or ham, and beer. Once we captured some onions and for days we had nothing but onions. We were issued with Italian olive oil but it was terrible stuff to try to put on bread, terrible, terrible.

'After the capture of Tobruk in 1942 we had our best time for food. There was tinned meat and fruit stacked up to the ceiling. People snapped them up and it was soon all gone, tanks and trucks were well packed up.

'Water was always the scarce commodity, and everyone guarded his water carefully to make sure there was no spillage. At the front we tried to carry two water canteens, and we always hoped that after that was gone there would be more. When we were in Egypt I can remember trucks going back as far as Derna – that's 500 kilometres – to pick up water. And once while I was driver for the General there was an uproar at some water filling station. People were running around yelling "the British are here", but it turned out to be only one truck. We went over and saw two British soldiers being pulled out of the truck, which was a British truck with a *Balkenkreuz* (German cross) painted on its side. This was common enough – we used more British trucks than German – but these were Tommies who had joined our line of trucks getting water rations. When they were asked what unit they belonged to they could not give a satisfactory answer and so we caught them. This was way behind the front line – these two Tommies just drove in out of the desert. It always used to amaze us how the British could do this, how they managed to live in the desert, but they had better training for this and they had supplies of food and water and petrol buried in the sand which we had no idea existed.

'As for equipment – it amazes me now when I look at photos and I wonder how the dickens we carried all that stuff around. I remember the most important things we kept and the rest we left behind whenever we had to move. We just could not carry all the stuff we were issued with. The most important thing was always to keep your rifle and ammunition. It was a court martial offence to lose these. And the other pieces you tried to hang on to were your messkit, your cap and woollen overcoat (the nights were cold in the desert) and a bit of spare underwear. Everything else was excess. The first stuff we used to get rid of were things like the mosquito netting and the gas mask. Some men used to keep the gas mask canister, it was useful for filling up with ammunition or any spare food you had. The *Zeltbahn* (canvas shelter quarter) was not much use either – the overcoat was a far more useful item, you would be surprised what you could do with an Army overcoat to give protection and comfort. A shovel was a handy thing to hang on to, too – in basic training in Germany I used a rigid type but in Africa I was issued with a little folding one.

'The uniform we were pretty happy with, except the high lace-up leather and canvas boots. I cut the tops off mine down to the level of ankle boots. It was too much bother wearing them with those long high laces. We wore a lot of bits of English uniform that had been

A typical Italian settler's house in the arable coastal area of Libya near Misurata. (Author's collection)

captured. Our shirts used to disintegrate with so much wear and washing so I used several British shirts. We could not afford to be fussy or formal about dress and we had to make the best of what could be found. I was lucky enough to get a pair of British boots with rubber soles, desert boots, and I wore these all the time. Those were sought after and if you found a pair you put them on quickly.

'When things became really drastic at the front, after we had reached El Alamein, I decided I had done enough sitting around at HQ, or driving around. I wanted to make myself useful so one day when we were driving up to Tobruk I asked my General if he could get anyone else to be his driver. He was Bavarian and came from Munich and he said to me in his Bavarian dialect: "What – do you want to go to the front to do some shooting?" But he understood and I got my papers which posted me to a front-line unit. I had to make my own way as best I could, asking directions and getting lifts as I went along. I was sent to join the 90th Light Division. I went into Infantry Regiment 200, commanded by Major Briel.

'When I arrived at my new unit, 1st Company in Infantry Regiment 200, the men took me under their wing and looked after me. When I heard the first artillery shells come over I dived for the nearest hole and covered myself but the other fellows just went on eating and smiled a bit. Later we had quite a laugh.

'There were quite a few former French Foreign Legion members in my new company, and one oldish fellow made a strong impression on me, Otto Kindereith. He came from Hamburg. He looked old but he really was not all that old, he was just skin and bones, leather faced. He was the one who always replied to our

Hans Schilling in Athens, August 1941 (note the modified French Army tropical shirt with button-down collar that he is wearing). (Hans Schilling)

Hauptmann (Captain) with "*Oui, mon Capitaine.*" He always did it and in the end the *Hauptmann* had to accept it. Still Kindereith used to spend a lot of time serving punishment. I can still remember the Captain saying, "Sergeant, teach this man how to speak properly – I've told you a hundred times."

'"*Oui, mon Capitaine,*" was Otto's stock reply.

'I watched an attack go in one day during the El Alamein battle, and Kindereith was the one in an attack. The Captain got out of the trench first and everyone followed him but he was shot as soon as he started running. There was nothing we could do where we were but Otto Kindereith was closer and he just walked out with an MG 34 (machine gun), firing it over his arm. Everyone gave him all the cover they could while he stooped down and picked up the Captain and brought him back to the trench. In our Company it was Otto Kindereith who always told the stories of other days and other battles.

'Supplies were our main problem. Before we left Alamein, during the battle, after the retreat, we kept waiting for supplies to get through. The British had our lifeline throttled. We used to wonder how the British had so many submarines and planes to sink our ships. We especially needed petrol – there was constant rationing and any unauthorized use of a vehicle was heavily punished. El Alamein was a hell, but we managed to hold together. Rommel got us out and even though we knew the Americans and British were behind

us now we still hoped that one day our ships would get through with supplies and reinforcements.

'On the way back, near the Egyptian border, we found a cache of petrol through a simple accident. One of our men had gone for a walk with a shovel and when he dug his hole he found these cans. It was a British petrol dump and everyone worked all night to dig it up. But these were only drops in the bucket. We kept losing our equipment, leaving our vehicles behind – setting fire to them or shooting the tyres out. From this time we wondered just how far back we would have to go. We knew we could still lick the other side, but not until someone turned the tap on for us. We were told they were preparing the Mareth Line for us already. But we went on and on, through Tripoli for the last time, and there was nothing at the Mareth Line inside Tunisia, nothing behind it. We heard only scraps of what was happening on the other side of Tunisia with the 5th Panzer Army, and now there were rumours we would be taken back to Italy.

'When I got to Tunisia we fought close to the Italians for the first time. One night we heard a great uproar in the line beside us, it was Italian soldiers. They were going to make their night-time meal from a couple of goats they had procured from somewhere. The goats got loose and the noise we heard was the sound of all the Italian soldiers chasing after them. In the end they were caught and a great cheer rose up. The goats were butchered and this was their meal. We Germans watched a few Italian officers and NCOs looking on and not helping – they had already eaten. Good food they kept for themselves. I do not think anyone could blame the Italian soldiers for their behaviour. We Germans did not regard them as disciplined soldiers, but they were given very little and their officers looked after themselves first.

'Near the very end I was told that I would be recalled to Germany to attend an officer training school, as soon as things had settled again and the Ju52s could get through. However, a week later, this was at Enfidaville in the last month, our only officer, the Company Commander, told me he had a message from HQ. I had no idea what this was about. He had only arrived recently from Germany, sent over to us from the 5th Panzer Army. This *Oberleutnant* (First Lieutenant) stood there in his spick and span new uniform and gave me a piece of paper saying I was now an officer, a *Leutnant*. He apologized that he could not get me a new officer's cap or a new tunic with officer insignia. So I kept wearing my old NCO rank on my tunic, but everyone in the company was told that I was now a *Leutnant*.

Letters from home – 15PzDiv, summer 1941. (Author's collection)

Wartime officer promotion

As a result of casualties that depleted the ranks of officers and NCOs, the war created conditions for promotion for those who had the aptitude or ambition. In extreme conditions an NCO could be promoted in the field to officer rank, but the usual procedure was for someone with NCO rank to be given the rank of 'officer aspirant'. Then, after extra time for evaluation as officer material, the candidate would be sent to an officer training school in Germany.

Such an evaluation was made on 26 September 1942 on Feldwebel Rudolf Nolte, who was a member of Infantry Regiment 155 in the 90th Light Division. At this time his aspirant designation was *Kriegsoffizier Bewerber* (War Officer Applicant). The following are the comments made by a captain in his battalion acting as an examiner. The remarks, and the headings on the standard Army form for this type of assessment, say something not only about Rudolf Nolte, but also about the criteria used by the Army in selecting officer candidates. The part of the form containing the comments and the headings under which they were made are quoted in full:

1. **General Assessment of Character and Personality**:
   Medium height and normal appearance, open and impeccable character, reliable, somewhat reserved in manner, positive attitudes but still needs guidance and leadership.

2. **Service Aptitude**:
   a) *Performance in Command and Voice in Command*:
      Sure and versatile in himself when in front of a unit. Good voice of command.
   b) *Achievements and Bearing as Leader*:

Vigorous and full of élan as a leader. He acts without regard for himself, and holds his men strongly in hand and gives orders clearly.
   c) *Service Expertise (Also Weapons Knowledge)*:
      In tactics – sufficient knowledge and performance. In combat – and in self-instruction – he has the required education. He has a good familiarity with service regulations and with weaponry.
   d) *Mental Ability and Physical Capabilities*:
      Just average mental ability. His performance in this area is quite acceptable though because of his great enthusiasm. He is realistic in his thinking and reliable in his work. Physically he performs well.
   e) *Personal Conduct*:
      Very good.

3. **Behaviour Apart from Daily Routine**:
   Behaviour towards his superiors is impeccable. He is popular among the circle of his comrades. His social manners are just sufficient.

4. **Concluding Assessment**:
   Suitability:
   a) *For officer:* Recommended for War Officer
      To which employment: Infantry Platoon Leader
   b) *Appointment to Officer Aspirant:* 1.9.42
   Suitability for placement on the permanent officer list: NO.

   signed: Kügendorfer
   Captain, and Assessor.

Many NCOs were promoted to officer rank, though one common handicap among such men was their level of education. Men drafted straight into Officer School after their basic training, were required to have as a minimum edu-

cational requirement the equivalent of University Matriculation. An officer was expected to be familiar with the great number of Army regulations, and to be able to read easily and disseminate regulations as well as carry on the daily 'paper war' of reports and recording. In Rudolf Nolte's case his enthusiasm was considered to balance any lack of mental abilities. However, in the important last entry, he is thought to be fit only for the role of 'War Officer'. Under this classification he would not have been able to advance beyond the rank of captain, and he would not have been eligible to continue as an officer in a postwar peacetime army.

As a result of this assessment, Rudolf Nolte would have been sent to the Officer Training School at Döberitz near Berlin for a course of training which would have taken about six months.

Officer Aspirants, with NCO rank, wore two loops of braid (tresse) around their shoulder straps. Private ranks could also be elevated to this status, but it was more common for the step to be taken from an NCO rank. (There was also an 'NCO Aspirant' status, and this was indicated by a single loop of braid around a private's shoulder straps.)

The status of Officer Aspirant, indicated by the double loops of rank braid worn on the shoulder straps was used only in connection with the elevation to 'War Officer' and all candidates for a commission – unlike those in the British Army where suitable applicants went straight into Officer Cadet Schools – had to serve in the ranks before going on to officer training school. So every German officer, regardless of the path he took to becoming an officer, knew what it was like to be the lowest rank in the Army before being commissioned. Not only did German officers share the same rations as their men, they also shared a common experience of going into the Army at the bottom rung.

Men of the 5th Light Division in a typical camp constructed of tent sections south of Tobruk in the summer of 1941. (Author's collection)

'In these last weeks we fought against the French as well as the British. We were careful and cautious fighting the French – there were no holds barred with the French. They were African French, Senegalese, with French officers.

'At this time we held a terrific position, near Enfidaville, a perfect defending line and very secure. There was a long gradual slope in front of us and an abrupt steep fall behind us, about sixty or eighty metres. We were dug in just behind the top of this ridge, out of sight of the enemy in front of us. The French attacked us twice, coming up the slope screaming with their officers behind urging them on. We cut them down.

'The last attack was put in by the British. There was a fantastic artillery bombardment this time to soften us up. They didn't appreciate the situation we were in – the shells whistled five or ten metres over our heads and exploded harmlessly down below us, so nothing happened to us. We could sit there with our backs against the top of the ridge and throw stick grenades over, and they just rolled down.

'We were on the back side out of view and safe from the British artillery. Then, when we looked over the top, we let them have it with everything, machine guns, machine pistols, carbines, grenades. It lasted for about half an hour and then it all died away. Voices went up from our chaps:

' "Anybody break through?"

' "No!"

' "All clear this side!"

' "Good, keep your eyes open!"

'The other sounds we could hear were some cries of help from the British wounded lying out on the slope. When the sun came up we saw a white flag and ambulances among a group of men at the bottom of the hill. We saw the British needed help and our white flag went up too and we could see people walking out of the trenches. British came up, and we walked down the hill.

'We helped as much as we could, helped them locate the bodies, tried to find any still alive, carry them down. A British major walked over to us and threw a snappy salute. He asked if anyone spoke English and when I said I had school English he pointed to his watch and indicated that at 0900 the flags would come down. The British gave us chocolates and sweets. In return we gave a few cigarettes. We had nothing else.

'We walked back and at 0900 the flags were pulled down and the war was on again. I suddenly thought for the first time how ridiculous it all was. But it did not hit all that deeply because we were so entrenched in what we were doing.

'We were still on these hills when the fighting stopped, on 12 May. We saw the British coming up, and further over the Italians were running out with big embraces. The war was over for us. We smashed our weapons, and threw them away except that I kept a PO8 (9mm semi-automatic pistol). I had had it since the beginning and I kept it for a while just in case, so as not to let my men down.

'It was a strange thing walking up to someone you had been shooting at a few minutes before. Some were trying to speak German; I was trying to speak English.

'"Do you speak English?"

'"Just a little."

'"You are good. You are the 90th Light. You will go to England."

'They gave us food saying we must have something to eat. The white flags were up and we just followed the line down the hill. There was nobody asking for our guns, but one British soldier wanted the AFRIKAKORPS sleeve band on my tunic. One British officer told us that the further back we went from the front line the more "base wallahs" we would find, people who thought they had won the war but had probably never heard a shot fired in anger. And that is what we found when we went into the POW cages. I still had no officer insignia, so I was not separated from my men. We stayed together, and in the first POW camp we still had a closeness, everybody pulled together. But later we were all split up and mixed up with the men from the 5th Panzer Army.

'We saw our first American soldiers, and they were not what we thought soldiers should look like. When we had the choice to go to America or England I decided to go to America. The English kept asking for all the old *Afrikakorps* division men to go to England – 90th Light, 164th Light, 21st Panzer, 15th Panzer. But I was young and on impulse I decided to go with the Americans. There were still five of us who managed to stick together, and we all decided to go to America. We had survived, and we had grown up through everything that had happened.'

* * *

Another typical member of the *Afrikakorps* was Paul Erich Schläfer. He too came from Sömmerda in Thuringia and was a classmate of Hans Schilling, but the two friends lost contact in the Army and neither was aware the other was also in Africa. Today Paul Erich Schläfer lives in West Berlin.

'I volunteered to join the Army when I was eighteen

Burying a cache of petrol canisters ensured an emergency supply behind the front line. (Author's collection)

and it was a privilege given to volunteers to select their special unit. I wished to join the unit my brother was in, AR69 (Artillery Regiment 69, *bespannt* – drawn by horses). Later my brother, *Oberleutnant* Valentin Schläfer, and I both successfully requested a transfer to the unit of my brother's best friend, *Oberleutnant* Dröber, PzArtlRgt33 in 15PzDiv. In my first regiment we had trained with the 15cm howitzers and I had no idea what to do with the new 10.5cm howitzers. This

February 1941: two members of PzJägAbt39 in newly issued uniforms stand beside their vehicle, a 3-ton Opel 'Blitz' still in its original blue-grey colour. (Author's collection)

Two Panzer III tanks of the HQ Panzer Company of 15 PzDiv clearly showing the unit's emblem, an ace of spades inside a single or two concentric circles. The MG34 light machine gun mounted for use against aircraft beside the Panzer III in the upper picture has been removed from the tank (note absence of air cooling jacket around the barrel). Photos taken at El Alamein, July 1942. (Karl-Heinz Böttger)

was in early April 1941, and I had to do some training during the seven days we spent in Naples.

'We were issued our tropical uniform at Baumholder, in the Pflaz near Kaiserslautern. Before we left Baumholder all the vehicles of our regiment were painted a special camouflage colour for the desert.

'We went in a convoy to Africa, and I was in a German ship called *Wachtfels*. It had a German crew and *Kriegsmarine* gunners manned its guns. We started out only to return to Naples after one night. A few days later we went out again and managed to reach Tripoli without any trouble. One night there was a loud bang on the hull of our ship and we must have hit something. Because I was afraid that we might be hit by a torpedo I never slept below deck, assuming that if we were blown up I might have a chance to fly through the air into the water. We had only two nights in Tripoli after arriving on 20 April (I remember this because of the date, Adolf Hitler's birthday) while our supplies and vehicles were unloaded.

'Five days later we reached Benghazi where I had to enter hospital with a very high temperature. Obviously my typhoid injection, which I was given rather late, was not working properly. In any case I had paratyphoid but I did not realize it at the time. I was diagnosed as having angina. We were not supposed to stay longer than three weeks in hospital otherwise one could be sent back to Germany. When my temperature had not gone down after two weeks I pulled the thermometer out as soon as it reached 36.8 degrees! A few days later I was on my way to join my unit.

'My unit had passed Tobruk without any fighting and had taken up position near Fort Capuzzo. I joined my unit shortly before the Sollum Battle of June 1941. At first, I had the job in my gun crew of carrying the ammunition because I was still unfamiliar with the gun. During the battle, though, I advanced from K5 (*Kanonier* number 5) to K2, the one who actually loads the howitzer, for the simple reason everyone else was lying flat on the ground and nobody was loading the howitzer. So I did it and it worked fine from the first time.

'This is what I remember of my first battle. I was on guard duty during the night when the coloured signal flares from the attack went up. Our battery had six guns, two captured British 25 pounders and the usual four light German howitzers. Around 1000 hrs, the British tanks advanced in front of us, but we managed to stop them and force them back. The British tanks then started coming at us from one side and from the

rear and I have forgotten how many we shot up in all – my friend H. Köllenberger got two with his British gun and my howitzer also got two. The tanks kept coming and when they were only 50 metres in front of us we quickly got our things together and escaped south, the only side left open to us. Our first battery had been overrun and had suffered heavy losses. *Oberleutnant* Wild, the leader of this battery, had lost a leg. I saw him stand up to give orders but a British tank rolled right over him. Somewhere in the desert we stopped. We saw one British vehicle after the other rolling on towards the west and we were all expecting to be taken prisoner. We could not drive off to the west, nor could we drive to the south so we stayed the night where we were.

'Next morning Rommel flew low over us in his plane. He did not land, but about half an hour later three German PzIVs came up with Rommel's order to attack, which we did. We moved forward and captured a British camp, where I picked up a New Zealand overcoat because I had lost my German one. Then we linked up

A Sd.Kfz.139 Marder III self-propelled gun carrying a modified captured Russian 76.2cm gun used in an anti-tank role knocked out near Tel El Eisa in the last days of the El Alamein battle in November 1942. (Author's collection)

with some 88mm gunners who were part of a force commanded by *Hauptmann* Bach. Fortunately we did not have heavy casualties, four dead and some wounded. We were all completely surprised when we were told we had won the battle.

'Whenever Rommel flew over our unit we always cheered and shouted "Erwin". Rommel could not hear this of course – otherwise we would not have dared to do it. Though Rommel was loved by all his troops, he kept us under a very strict discipline. We would have been disillusioned if this had not been the case.

'We were luckier in many ways than the Infantry because we always moved around in our vehicles and did not physically have to carry any of our equipment or personal kit. What we did not carry around with us on the vehicles we had stored at the rear base used by our unit.

'We were very satisfied with our uniforms except the high boots which we never wore in action, or the breeches. We much preferred to use the low boots and long trousers and we put string through the bottom of our trousers to pull them tight over the tops of the low boots. We all liked the caps – I never bothered to bleach mine – but thought the tropical pith helmet was useless. We did not have steel helmets in Africa. Only the front-line infantry and sappers, *Pioniere*, had steel helmets, but I think we should have had them too. I did not wear a steel helmet in action until I fought in Russia in 1943.

'In the German Army there were very strict regulations about uniform and equipment, but in a battle it was not like this. You may only have saved what you were wearing on your body, and your weapon, so at least in Africa the rules could not be enforced about things no longer in your possession.

'In hot weather we wore only shirts above the waist, but in winter we wore our tunics with a woollen sweater and the warm woollen overcoat. I had my New Zealand overcoat which was also good and I wore it when I went back into hospital in December 1941. In fact I was mistaken for a New Zealander in hospital, but the Germans and British were put together anyway so it did not matter. The Italians were always segregated from the German and British patients. Strangely enough, whenever we had arguments with the Italians the British were on our side. I must say we felt sympathy for the Italian soldiers, who lacked good leadership.

'I find it hard now to remember much about the food we were given in Africa, only that on the whole it was miserable. We preferred British food when we could get it. I do however remember with disgust the Italian food we were given occasionally – especially their tinned meat. We called it 'Old Man' (*Alter Mann*) and I could not swallow it. We did gets lots of beans and peas, dried of course, and also rice. But the basic food was bread, German *Kommissbrot* and Italian *Maisbrot*. In November 1941 we were given a pig to feed and fatten up on scraps for our Christmas feast, but one night there was a big flood after a cloudburst and our pig was washed away, along with a lot of our gear that had also been placed in a wadi.

'For most of the time there were little jobs to do, and training. During our spare time we read, wrote letters, learnt the Italian language, played football and occasionally we went for a swim or to a cinema, open air of course. The only souvenir I had of my time in Africa was a silver ring I bought in the market (Arab bazaar) in Benghazi. It had the *Afrikakorps* symbol on the top.

'I left Africa at the end of 1941 when I again came down with a severe case of paratyphoid, and I was flown to a big hospital in Athens.

'The *Oberleutnants* Dröber and Wild had been with my brother at the *Kriegsschule* (War Academy) in Potsdam before the war and had been instructed by the then *Oberst* (Colonel) E. Rommel. All three of them were enthusiastic soldiers, and all of them died in Africa in 1942 in courageous actions.'

*   *   *

The men of the German Army in Africa fought believing that their fight was right; that their presence in Africa was necessary to confront the British enemy and to assist their Italian ally. There were also other factors – patriotism, a strong nationalism fostered by state propaganda, a conditioning inculcated by military training and knowing your place in the functioning of an army machine. All through the ups and downs of the North African campaigns these Germans preserved a steady faith in their leaders, not only in the immediate military sphere but in their political leadership as well.

Allied servicemen taken prisoner by the Germans in Africa have spoken warmly of the care and consideration shown them by their captors, though something quite different might have been anticipated. The usual sort of comments heard from ANZAC servicemen about the *Afrikakorps* were: 'they were bloody good soldiers; professional; they were tough and hard to fight; we respected them.'

Remarks like this gloss over the ugly side of war, the horrible deaths that came to men burnt in a tank, smashed by exploding artillery shells, maimed and

The pig given to 2nd Battalion, PzArtlRgt33, as a Christmas feast – before the flood that washed the unfortunate animal away, November 1941. (P. E. Schläfer)

broken by the blast of a mine or cut down by machine gun fire. That respect and some sense of honour survived the ugliness of war is shown by the regard of both sides to the other's dead. Bodies were properly buried and care was taken to record grave sites and the names of those who died.

All wartime propaganda attacks the real and true, and substitutes in its place a basis for hating and killing. Many former members of the *Afrikakorps* still today wince at stories of the war that labelled Germans as the Boche, the Hun, or the Nazis. Those who perpetrated these stories created the ambience for the isolated instances of prisoners being killed. Such things did happen, for several New Zealand and Australian servicemen did witness the killing of prisoners. These dead lie in unmarked graves, their deaths unrecorded.

War creates its own cruelties. A former member of *Afrika-Regiment 361* in the 90th Light Division related how his company was captured on 24 November 1941 near Point 175, south-east of Tobruk. The New Zealand troops loaded their prisoners into trucks and took them out of the battle area to spend the night in the open. Before being allowed to bed down, the German soldiers had their boots taken from them to stop escapes in the night. Next morning before the boots could be returned

an approaching German column on the horizon prompted the New Zealand escort to move immediately. At the moment of departure the hundred or so boots were thrown on to the ground and the scrambling German POWs had to pick up the nearest two boots to hand. Very few managed to grab even one that fitted and an agonizing march across miles of rocky ground followed. When the party of prisoners and guards stopped hours later, the Germans were limping from lacerated and swollen feet. It was more usual, however, for both sides to treat their prisoners with some consideration.

The total number of German troops in North Africa between 1941 and 1943 was around 260,000. Most became POWs, some were killed – the official figures are 18,594 killed and 3,400 posted missing – but a significant number of veterans of the *Afrikakorps*, who had been evacuated because of wounds or sickness, or because they had been transferred to other units, fought on in Europe on other fronts until the end of the war.

Burials and graves

Whenever Allied troops in Africa advanced into territory previously held by the *Afrikakorps*, one thing that always attracted their attention was the carefully built and tended German cemeteries. If an Allied soldier had a camera, he often used it to record some of the more ornate-looking grave markers and the neat symmetry of the stone-bordered grave plots. To an Allied soldier these German military cemeteries were overly decorated with prominent representations of outlines of the Iron Cross, swastikas, often some unit design (for paratroops, etc.) and patriotic inscriptions. However, to the German soldier it was a matter of following a tradition, of honouring the dead and holding respect for the memory of a fallen comrade.

In a fast-moving battle the dead very often had to be left for the enemy to recover and bury. If time and opportunity allowed in battle all that could be done was to bury bodies quickly in shallow graves noting the place of burial. It was not often that bodies could be evacuated for a decent burial. However, when the fighting was static and both sides occupied prepared positions, such as at Tobruk in 1941, at El Alamein in 1942 and for much of the campaign in Tunisia, the dead were normally buried by their own side with proper attention to military protocol. Both sides in the African fighting showed respect to the dead of the other side. If the North African campaigns have any claim to being a 'civilized' war, it was in the treatment of the dead rather than in the killing of the living enemy.

Because of the high temperatures and

The body is carried to the waiting open grave as the guard section stand to attention and the attending officers salute. (Dieter Hellriegel)

swarms of flies that accompanied the troops it was of paramount importance for reasons of hygiene to bury corpses as quickly as possible. Burial parties handling corpses that had been in the open sun for more than a day had to hold moist cloths over their faces and to wear gloves to touch the bloated and fly-blown bodies. This was a particularly distasteful exercise and no one would have done it willingly. It was very uncommon for corpses in this condition to be looted – the stench of death was attached to everything that came from these dead bodies.

After the fluid battles in the open desert of 1941 and 1942 there were large numbers of temporary and shallow graves scattered over a wide area. It was the responsibility of whichever side occupied the battleground to disinter these corpses and to collect them for burial again in one of the larger and permanent cemeteries closer to the coast. These cemeteries were dug up yet again after the war and the bodies were concentrated in the three permanent German cemeteries at El Alamein (Egypt), Tobruk (Libya), and Bordj Cedria (Tunisia).

In the German Army during World War II the customary form of military burial involved the presence of a chaplain, the dead soldier's company commander, the battalion or *Abteilung* Medical officer, and a guard of approximately section strength drawn from the dead man's unit. Personal friends would also normally be present. The actual service was short in length and there were sound military reasons for this. In any case, soldiers did not appreciate long and drawn-out ceremonies.

Military chaplains wore an identical uniform whether drawn from the Lutheran or Roman Catholic churches though a different prayer or hymn book was used (the Lutheran book was entitled *Gesangbuch* and the Catholic equivalent was known as the *Gottesdienst*). There were small differences in the graveside readings but both services included a reading from the New Testament, usually from one of the Gospels, a standard burial litany, and the Lord's Prayer which was spoken aloud by everyone present. At the end of the service the traditional German military funeral march, *Ich hatt' einen Kameraden* (I had a Comrade), was sung and, whether accompanied by a military brass band or just sung by the mourners, it was always emotional.

The body wrapped inside a blanket lies draped in a swastika flag below a pith helmet in the shallow grave. (Dieter Hellriegel)

The Field Chaplain starts to read the Burial Service from the Gesangbuch. (Dieter Hellriegel)

The identity disc – the top half was buried with the soldier, the lower half was returned together with all personal belongings to his company commander. (Author's collection)

The Company Commander speaks his last words about the life of the fallen soldier. (Dieter Hellriegel)

German dead were buried in full uniform, down to and including the boots. Dress for the funeral party was as formal as circumstances would allow, and it was common in Africa for the tropical pith helmet to be worn. It seemed more appropriate as an item of dress or formal uniform than a faded and often dirty field cap.

It was the responsibility of the Field Chaplain to supervise the erection of a grave marker. This normally took the form of a simple wooden cross with a standard form of inscription, unless there were supplies of a more elaborate grave marker. Medical units were also involved in this work of attending to graves, which suited many of the medical orderlies and stretcher bearers who had been theology students and had volunteered for their non-combatant medical roles in the Army. However, in the German military cemeteries there was a great variety in the styles and sizes of the grave markers. This came about because it often depended on just what pieces of wood could be scrounged from broken crates and boxes and how much time could be given to making them. More ornate grave markers were possibly erected because comrades of the dead soldier, or his personal friends coming from his home town, took the time and effort to construct a grave marker that attracted the attention of Allied troops and their cameras.

After a death had been noted, and before burial, the identity disc which had been worn around the neck of the dead soldier was broken in half. The top half, still attached to the neckcord, stayed with the body. The separated lower half eventually went back to the dead man's company as evidence of the death, along with any personal belongings recovered from the body such as rings, watches, wallets, papers, letters and photos. The company commander had the task of writing a personal letter to the next of kin of every soldier from his company who had been killed. This

The Field Chaplain stands to attention while the burial party sing the military funeral march, 'I Had a Comrade'. (Dieter Hellriegel)

letter did not follow any prescribed form and its contents were left to the discretion of the company commander who sent it to the man's family in Germany along with a parcel containing the dead man's personal belongings.

The identity disc carried by all members of the German Armed Forces bore the soldier's personal number assigned to him by whatever basic unit he happened to train in, unlike the disc carried by the various Allied armies which had the soldier's master military service number as well as his name. The German discs carried no such master serial number, nor the soldier's name. The information related to the man's

The end of the service, and with headgear removed a minute's silence is observed. (Dieter Hellriegel)

original depot which had received him for training, and issued him with his paybook, and was not the unit he served in at the front. However, if a soldier lost his identity disc or was transferred to another branch, the replacement disc would show the actual unit in which he was serving.

While the German troops themselves had no difficulty in understanding their system of identification, it was not so easy for Allied soldiers to comprehend. Some of the thousands of Germans listed as 'missing' were recorded as such because Allied troops handling them incorrectly transcribed the information on their identity discs if there was no corroborating reference such as a paybook on the corpse. In these cases Allied troops confused the German prefix letters used to identify units and unit numbers. German identity discs also usually carried a letter indicating the wearer's blood group and this was sometimes read by Allied soldiers as a part of the German soldier's unit, which further complicated the matter of recording the information contained on the disc.

The last act in formally acknowledging the death of a soldier was taken by the next of kin of the dead man in Germany. Upon receipt of the official advice from the High Command of the Army that a husband or a son had been killed – couched in a set announcement indicating that he had 'fallen for the freedom of Greater Germany dying a hero's death for Führer and Fatherland' – the family prepared their own death notices and the Catholic families usually took the further step of making up a funeral card.

A German cemetery behind the northern part of the Alamein line overrun by Australian troops in early November 1942. The grave of an airman is marked by a propeller blade which serves as a tombstone. (Author's collection)

The last act: the guard section, on command of the Unteroffizier *leader, fire a volley over the grave. (Dieter Hellriegel)*

The aftermath: the company medical officer, in old style field cap, and the Company Commander (in his tropical field cap again now that the service is finished) walk away from the covered-over grave. (Dieter Hellriegel)

Narrative of Campaigns

THE WAR in North Africa, as it took place in the wide empty desert of Cyrenaica in eastern Libya and in western Egypt in 1941 and 1942, had no parallel with other previous wars. In the fighting it was impossible to know the overall position at any one time, and possession of disputed territory was always in a state of flux. Conventional ideas, of front lines and space that had been occupied in the course of fighting, had no meaning here because of the constant flowing tide of battle which moved over great distances of the desert. In reading about such battles, this factor has to be borne in mind.

The 10th Panzer Division arrives in Tunisia: Panzer IIIs move out from the Tunis bridgehead to consolidate the German presence in December 1942. (ECPA)

1941

When the Italians had been pushed back to El Agheila on the lower Gulf of Sirte in early 1941 after Wavell's spectacular advance from Sidi Barrani through Cyrenaica (culminating in the annihilation of the remaining Italian forces at Beda Fomm), the Germans were forced to consider involving themselves in the North African war. Hitler had offered German assistance (specifically, one Panzer division) to Mussolini in the autumn of 1940 for the Italian advance into Egypt. The proud Mussolini had declined this offer, but because the proposal had come from the Führer, the German Army prepared for the employment of a Panzer Division, the 3rd, in North Africa, had ordered tropical uniforms and made some preliminary research into conditions for fighting in Libya.

The consequences of a British victory in North Africa, coupled with the Italian reverses in Greece and the known British intention of involving themselves there, would have put Italy under a serious threat. The first German involvement in the Mediterranean came

General Johannes Streich, Commander of the 5th Light Division, in conversation with officers of his division south of Tobruk, April 1941. (Imperial War Museum)

in January 1941 when *Luftwaffe* units were sent to Sicily. From there they were in range of Cyrenaica and within days *Luftwaffe* strikes were being made against the British around the eastern Gulf of Sirte.

Despite the pessimism of the German General Staff, Hitler went ahead with his decision to rush German aid to Libya and the first units arrived in Tripoli on 14 February 1941. These were the advance units of the 5th Light Division, a unit made up of a Panzer regiment taken from the 3rd Panzer Division and augmented with two machine gun battalions, a reconnaissance battalion, one part of an artillery regiment, and pioneer, anti-tank and auxiliary units, such as signals and transport. It was very weak in infantry, but it was fully mechanized and in its Panzer regiment it had a powerful fist. Just as powerful as the division itself was the new commander of the German forces (shortly to be named the *Afrikakorps*), General Rommel, who had a reputation as a brilliant exponent of armoured fighting and as a leader was prepared to take risks in bold strokes through enemy lines. As well as the 5th Light Division, which did not fully arrive until the middle of March, Hitler had also earmarked a complete Panzer Division, the 15th, which would be ready for shipment to Libya in mid-April. This was all that Hitler was prepared to release for action in Africa, because everything else was needed for the approaching invasion of the Soviet Union.

Rommel's primary function was to act as a blocking force in Tripolitania to prevent an Italian collapse and to keep the British at bay. Hitler had known when he picked Rommel that he would act aggressively, would try to keep the British off balance, and would give the greatest return for the smallest force. Though ULTRA was still in its infancy, enough of the signal traffic between Berlin and Libya was being intercepted to inform Churchill that the Germans had no plans for offensive action against the British for at least two or three months. Churchill knew that the 15th Panzer Division would not be completely shipped across until early May and he anticipated a further breathing space while it was being acclimatized and trained for action in the desert. Thus lulled, Churchill weakened his forces in Cyrenaica and supported Wavell in sending a strong expeditionary force to Greece. Churchill at this time did not know much about Rommel, though he was soon to learn.

The very first German troops to reach the front, the anti-tank units, were soon digging trenches and deploying against a possible resumption of the British advance. It did not take Rommel long to realize that

Members of Machine Gun Battalion 8 captured in the attack against Tobruk on 1 May 1941 – here gathered by their Australian captors before being marched into a POW cage inside the fortress. (Australian War Memorial, Canberra)

the British in front of him were thin indeed, and he thought of how to turn this to his advantage – he was not one to let such an opportunity go by without striking first. What followed was a stunning example of how mechanized units used quickly and with confidence could completely throw an enemy off balance and economically win a battle against a numerically stronger force. What the British had done to the Italians only a few short months earlier, Rommel now forcefully repaid in kind.

After the El Agheila fort had been easily occupied, Rommel probed forward at first cautiously, but as soon as he sensed the British were reluctant to engage him he threw caution to the wind and, disobeying orders to limit the scope of his 'reconnaissance', the 5th Light Division was unleashed. Confident that the British were

already off balance he also took the risk of dividing his meagre force by sending one column north to take Benghazi while the remainder, including his Panzer regiment, struck out towards the inland position of El Mechili.

Despite sandstorms and some confusion in the leading German units, Rommel's gamble paid off. He drove his forces on with a desperate urgency, always flying over the battlefield to keep the momentum of his advance moving. Once he flew over a company that had paused for no apparent reason, and all that it took to get it moving again was a terse message dropped from the plane to the ground: 'If you don't advance at once, I'll come down . . . Rommel.'

* * *

On 12 April 1941, Rommel launched an assault on Tobruk by attacking the south-west sector of the fortress perimeter, after an earlier probe against the south-east sector had failed. His forces were not strong – what remained of the 5th Panzer Regiment, a small number

of Pioneers and the 8th Machine Gun Battalion. The Italians were also meant to help in this attack but in the end their support did not count for much.

During this critical period a Panzer *Leutnant*, Joachim Schorm, kept a diary which vividly described Rommel's assault and its aftermath. The diary begins on 14 April, the date of Rommel's main thrust to enter Tobruk. Already his assault had been stalled for two days, and the machine-gunners were pinned down inside the breach that had been opened inside the outer ring of the Tobruk defences. The heavy artillery fire of the British and the skilful defence by Australian Infantry had by this time shown the weary Germans that their attempt to seize Tobruk had failed. But Rommel

A dead Panzer crewman lying beside his knocked-out tank. Death for Panzer crews was often a terrible combination of wounds and burns. (Imperial War Museum)

doggedly decided to continue the attack, and in any case he was bound to try to rescue the survivors of the 8th MG Battalion who were still holding the gains made in the previous two days' fighting.

This then was the background to the fighting recorded in the diary of Lt Schorm. It is not an account of a straight tank-versus-tank battle, but much of the tank fighting in North Africa was like this – tanks pitted against anti-tank guns, or heavy artillery used in an anti-tank role. The British originally envisaged using their tanks primarily in a tank-fighting style of battle, but the Germans always preferred to use anti-tank guns, or minefields first against enemy tanks to preserve the strength of their tank forces for the decisive end-fighting in a battle. It is ironic, therefore, that in this particular engagement Rommel was forced to use his precious tanks against strongly fortified positions, in a frontal attack which went against the doctrines of armoured warfare.

The stopping of this German attack was Rommel's first serious setback in Africa, and it was the first occasion that the forces of the German Army had been *decisively* blocked in World War II. In the aftermath of this battle, as mentioned in a previous chapter, Rommel blamed his Panzer commanders for not pressing the fighting hard enough and for not following his orders. However, the blame must lie with Rommel. He sent a weak force against a strong defence about which he had little information, and he persisted in the attack after it was evident that his forces were unable to make the deep breakthrough necessary for the capture

A Panzer III knocked out in the attack of 1 May 1941 being examined by an Australian member of the Tobruk garrison. (Author's collection)

of Tobruk itself. The losses suffered by the 8th MG Battalion were very heavy – of the 500 men committed to the original attack just over a hundred were to eventually escape encirclement on the night of 14 April. Among the dead was the Battalion commander, Colonel Ponath.

The second attack alluded to in the diary – on 1 May – was very nearly a carbon copy of the earlier attack, with heavy losses of tanks and men of the Pioneer Company and MG Battalion. The heavy artillery fire from inside Tobruk and the strength of the defensive lines proved too strong for Rommel's men to crack. A stalemate had been reached which was to continue until the battles of November 1941 when the 8th Army launched its offensive from Egypt to relieve the Tobruk garrison.

The diary of Lt Joachim Schorm around Tobruk 14 April 41 to 14 May 41

14 April 41

At 0100 hrs I am called and ordered to report to the Company Commander. Situation: MG Pioneers have worked a gap through the anti-tank defences; 5 Tank Regt, 8 MG, PAK(A/T), Flak-Artillery will cross the gap under cover of darkness and will overwhelm the positions. Stuka attack at 0645 hrs.

0715 hrs. Storming of Tobruk. With least possible noise the 2nd Bn, Regt HQ Coy, and 1st Bn move off with cars completely blacked out. Bitterly cold. Of course the opponent recognizes us by the noise, and as ill luck would have it, a defective spotlight on one of the cars in front goes on and off.

Soon arty fire starts up on us, getting the range. The shells explode like fireworks. We travel 10km, every nerve on edge. From time to time isolated groups of soldiers appear – the tank support men of 8 MG – and then suddenly we are in the gap. Already the tank is nose first in the first ditch. The motor whines; I catch a glimpse of the stars through the shutter, when for the second time the tank goes down, extricating itself backwards with a dull thud with engines grinding.

We are through and immediately take up file in battle order. In front of us the 8th Coy, then 2nd Bn HQ Coy (Abt.Stb.II), then the 5th Coy.

With my troops I travel left of the Coy Commander. With the 2nd Bn HQ (Abt.Stb.II) about 60 men of the 8 MG are marching in sparse groups with Lt Col Ponath. Tanks and Inf – against all rules. Behind us follow Regt HQ Coy (R.Stb) and the 1st Bn, likewise the other arms. Slowly, much too slowly, the column moves forward. We must, of course, regulate our speed by the marching troops. In this way the enemy has time to prepare resistance. In proportion, as the darkness lifts, the enemy strikes harder. Destructive fire starts up in front of us now -1 -2 -3 -10 -12 -16 and more. 5 batteries of 12cm calibre rain their hail upon us. The 8 MG Coy presses forward to get at them. Our heavy tanks, it is true, fire for all they are worth, just as we do; but the enemy with his superior force and all the tactical advantages of his own territory makes heavy gaps in our ranks.

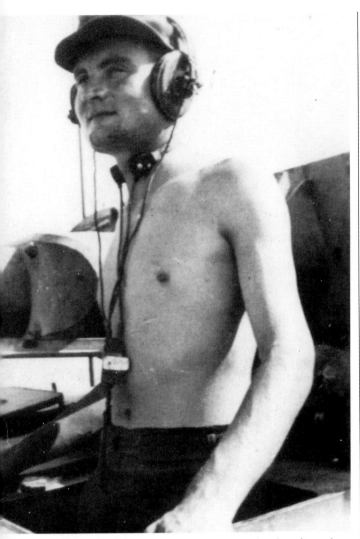

A Panzer commander standing in an open hatch and wearing radio headphones. (Charles Hinz)

Shortwave services

An immediate link with home was provided for German troops in Africa by the shortwave services of the *Reichsrundfunk*, which transmitted programmes from Berlin and Köln/Hamburg (the same station transmitted from both these cities). The troops had only their military shortwave receivers, the most common in Africa being types Fu.11 and Fu.19. Although these sets could pick up broadcasts on the 28m, 41m, 49m and 60m bands, the main one tuned into in Africa was the 41m band, which was the band in general use for broadcasting to Europe. Another station easily picked up in North Africa was the German-controlled radio station in Belgrade. This station soon established a special identity for the *Afrikakorps* when it regularly featured the song that was to become their own marching song: 'Lili Marlene'.

The programmes received in Africa were not always specifically made for reception in Africa, being received everywhere in Europe that German troops were stationed. The programmes were a mixture of light and classical music, news reports, and a lot of propaganda items. The best times for reception of these broadcasts in the desert was between 1530 and 2030.

There was one shortwave transmitter, though, which was set up specifically for the benefit of the *Afrikakorps*, but it was not a German station. The British established a special radio transmitter in Palestine under control of Middle East General Staff Intelligence. This station broadcast on a wavelength that could be picked up by receivers built into German tanks, and also used by signal units attached to artillery and HQ bases. Listening to this station was strongly discouraged, as was tuning into the BBC broadcasts which could also be picked up easily.

This photo taken on 24 February 1943 inside Tunisia shows a group of desert veterans gathered around a radio receiver listening to a political speech broadcast from Germany. (Graeme Brailsford)

Wireless: 0900 hrs anti-tank gun – 1,700 metres, tank. We are right in the middle of it with no prospect of getting out. From both flanks armour-piercing shells whizz by at 1,000 metres per sec.

Wireless: turn right, left turn. Retire. Now we come slap into the 1st Bn which is following us. Some of our tanks are already on fire. The crews call for doctors who alight to help in this Witches' Cauldron. English anti-tank units fall upon us with their machine guns firing into our midst; but we have no time. My driver, in the thick of it, says, 'The engines are no longer running properly, brakes not acting, transmission working only with great difficulty.'

We bear off to the right. 600 metres off on the reverse

Loading ammunition into a turret of a Panzer IV. This tank belonged to Panzer Regiment 5 in 1941. (Charles Hinz)

slope, anti-tank guns. 900 metres distant, in the hollow behind is a tank. Behind that in the next dip, 1,200 metres away another tank. How many? I see only the effect of the fire on the terraced-like dispositions of the enemy. Judging from their width and thickness there must be at least 12 guns. Above us Italian fighter planes come into the fray. Two of them crash in our midst. The optical instruments are spoilt with the dust. Nevertheless I register several unmistakable hits. A few anti-tank guns are silenced, some enemy tanks are burning. Just then we are hit, and the wireless smashed to bits. Now our communications are cut off. What is more our ammunition is giving out. I follow the battalion commander. Our attack is fading out. From every side the superior forces of the enemy shoot at us.

'Retire.' There is a crash, just behind us. The engine and the petrol tank are in the rear. The tank must be on fire. I turn around and look through the slit. It is not burning. Our luck is holding.

Poor 8th Machine Gunners! We take a wounded and two others aboard, and the other tanks do the same. Most of the men have bullet wounds. With its last strength my tank follows the others which we lose from time to time in the dust clouds. But we have to press on towards the south, as it is the only way through. Good God! Supposing we don't find it? And the engines won't do any more!

Close on our right and left flanks the English tanks shoot into our midst. We are struck in the tracks of the tank, which creak and groan. The lane is in sight. Everything hastens towards it. English anti-tank guns shoot into the mass. Our own anti-tank positions and the 8.8cm anti-aircraft guns are almost deserted, but the crews are lying silent beside them. Italian arty which was to have protected our left flank lies equally deserted. English troops run out of their positions, some shooting at us with machine pistols, some with hands raised. With drawn pistols they are compelled to enter our tanks. The English MGs start up and the prisoners fling themselves to the ground. 1st Lt V. Huelsen and my machine gunner lie on that side of my tank which faces towards the machine gun battalion. We go on, now comes the gap – now the ditch! The driver cannot see a thing for dust, nor I either. We drive by instinct. The tank almost gets stuck in the two ditches, blocking the road; but manages to extricate itself with great difficulty. With their last reserves of power, the crew gets out of range and returns to camp. Examine damage to tank. My men remove an armour-piercing high-explosive shell from the right-hand auxiliary petrol tank: 3cm of armour plate bogie (*Laufrollenhalter*) cut clean

through. The petrol tank shot away. The petrol had run out to this level without igniting! Had it not been for the bogie we should not have got out alive.

At 1200 hrs we retire into the wadi to the south of us. Impedimenta follows. We cover up. Heavy cumulus clouds cover the sky. At intervals of from 10–30 minutes, two or three English bombers swoop out of them among the tanks. Every bomber drops four to eight bombs. Explosions all round. It goes on like this until 1900 hrs without a pause. The Lion has Wings; we have one, in fact several, above us, 'Egons' (spotter aircraft). These hateful birds immediately direct arty fire over our post. Likewise smoke bombs, which sail down on parachutes, producing a streaming veil.

At 1900 hrs I am invited to accompany Lt Franke-Undheim to the O.C. Colonel Olbrich. For the tank battle near Agedabia 2.4.41 the Iron Cross 2nd Class. Ordered to the Battalion Commander; The Div Officer (Offrs V.D.) proposes a short toast.

A Panzer III of Panzer Regiment 5 in a laager south of Tobruk in the early summer of 1941. (Author's collection)

In the first days after arriving at the front the leading elements of the 5th Light Division anticipated fighting defensively and set up a network of trenches in front of El Agheila. (Author's collection)

Award citations

Among the papers carried by individual German soldiers, usually inside their paybooks, two common examples were the official and provisional documents for the award of a decoration. The provisional document was a simple typed text on plain paper listing the recipient with the award and date. The official document was printed on heavier-quality paper, often with a representation of the decoration or medal printed on the paper. The official document was presented together with the actual badge or medal, but the provisional award paper was often presented in lieu of both the official award document and the award itself at the time, usually in the field. The signature of the officer presenting the document was mostly that of a company or a battalion commander, but in some cases a divisional commander's or even Rommel's signature appeared on either provisional or official award documents. There appears to be no significance in this, it would be merely a matter of whether a ranking officer such as Rommel had time or opportunity to spend signing these papers – keeping in mind the obvious morale factor felt by a soldier receiving his award document signed by Rommel himself, or some other well-known and famous commander.

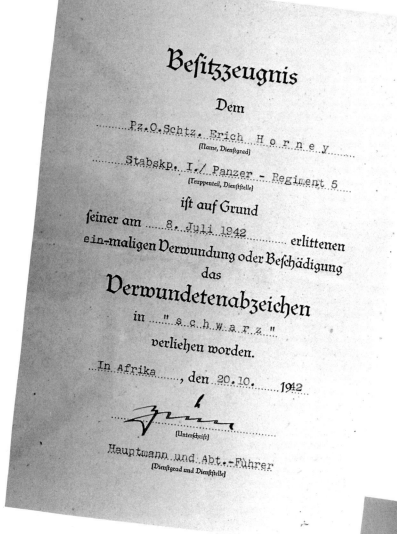

Official award document for a black Wound Badge. (Author's collection)

Provisional award document for an Assault Badge. (Author's collection)

Major Hohmann says: 'Let's drink first to today.' How fortunate that the Regt got out again. How splendidly the men fought – indeed.

Casualties in the 2nd Bn of the 5 Tank Regt (*bei II/s*) 10 tanks, a few dead, several wounded, more missing. It went badly with the A-Tk units, the light and heavy AA, but especially with the 8th MGs. The Bn has lost all its doctors, presumably captured. The Bn is practically wiped out.

15 April 41
Artillery fire from 0700 hrs. The bombers repeat yesterday's game.

My platoon has two heavy tanks again. Tank No. 625 doesn't go any more, however. It only serves as a pill box. According to orders, Frank and I report at the Brigade Commander's office at 1200 hrs. Once more the principal subject discussed is the action in front of Tobruk on 14 April. We simply cannot understand how we ever managed to get out again. It is the general

Early days in the desert, men of a MG company take a rest during a route march intended to acclimatize them to Libyan conditions. (David Hunter)

opinion that it was the most severely fought battle of the whole war. But what can the English think of us! A weak battalion, only two companies strong, bursts through the complex defence system until it is just on 2 kilometres from the town, shoots everything to bits, fights the enemy on all sides, and then gets away again.

The day will go down in the records of the regiments, and deserves a special mention.

In the afternoon, I go down with Frank to inspect the baggage. We have just reached the Commander's tank when there is an air-raid. 5 bombers in close formation. The British are daring since they met very little defensive fire. They have complete mastery in the air, not to mention mastery in other directions.

We dash under the tank; but it has no trench below it. The bombs drop very near . . . then more air-raids.

Had some food at the field kitchen, and then continued our inspection of the soldiers' quarters; also of the Italian camp. The Italians are also to attack today with 3 divisions. I wish they would drop it, otherwise we shall have to give them half our clothing and rations again.

Yet another air-raid. How quick they are! They come right over our car. On the way back, two more air-raids.

16 April 41

Two night alarms. Ordered to the Major once more. We are to march back. Bombs. New start. Received congratulations on my Iron Cross – healths drunk in Chianti. Conversation on the 'Hell of Tobruk' (14.4.41) as the survivors of 8 Machine Gunners, Anti-Tank Gunners and AAs call this day.

38 tanks went into 3rd attack. 17 of them were shot up, many more including my own put temporarily out of action.

Then we go back to get a wash. Two basins, half-filled with water for a rub-down. I am still in my underclothes when there is the first air-raid. To action stations at once! The British intend attacking the Machine Gunners. From now on air-raids every 20 minutes. Just now, 1600 hrs, we hear that Sgt Tollmer of the 5th Coy has been killed; he was lying under the tank.

The war in Africa is quite different from the war in Europe. That is to say, it is absolutely individual. Here there are not the masses of men and material. Nobody and nothing can be concealed, whether in battle between opposing land forces, or between those of the air, or between both, it is the same sort of fight – face to face, each side thrusts and counter-thrusts. If the struggle was not so brutal, so entirely without rules, one would

Generals O'Connor and Neame, captured on 6 April 1941 by Colonel Ponath's advance with MG Battalion 8, about to be flown back to Europe from Derna on 16 April. (Author's collection)

be inclined to think of the romantic idea of a Knights' Tourney. It was like this at Marsa el Brega, at Agedabia, and now before Tobruk.

The airmen get on our nerves. Ten raids or more a day. No AA, no fighter planes. They attack only according to plan – only tanks and Div HQ. We remain on the alert, but nothing happens. At night, two raids.

17 April 41
The day begins with the usual shelling and bombing, but now it has become a little quieter. The rumour is going round that Lt Col. Galland is coming with his squadron. It would be splendid if it were true. No German troops up to the present have had such a drubbing as we . . .

The news isn't very encouraging. The British have attacked the Italians, whose counter-attack was repulsed. Communications with Bardia have been cut off. The Reconnaissance Unit 3 in Sollum was struck down. I don't believe that the 5th Div can have lost itself on the way from El Agheila to Sollum.

On the Commander's order, I now take over tank No. 602 in order to cover the northern part of the Tobruk–Giarabub road. I had no sooner left in it than I was fired at – from only 300 metres away. How can they have noticed so soon! The night attacks on us are directed chiefly at the landing ground . . .

18 April 41
From 0200 hrs–0500 hrs our Air Force attacked Tobruk. It was grand, and very soothing to us . . . strong defences put up a real fireworks display. With the beautiful morning light came shells and bombs. As usual, no artillery or air activity. Yugoslavia has capitulated. Who will get here first: the German forces thus set

Many of the merchant ships that ferried German units to Libya were crewed by German naval personnel. Here men of a Flak unit with 88mm guns belonging to 15PzDiv make the crossing in April 1941 on the Wesermünde. *(Author's collection)*

free to act, or the British from Abyssinia?

Replacements for the 13 tanks which were lost through the steamer *Leverhusen* being set on fire are now on the way.

19 April 41

Bombs on Tobruk. Our dive-bombers seem to be putting in good work. They begin at 0200 hrs and go on the whole day, on and off. Temperature risen. Pulse increased since I had some real coffee at 1500 hrs. . . .

20 April 41

In the afternoon tank No. 623 rolls up with new engine. Now I have the strongest company in the regiment; 4 Mark II tanks, 4 Mark III. Gradually, however, the job of Company Commander is becoming difficult. I have absolutely no support of any description, everything is in the desert. Where are the tanks, where the motorcycle sections of HQ's Combat Group, where the 1st and 2nd baggage convoys, where the Company office? And I have no motor car and no motorcycles – and then the reports, and the paper-war which begins as soon as the last shot has been fired.

22 April 41

In the small hours of the morning artillery fire starts up. At 0550 hrs, alert, and ready for action – then there is a humming in the sky. Hurrah! 6 German Me 110s protected by 4 Me 109s bomb and harass the enemy's defences 2–3 kilometres from here. Then a long row of dive-bombers follow. They form themselves into formations of three. Their objective is the harbour. The dull thuds of heavy bombs detonating roll over us. 'Give it to him,' my men shout. They will do that all right without our pious wishes, and despite the strong defence.

I present the War-Wounds Medal to two of my men and tell some others that they have been mentioned in despatches for bravery in face of the enemy. These are the joys of a Company Commander.

Sgt Brauchmann hands over the captured car. Now at least I can get about and look after the equipment which was sadly neglected before.

23 April 41

The journey I planned has been postponed owing to the arrival of Lt Grim, who has brought 6 tanks, of which 3 belong to our Company. 621 and 624 are mine – so I change from No. 602 back to No. 621 again. The engines of the tanks are in part new, in part overhauled in the factory. They have new gears, transmission, brakes, etc. The British do not miss a chance of sharing in the welcome by means of well-laid fire. The faithful 625, which is the only heavy tank of the Company which stayed with us, will now be sent back to have its 6 wounds, caused by shell fire, cured. While in the workshop it will have its engines changed.

28 April 41

Splendid weather. Dive-bombers over Tobruk. The second bird has made a forced landing behind us with a broken oil pipe. The Div Intelligence makes amazing assertions. According to it there are 15 different batteries in Tobruk, 1 A/T Bn, 50 tanks, of which 20 are Mark II, and in addition all Italian old fixed guns etc. This estimate must be at least 50 per cent too high. The British are also said to have seen some 120 tanks of ours

The tank killer: an 88mm gun of 15PzDiv dwarfs an anti-aircraft mount of two machine guns. (David Hunter)

Documents

The 'paper war' was a heavy load on all officers, especially company commanders who had many other duties to perform in the front line. The list of subjects requiring this sort of written treatment is almost endless – weapons and ammunition returns, sickness figures, daily reports of action and normal routines, indents for food and equipment needed, the number of flares by colour fired in a day, answering the constant stream of requests for information on individuals in the unit (sometimes this type of request originated from the replacement depots in Germany who kept up-to-date files on troops in the field), submitting requests for replacement troops to cover attrition through sickness or wounds, copious reporting on anything to do with disciplinary measures meted out to members of the unit, answering correspondence from other units – and so it went, on and on. These returns dating from the time spent on the Alamein line show that the numbers going out of the line due to sickness were unusually high, and that as a consequence units were always under strength.

Often this continuing correspondence on the one subject has its humorous side, at least when read today. One such exchange involved the 2nd Battery of Artillery Regiment (Motorized) 190, in the 90th Light Division, concerning an order originating from Regimental HQ that all guns were to be covered with a certain type of camouflage sheet (Regimental Order No. 24/9 of 7.9.42). On 13 September 1942 the Battery Commander is writing to the Regimental HQ pleading that the order could not be complied with because the special sheets of camouflage and dust-protective material had not been received. The next letter in this correspondence, on 25 September, has the Battery Commander complaining that the order could still not be fol-

lowed – even though the sheets of camouflage and dust-proof material had arrived at the gun positions, there were no needles or thread with which to sew the material.

The 'paper war' continued right to the very end, and even when the defeat of the German and Italian Armies in Tunisia was drawing closer and closer, all routine work continued as if nothing was amiss. In the very last week of their existence, all units continued to send out and receive written reports. Transfers between units went on, those selected for officer training in Germany were recalled, ration returns were filled in, intelligence information was forwarded to higher commands, and whenever a retreat was made the typewriters went along too.

On 5 May 1943, the remnants of the 334th Infantry Division were holding its last position. On that day the division submitted a summary of the reports to the divisional HQ from its main units, Grenadier Regiments 755 and Buhse (the name of its commander), *Gebirgsjäger Regiment* 756, and Artillery Regiment 334. At hourly intervals the reports came in and were recorded, along with the name of the officer who prepared the report and the name of the NCO who transmitted the messages.

Each regimental entry in this daily report mentions by name the various battalion commanders and the news from

their section from the front. All artillery fire against their units is recorded as falling in sector numbers, along with sightings of enemy troops and their strength, attacks by aircraft, details of any response by way of fire from the German side, an appreciation of enemy intentions, and finally a list by number of men lost as a result of enemy action.

The last entry of this two-page divisional summary is a report received from Regiment Buhse, timed at 0715 the next morning. After a day of heavy artillery fire, tank attacks, infantry attack and counter-attack, there is something of an understatement in its last sentence. 'During the night, on the right wing of the sector, there was light disturbing artillery fire. 30/82 (co-ordinates on a map) is reported as being heavily reinforced by the enemy. Otherwise, nothing out of the ordinary.'

This was written only days before the entire division was forced to capitulate, and came at the end of some of the heaviest fighting in the whole Tunisian theatre over a feature known to the Allies as 'Longstop Hill' and to the Germans as 'Christmas Hill'. It says something for the conditions experienced by the long-suffering German units still fighting at this time that the last entry in the divisional report of the 334th Infantry Division on this day should end that there had occurred 'nothing out of the ordinary'.

A joyful Hauptmann *Bach and men of 1st Battalion InfRgt 104 greet the relief column from 15PzDiv in Halfaya Pass on 17 June 1941, ending the isolation of Bach and his men in their position behind the British lines. (ECPA)*

in Sollum. On learning this, one tank each of models I, II, III, will be sent to the spot immediately. The Regiment, whose commander is ill, will be divided into a mobile and stationary battalion. We have now been away from Germany for two months, and without butter, etc. into the bargain. Our principal food is bread and 'something' spread on it. In this heat every single bite needs a sip of water or coffee to help it down.

If one stops to think, one realizes that one drinks three times as much in Germany as here in the heat. Hence the body has to adapt itself quite a lot. But we manage. Where would you find anybody in Germany who would drink water of this colour and taste? It looks like coffee and tastes horribly of sulphur. But that's all to the good for otherwise it would stimulate one's thirst.

We are still waiting for the 15th Panzer Division, which should be following us. The men call it 'the 5th Column'.

At 1900 hrs we draw more to the south-west: at 2300 hrs bivouac.

29 April 41
50 dive-bombers circling over Tobruk. Tank 622 turns up. They tell us about the desert – of hunger and thirst, of Benghazi and of Derna. Since No. 625 is still in the workshops, I am getting No. 634 as my fifth tank, with Sgt Schäfer, my driving instructor from Wunsdorf. In the evening I drink a glass of Chianti with the Commander – our last drop. In Tobruk there is more of the stuff, so we shall have to restock there.

30 April 41
Finishing touches on our preparations for battle. 1745 hrs. March to assembly place. Strong Stuka attacks. 2000 hrs. Our own strong arty bombards the enemy heavily; x/115 and x/114 left of us; 8th Machine Gunners in front. 1 Pioneer Bn and 1 Bn Assault Pioneers (*Sturm Pioniere*) break through and demolish the barriers on either side. The flare signals show that the attack has begun.

At 2200 sleep under the tank.

A knocked-out British Crusader Mk I is examined by a German anti-tank crew after the Sollum Battle of June 1941. (Author's collection)

1 May 41

We intend to take Tobruk. My 4th attack on the town. Up at 0330 hrs; leave at 0430 hrs. We lose touch in the darkness and dust – and join up again. We file through the gap where many of our comrades have already fallen. Then we deploy at once – 6th Coy on the left, 5th Coy on the right. Behind HQ, 8th and 7th Coys. The regiment is now Hohmann's Mobile Bn, and consists of 5 (1 and 2), 6 (5 and 6), 7 (the remainder), 8 (4 and 8) Companies, altogether 80 tanks.

The English arty fires on us at once. We attack. No German patrol goes out in front to reconnoitre. Tier on tier of guns boom out from the triangular fortifications before us. The two light troops of the Coy and my left section are to make a flanking movement. I attack. Wireless message: Commander of 6th Coy hit on track. Then things happen suddenly ... a frightful crash in front and to the right. Arty shell hit? No? It must be a mine. Immediately send wireless message: 'Commander Schorm on a mine', try to turn round in your own tracks. 5 metres back. New detonation – mine underneath to the left. On reversing, went on a mine again. Now mounting tank 623. Back through the artillery fire for 100 metres. Got in. Wireless order: 'tanks to go back behind fight.' The men of the mined tank all right. Enemy is attacking with tanks, but will be put to flight.

Back carefully. Then, with the last tank of the Coy and Lt Rocholl, I will cover to the north. 9 heavy and 3 light tanks of the Coy have had to abandon the fight owing to mines. Of my troop, the Commander's tank and both of the Section Leader's tanks. Of course, the enemy went on shooting at us for some time.

A slight change of position: forwards – right – backwards – left! With the Commander's approval, I am to go with Lt Grim up in front to salvage tanks. While we are on the way, we are fired at by MG and anti-tank guns at 550 metres range. I silence them with HE shells and drive on the tracks of 624. I bring up the rear, and then the laborious work of salvaging begins. The anti-tank gun fire starts up again, and has to be kept in check by Lt Grim by constant MG fire. Grim himself goes on to a mine, and damages the track. At last, I move

A captured British Matilda tank being repaired in the German field workshop near Bardia in July 1941. When ready to fight again this tank would be given German markings. (Author's collection)

off slowly with No. 624 in tow, through the gap, and a further 800 metres 250,000 Reichmarks are saved! The crew is really delighted to have its tank back. Continue on to the Bn. It is now late afternoon.

Dive-bombers and twin-engined fighters have been attacking the enemy constantly. In spite of this, the British repeatedly counter-thrust with tanks. As soon as planes have gone, the arty starts up furiously. It is beginning to grow dark. Which is friend, which is foe? Shots are being fired all over the place, often on one's own troops and on tanks in front which are on their way back.

Suddenly – a wireless message: The British are attacking the gap with infantry. It is actually true. Two Coys get off their motor lorries and form a skirmishing line. All sorts of flare signals go up – green, red, white. The flares hiss down near our MGs. It is already too dark to take aim. Well, the attack is a failure. The little Fiat-Ansaldo cars go up in front with flame throwers in order to clean up the triangle. Long streaks of flame

of masul oil (*Masul-oele*), thick smoke, filthy stink. We cover until 2345 hrs – then retire through the gap. It is a mad drive through the dust. At 0300 had a snack beside the tank. 24 hrs shut up in the tank – with frightful cramp as a result and a thirst!

2 May 41
Salvaging tanks. We got both of the Mk II tanks. 800,000 Reichmarks saved. . . .

3 May 41
12 hrs sleep. Refreshed. The arty duel goes on. Dive-bombers and twin-engined fighters. General Rommel has commended the 5th Tank Regt. I consult the Commander about the possibility of rescuing the last Mk II tank of the Company. We shall do it tomorrow . . . Stukas go off to the attack. The 'bird' which made the

forced landing and which was towed here from near the wire entanglements by a Mk II tank, is once more up and away.

Arty fire very severe. 10 batteries are firing ceaselessly. Something is in the wind. Naturally the enemy answer equally briskly. At 2200 hrs, ready to move off, and out we go into the desert. Then the order to break off comes. Not until 0100 hrs does the firing stop. At 0115 hrs to the Commander immediately. Australians have penetrated the defences R.1–R.7, which were captured and occupied by *Ariete* and *Bersaglieri*. Immediately, counter-attacks and cover with tanks. Alarm. March.

Wireless message: 'ready for action. Captain Santo Marro will lead.' Oh hell! Where to? No idea! Italians argue and gesticulate wildly. Oh well, I start by going as far as the gap, and then turn right. No officer knows the position. Near R.7 an Italian tank is burning.

The Australians have gone back, leaving 36 dead behind. The Italians are absolutely in confusion. They have been under heavy arty fire. Of 150 men occupying R.7, there are over 100 dead and wounded. I cover toward the east.

Wireless message to the Battalion: 'I am coming back

One of Rommel's effective improvisations – turrets and guns removed from captured Matilda tanks set in concrete and sited above Halfaya Pass. (Author's collection)

at 0530 hrs in daylight, so as to avoid drawing renewed fire on to the Italians through my movements.'

4 May 41
0600 hrs. I inform Bn that my task has been carried out. Sleep. At 1200 hrs summoned to the Bn again. At 1400 hrs, I hand a report to the Division – General Kirchheim. Naturally, I have to go out once more after dark; for, of course, there is only one troop in the Regt. Captain Prossen and the other officers who served in the Great War are all saying: 'Yes, it was like that between 1916 and 1918.' What we experienced in Poland and on the Western Front was only a promenade in comparison.

After listening to the Führer's speech to the Reichstag, 1800–1900 hrs, I am to take 5 tanks out. This time to R.5. Once again, none of the Italians know the way for certain, but I know the terrain inside out by now. My Italian *Bersaglieri* doubles back suddenly. 'English everywhere!' Nonsense!

Near Point 125 I meet 2nd Lt Kalk of the 2nd Machine Gunners, who is to go to R.7 with two guns. Naturally the Italians have misdirected him, and I show him how the land lies. We agree how we are going to co-operate. From time to time, the arty lays down harassing fire. Our 8.8 AA succeeds in setting a munition dump on fire. From 0200 to 0400 hrs, the shells go high above us.

Heavy German artillery emplaced outside Tobruk in the autumn of 1941. This large powerful ex-naval gun shows the siege conditions after six months of fighting around the fortress port. (Author's collection)

5 May 41

At 0600 hrs I withdraw. Report. Sleep. At 0900 hrs I wake up. An Italian fighter plane shoots down an English bomber – much noise.

Up at 1500 hrs. A commission is to inspect arms to see the effect of sand. Of course, there is only *my* tank. At the Bn, I arrange about reliefs.

6 May 41

In the night, such a severe sandstorm blew up that by morning visibility was reduced to 2 metres, and it forced us to get into the tanks . . . in the midst of these troubles, the rations have become even shorter. Everything is

waiting in Tripoli, but Rommel needs soldiers and munitions. Clears up in the evening.

7 May 41

Plenty of sunshine, little food. . . .

Dive-bombers begin their work again. Let us hope they will accomplish something this time. Up to the present they have done nothing to speak of. It is only over the harbour of the town that there are strong defences. In the fortified area, they could circle around quietly and make out quite a lot, and then pop in – so what! The commander dives, chucks his eggs haphazardly, and of course the other 30 follow his example.

And they've got a 1/200,000 map into the bargain! Blockheads. *Then, for three whole days they haven't any bombs.*

I am thinking again of the Italians. Lt Col. Marelli and Major Gatelli are really fine fellows. Capt Santo Marro as well. Colonel Brinelli I have not yet met ... from the *Ariete*.

A typical desert airfield, ready-made on the flat desert surface, with a necessary anti-tank gun deployed on the perimeter in the foreground (50mm PAK38) under a camouflage net. (NZ National Archives – Alexander Turnbull Library)

8 May 41

At noon, sandstorm began. In the chief's tent there's a good deal of grumbling. What is there for a soldier to do when there is no fighting? And nothing to eat. This morning the bit of cheese wasn't even enough to go round for breakfast. The men want to attack, want to get into Tobruk. There, there's loot to be had. Replacements from Germany don't arrive.

They are going to send in a fresh indent for them in 8 weeks. What tripe. Boy! If only Göring knew. We have already been a month trying to reach Tobruk. Hour by hour our advance becomes more difficult. The British lay mines, construct obstacles and positions which we shall have to take again. The secret of our victory in the European theatre of war:

1. If advance troops were held up, the Commander-in-Chief called up fresh troops as reinforcements from behind the lines, and pushed on as quickly as possible, or kept the situation fluid. If we had been able to do that in the case of Tobruk, it would have been a mere bagatelle, and we should have been in Alexandria by now.
2. Our opponents are Englishmen and Australians. Not trained attacking troops, but fellows with nerves and toughness, tireless, taking punishment with obstinacy, wonderful on the defence. Ah, well, the Greeks also spent 10 years before Troy. In this war for positions, we no longer talk of vipers and scorpions, despite the fact that there are still some crawling about.

9 May 41

I drove over to the Pioneers with the Commander to consult them about the capture of the nearest concrete dugouts. While we are returning, the sandstorm springs up again.

New position: 1845 hrs preparation for the march. 1900 hrs we march off in wide detours – west – south – east – direction of Sollum through the desert. Thank God! We can regain our operational freedom.

Corporal Wilheim, the gunlayer on tank 624, has been ordered to the Regiment. He is to go back to Germany immediately to attend the Weapon School.

10 May 41

The usual stop to change the oil, clean the filters, etc. To the right there is a mountain rising sharply out of the dunes about 200–300 metres high.

After travelling 160 kilometres we reach Fort Capuzzo at 1800 hrs, and camp 1 km to the south of it. Of our own troops, 2 Recce Bns and 2 A/Tk Companies are in the neighbourhood. The British are in the habit of giving us a rough time at night with naval artillery.

Our next objective is Egypt. The frontier is to be seen 2km from here. I thank God from the bottom of my heart the 2nd troop has not lost a single man or a single tank. The only one in the Regt.

11 May 41

An English reconnaissance party wakes us. This time they noticed us. We are feeling hungry. The clever theorizers in Germany said: 'Make sure that the soldiers eat enough. The heat takes away the appetite with disastrous results.' A pretty theory, but we *have* an appetite, unfortunately a bigger one than we can satisfy, and we can't forget it.

It is said that the enemy has got a strong force near El Hamrah. We are to bring five fighting units against him. It is really not a job for tanks. I consider it a mistake to strike at an extraordinarily mobile and fast opponent in the desert after making a journey of 100km.

At 2100 hrs we start up. Shortly afterwards we pass the frontier. Plain, as flat as a table. At Suleiman we stop to fill up at 0100 hrs.

12 May 41

We set off again at 0230 hrs. Already as dawn comes, we see little points on the horizon: in front of us to the right, to the left and behind us, which strangely never get any nearer. These are English armoured cars which are watching our movements. They are afraid of our own armoured cars, but not of our much slower tanks so long as they keep out of range of their guns.

Nevertheless, from time to time they pop out as quick as lightning from behind a rise in the ground, fire off a cone of MG bullets into the column, and are off again. Meanwhile we have taken up attacking formation. To the left the 6th Coy, to the right the 5th Coy, in the middle behind HQ and 8th Coys. It makes a wonderful picture as the tanks roar along in a front over 1 km long, even more interesting owing to the explosions of the shells. The British have mounted guns on light lorries. They let us get to within 3.5km and then open fire, letting us have what is in the barrel, and getting away again at full speed. Then they stop 8km away and the game begins again. They make no impression on us. They use their heavy field guns, which serve as anti-tank guns in the same way.

The munition limber is drawn by a stable tank.

The enemy came to meet us, but now travels along beside us.

When we had approached a little the order came: Attack – greatest strength in front. Very well, but that's the way to ruin tanks very speedily. At 40km an hour we rush off, approach. The British prepare like fury.

We are already within 2km. 'Halt!' High-explosive shells, and machine guns open up. A light truck and a munition limber on fire. Behind those in flight our shells burst. Rally. A couple of Tommies dead, a couple captured; but it is impossible to go further. The petrol is barely enough to get us home. It is frightfully hot; 58°C* on the battlefield.

Four English guns are being towed by our tanks, also some cars and limbers. On the return journey some men of the 7th Section are wounded by machine gun fire of the English armoured patrol cars.

As we near the frontier, air attack in depth. The 2cm AA brings down a plane. New attack 0500 hrs, MG sights at 1,000 metres. Ready to fire. Aim more ahead. If you aim 5 lengths ahead, it will hit the mark. The last 50 rounds on the belt are well laid when the Englishman turns out of the line of fire. New belt. New attack. A few more times and then it is all over.

At our meeting point we hear that the airman went on to the 7th Section. Several wounded. We go to our tents very tired.

*The accuracy of this temperature must be open to doubt. The highest ever recorded temperature on the earth's surface was 58°C, in Libya.

13 May 41

At noon I hear that Hess is missing. He is supposed to have made a parachute jump over Scotland in a fit of madness. Then comes the report that Sgt Malinowsky has died of his wounds. Lt Frank has gone off in an armoured car to haul back the tanks of Sgt Steen, since tanks Nos. 614 and 615 have remained outside inexplicably. My tank No. 622 ought to be the first to run out of petrol.

At 1800 hrs Frank returns. Absolutely impossible, he reports; already it is buzzing with English armoured patrol cars and artillery behind Suleiman. It is pointless, since the British have been there for a long time with armoured cars.

In preparation against attack, November 1941. Machine guns were set up on tripods in pits and set to fire along predetermined lines of fire, worked out with other nearby machine guns. (NZ National Archives – Alexander Turnbull Library)

Members of 361 Afrika Regiment from the 90th Light Division captured by NZ troops on 25 November 1941 south of Point 175 during the Sidi Rezegh battles. (Australian War Memorial, Canberra)

With the last light of the day we retire to Fort Capuzzo. Before a great archway, which is over the main street, bearing the Fascist symbol, is the newly dug grave of Sgt Malinowsky.

According to reports, the British are restless. We bring up tanks to the front for protection.

14 May 41

A strong wind brings a sound of gunfire with it. We hasten our preparations. English armoured cars make sure that we are still here . . .

DIARY ENDS

Postscript – Report by Colonel Olbrich

As an appendix to the diary entries made by *Leutnant* Schorm, the following is the official report submitted to Rommel by Colonel Olbrich after the failure of the first attempt to break the Tobruk perimeter. Rommel did not accept the negative criticism of his leadership and Olbrich joined General Streich in returning to Germany.

April 11

At 0730 hrs the Regt received orders to attack. It was to move up to Acroma from a point 32km west of Tobruk and sweep round on Tobruk from the south.

At 0830 hrs the Regt moved off and was met in Acroma by an orderly officer of the German *Afrikakorps*

under whose direction it turned off to the east about 10km south of Acroma and reached a position 12km south-west of Tobruk about 1500 hrs. As the assembly point came immediately under enemy fire, the surprise element was lost. The Commander of the Regt was shown the position personally by the G.O.C.

At 1600 hrs the Regt (Regt HQ Coy and 2nd Bn only) began the attack. The Regt was reduced to 25 vehicles. As it advanced across heights overlooked by the enemy, it met with heavy arty fire.

The advance of the Regt was unexpectedly held up by an impassable anti-tank trench which runs right round Tobruk. The Regt was ordered to 'right turn' to try and find a crossing place further to the east. It advanced for 4km along the trench under heavy anti-tank and extremely well-directed arty fire.

At 1715 hrs the forward units of the Regt reached the Tobruk–El Adem road where they discovered a thick minefield. The order was given to withdraw to the south and the light platoon of the 2nd Bn was sent out to reconnoitre in an easterly direction.

During this reconnaissance which went on till late in the night and penetrated to about 20km south-east of Tobruk, Lt von Hulsen distinguished himself by his great skill and circumspection. The Regt returned to its original position and drew up facing Tobruk.

Reports given the Regt had led it to believe that the enemy would retire immediately on the approach of German tanks. Nothing had been reported about the old Italian anti-tank trenches or about the large number of British anti-tank guns and arty.

April 12

An officer of the Engineers reported that 4km to the west of the point where the Regt was to have broken through on the 11th, there probably was no anti-tank trench. Acting on this information, the Regt was led up to the point to renew the attack at 1515 hrs (with 24 vehicles). On its approach, English arty began to fire into it with superb accuracy and at the same time a bombing attack was made on it with heavy-calibre bombs.

For this operation, an Engineer section had been detailed to destroy any anti-tank trenches there might be, under the protection of our fire.

As the Regt advanced, the enemy fire grew so intense that the Engineers could not follow, in spite of great dash and daring.

At 1600 hrs the enemy position could be clearly distinguished. At 1645 hrs leading units of the Regt reached the anti-tank trench, which proved to be com-

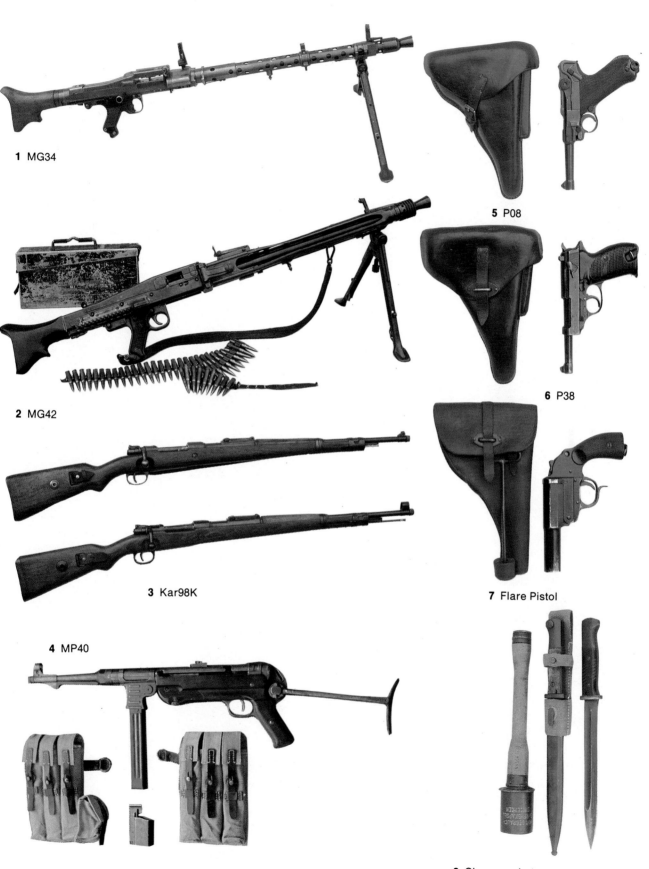

1 MG34

2 MG42

3 Kar98K

4 MP40

5 P08

6 P38

7 Flare Pistol

8 Close combat weapons

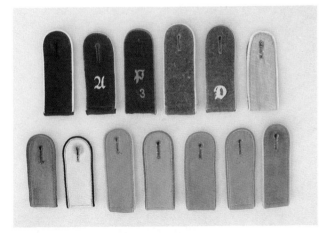

9 Shoulder straps – Private rank

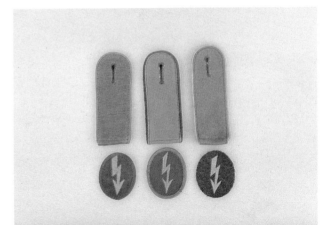

10 Comparison of green pipings

11 Shoulder straps – NCO rank

12 Trade specialist patches

13 Uniform national emblems and collar bars

14 Sleeve rank insignia

15 Officer silver bullion insignia

16 General rank insignia

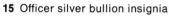

17 Officer Continental tunic and cap insignia

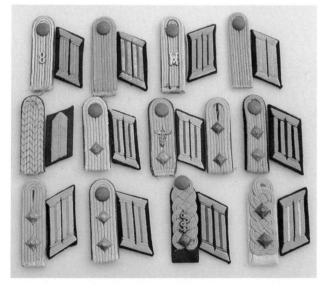

18 Officer shoulder straps and collar tabs

19 Metal insignia

20 Cufftitles

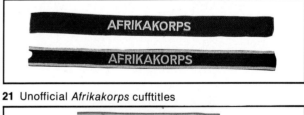

21 Unofficial *Afrikakorps* cufftitles

22 *Luftwaffe* cufftitles

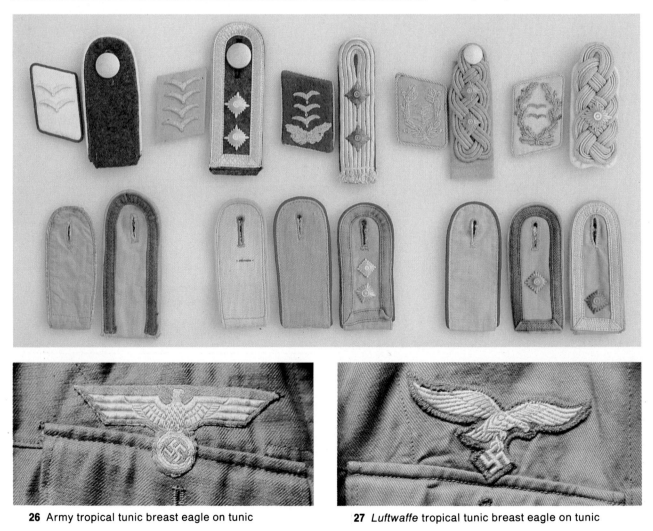

23 *Sonderverband* 288 (*above*)

24 *Luftwaffe* eagles and cockades (*left*)

25 *Luftwaffe* shoulder straps and collar tabs (*below*)

26 Army tropical tunic breast eagle on tunic

27 *Luftwaffe* tropical tunic breast eagle on tunic

28 Officer tropical field cap with red soutache denoting artillery

29 Officer tropical field cap with light green soutache

31 Other ranks cap with the lime-green of the *Panzergrenadiers*

30 Two other ranks caps very typical in that both have been well bleached

32 The two shades of blue used in the German Army in North Africa

33 Other ranks cap that was typical of those issued in the El Alamein position

34 Officer cap manufactured without soutache but with sweatband (*left*); and other ranks cap showing inferior standard of machine stitching

35 Officer tropical sidecap with silver piping and pink soutache for Panzer regiments

36 Underside view of two caps illustrating a sweatband on the lower inside edge (on right)

37 Two examples of other ranks tropical sidecaps showing a light green and a pink soutache

38 Example of tropical sidecap with white soutache

39 *Luftwaffe* peaked tropical field cap

40 An issue other ranks cap with the addition of privately acquired silver piping to give it the appearance of an officer field cap

41 Two examples of the standard *Luftwaffe* tropical sidecap

42 Detail of officer silver cording (*Luftwaffe* officer sidecap)

43 General's field service cap

44 Officer's field service cap

45 Officer's woollen M38 field cap

46 An unissued other ranks field cap with grass–green soutache (*left*); other ranks field cap with light green soutache (*right*)

47 Black woollen M38 sidecaps issued exclusively to tank crews as part of the special black woollen Panzer uniform

48 Other ranks field cap with copper–brown soutache

49 Field service cap of a General in the *Luftwaffe*

50 *Luftwaffe* General's summer issue field service cap (*below*)

51 The standard *Luftwaffe Schirmmütze* for officers (*above*)

52 Other ranks field cap with gold–yellow soutache

53 Two examples of the standard *Wehrmacht* helmet

57 The standard army cloth-covered pith helmet

54 Common camouflage colours

58 Dutch tropical pith helmet

55 Two further views of helmets showing the great range of paint colours used for camouflage

59 Standard *Luftwaffe* tropical pith helmet

56 Two *Luftwaffe* steel helmets

60 A Paratroop helmet

61 Roughly painted helmet with shrapnel gash

62 Tropical field tunic of a *Leutnant* in a Rifle Regiment

63 Tropical NCO tunic with pleated pockets and pointed pocket flaps

64 Tropical tunic with overcoat shoulder straps piped in lime-green (*left*)

65 Tropical tunic with a French-made shirt and cotton drill tie (*right*)

66 Continental woollen tunic in pre-war style with the dark green collar, here for a *Stabsgefreiter* (senior staff corporal) (*below*)

67 A later-styled NCO tunic with pleatless pockets

68 Tropical tunic for an *Oberkannonier* (senior gunner) in an artillery battery

69 *Luftwaffe* tropical tunic, as worn by other ranks in a Flak unit

70 *Luftwaffe* tropical tunic for a *Leutnant* in a Paratroop unit

71 Rare Paratroop variation of the *Luftwaffe* tropical tunic

72 Army tropical tunic for a tank crewman (*above left/left*)

73 Internal view of the Army field tunic

74 Front and rear views of the standard Army tropical overcoat

75 Tropical motorcyclist's or driving coat

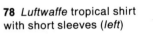

78 *Luftwaffe* tropical shirt with short sleeves (*left*)

76 Typical example of a German designed Army tropical shirt (*above*)

77 Modified French Army shirt (*right*)

79 *Luftwaffe* tropical shirt with long sleeves (*right*)

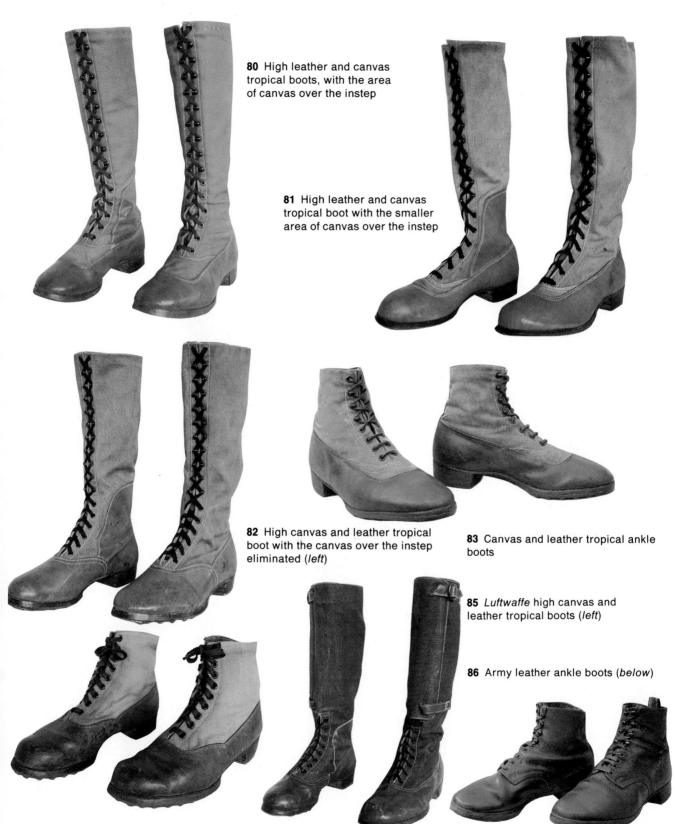

80 High leather and canvas tropical boots, with the area of canvas over the instep

81 High leather and canvas tropical boot with the smaller area of canvas over the instep

82 High canvas and leather tropical boot with the canvas over the instep eliminated (*left*)

83 Canvas and leather tropical ankle boots

85 *Luftwaffe* high canvas and leather tropical boots (*left*)

86 Army leather ankle boots (*below*)

84 *Luftwaffe* leather and canvas tropical ankle boots

87 The two styles of rucksack

88 Two styles of entrenching tools with their leather carrying frames

89 Gas masks/Canisters/Gascape bags

90 *Zeltbahn* (shelter quarters)

91 Leather map case and contents

92 Rear view of canvas combat Y-straps (*right*)

93 Canvas and leather Y-straps

94 Sundry items carried either in breadbag or rolled up inside the *Zeltbahn*

95 Pair of MP38/40 magazine pouches

96 Pioneers' equipment

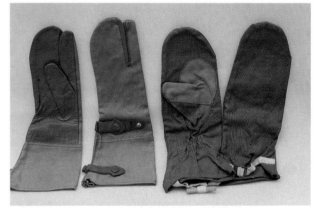

97 Two styles of canvas mittens worn with the motorcyclist's, or driving, coat

98 Officer belts/buckles

99 Other ranks belts/buckles

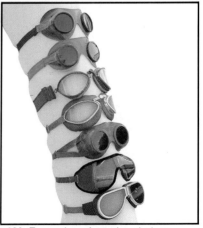

100 Examples of sand and glare goggles issued in North Africa by the German Army and the *Luftwaffe*

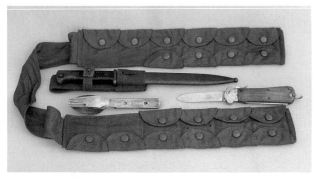

101 *Luftwaffe* items of equipment

102 Army waist belt arrangement

103 Four of the most common personal torches, issued for attachment to tunic or overcoat buttons (*left*)

104 *Dienstglas*, the standard issue Army 6 × 30 prismatic binoculars (*above*)

105 Water canteens (*below*)

106 Cover of the Army paybook

107 Cover of the *Luftwaffe* paybook

108 Stiff cardboard covers purchased privately for the Army and *Luftwaffe* paybooks

109 Cover of the *Wehrpass* (service record)

110 Cover of 'The Soldier in Libya'

111 Colour fold-out from 'The Soldier in Libya' showing guide to British Army uniforms

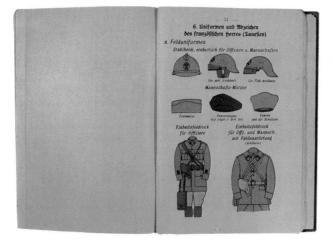

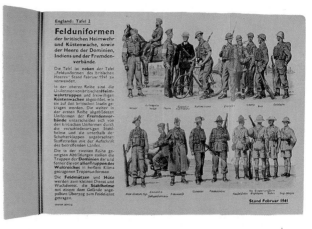

112 Colour page from 'The Soldier in Libya' showing French Army formations

113 Colour fold-out from 'The Soldier in Libya' showing different formations, and Allied armies

114 Covers of the 1942 and 1943 pocket diaries

115 Cover of the *Luftwaffe* magazine

116 Front page of the British Army propaganda paper

117 Typical page from a colourful propaganda magazine

118 German propaganda leaflet

119 Certificate of proficiency in first aid

120 Postcards and letters received by German troops in Africa

121 Pocket books taken from German POWs

122 Items taken from German POWs

123 One of the pages from scientific and popular magazines used as decoration (*right*)

124 Contents removed from tunics worn by POWs

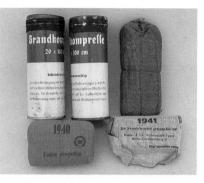

125 Dressings for wounds

126 Soldiers' field art items

127 Field art: a flattened section of brass shell case

128 Mess-tins decorated by German troops

129 Colour photo of Rommel

130 Adhesive stamp printed by the DAK field newspaper

131 Two examples of the stencilled DAK tactical symbol

132 Pennants from the North African battlefields

133 A representative range of medals and combat awards worn on uniforms in North Africa

134 General Neumann-Silkow's personal document stamp

135 Canvas rifle breech cover

136 A representative range of badges worn on uniforms in North Africa

137 Obverse and reverse views of the Italian-German Medal

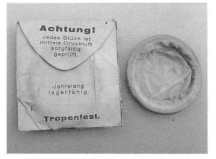

138 Condom as issued to German troops in Africa

139 Two examples of the *Afrikakorps* ring

140 Manufacturer's plate removed from a Messerschmitt Bf109F4–TROP

142 Contents of the standard first-aid chest carried in all vehicles in North Africa (*below*)

141 Camouflage colour on a 20 mm automatic cannon magazine canister

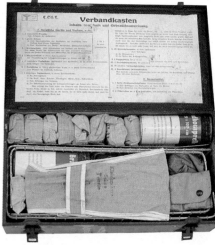

144 The famous 'Jerrycan' (*below*)

143 A piece of German shrapnel

The bitterly fought over feature of the Sidi Rezegh Tomb south-east of Tobruk, where the 2nd NZ Division suffered heavy losses in November 1941. (NZ National Archives – Alexander Turnbull Library)

pletely impassable at this point also.

Arty and anti-tank guns were firing at point blank range on the Regt, which first halted and then returned the fire while waiting for the Engineers. When, after 15 minutes, these latter failed to appear, the order to withdraw was given. The withdrawal was carried out in good order, accompanied by English arty fire.

April 14

In order to mislead the enemy, Engineers made a sham demolition of the anti-tank trench in the Western sector of the English positions round Tobruk. This took place on the night of the 12th.

On the night of the 13th, 8 MG and Engineers made a bridgehead at the road fork 7km south of Tobruk. Here, crossing places were to be made over the trench for the subsequent advance of the Regt. Anti-tank guns (from PzJägAbt.605) and a troop of AA

33 were detailed to co-operate with the Regt.

It was to assemble by 0230 hrs on, and to the south of, the bridgehead and to make its first attack in a northerly direction against P 99. It was planned that as the attack developed, the 1st Bn with PzJägAbt.605 would advance on a level with the Via Balbia, pursuing the retreating enemy to the west. The other Bn would turn off to the east and advance against Tobruk.

Actually, while the Regt was assembling, enemy arty opened barrage fire on it, but inflicted no loss.

At 0430 hrs the Regt crossed the bridgehead with 38 tanks and 4km west of the point it had been ordered to break through. The 2nd Bn was leading, followed by the 1st Bn and in turn by the three PzJägAbt.605 guns.

On first contact with the enemy 8 MG Bn went forward with a few units (2½ sections instead of 300 men). The situation seemed to be developing favourably with the enemy, taking them by surprise.

At 0530 hrs liaison between tanks and guns continued, but with the approach of dawn A/T fire concentrated on the Regt from all sides. The gunners were killed. At 0600 hrs, the Regt crossed P 99 and prepared to advance on the Via Balbia, completely alone, 6km deep in the enemy lines. It came under direct arty fire from near Fort Solaro, east of P 99, and from Fort Ariente. The enemy advanced his A/T units on both flanks and to the rear and succeeded in closing the gap in his lines. Hence the Regt was forced to fight on all sides at once.

At the same instant, six enemy fighters came roaring down in a low-level attack and enemy bombers dropped heavy-calibre bombs as well. While in this unpleasant situation an attack was launched from the right rear by 14 enemy tanks. Among them two Mark II were definitely identified.

Orders were given for an attack on these tanks. 1st Bn was to make a frontal attack and 2nd Bn a right flanking attack. During the combat, enemy A/T fire grew more and more intense. Visibility was considerably reduced by bursting grenades, burning tanks and the smoke of shells – adding considerably to our difficulties.

The Regt decided to withdraw for the losses in vehicles were far too great, which it did and in good order, firing in all directions and rescuing the wounded from the shattered tanks.

At 0800 hrs it reached the gap, now held by the enemy. On our approach they opened fire with A/T guns and from well-camouflaged MG posts. All concentrated their fire on the tanks passing through the narrow opening.

The 200 prisoners we had taken threw themselves on the ground to avoid the fire of their comrades, jumped into the trench and escaped. Several of our men riding on the outside of the tanks were wounded or killed.

1st Bn was detailed to cover the retreat against the A/T and MGs. The heavy well-aimed fire of the enemy pursued the Regt to a point about 2km south-east of the breakthrough. Here the Regt assembled, drew up its units in battle order, and prepared to receive the English counter-attack. This, however, did not take place. The enemy merely advanced a few tanks to the point where we had broken through.

The information about the enemy distributed before the action started told us he was about to withdraw, that his arty was weak and that his morale was poor.

Before beginning these three attacks the Regt had not the slightest information about the excellently constructed enemy positions, about his various arty positions and his enormous quantity of A/T guns. The presence of heavy tanks was also not known.

The Regt went into the fight with firm confidence and iron determination to defeat the enemy and take Tobruk. Only the enemy's great superiority, our great losses and a total lack of support, caused us to withdraw.

A German Sd.Kfz.222 armoured car driving off at speed from a New Zealand Field Dressing Station after arriving in the mistaken belief that the camp was in German hands. (Author's collection)

38 Tanks went into the battle
17 Tanks were destroyed by the enemy
 2 Officers are missing and 7 wounded
21 NCOs and men are missing
10 NCOs and men are wounded

That is a total loss of 50 per cent

Signed: OLBRICH

*　　*　　*

Cyrenaica was reconquered by Rommel in the space of twelve days (it had taken Wavell just on fifty days to cover the same distance) at a cost to Rommel of 1,300 casualties, while the British had lost well over two thousand prisoners and considerable stocks of military supplies, much of which had fallen into Rommel's hands. Among the prisoners captured by the advancing *Afrikakorps* was Lt General Richard O'Connor, the main architect of Wavell's victories, and one of the few

The cutting edge of a Panzer division: Panzers and anti-tank guns towed behind half-track prime movers, moving into battle together against British tanks, late November 1941. (Author's collection)

British commanders to know intuitively how to use the correct tactics for armoured formations fighting in the desert. By now Rommel was thinly stretched, with only weak forces on the Egyptian frontier and with not enough strength to take Tobruk, as Churchill knew from the intercepts of German signals he received from ULTRA.

One lesson that had been learnt by the Germans, and the British before them, was how an extended advance made a fighting force weaker and weaker as supplies (and in the desert this meant everything that an army needed) had to be carried over greater and greater distances. Vehicles – especially tanks with their exposed tracks and carriage wheels that wore down with sand, and high-revving engines that overheated and took fine dust and sand in through their air filters – very quickly came to the point where they needed maintenance. It was this process of diminishing strength that provided the pendulum effect in the fighting for the first two years as an advance took the attacking army further away from its supply bases.

Wavell's first attempt to dislodge Rommel came in mid-May, in an operation, known to the British as Operation Brevity, which resulted in some rather confused fighting for two days around Halfaya Pass and the border post of Fort Capuzzo. The British held Halfaya Pass after this short engagement but ten days later Rommel retook it in a sharp quick fight. Rommel was nervous about the strength of the Tobruk garrison to his rear and felt that Halfaya had to be in his hands if he was not to be threatened by the possibility of renewed action by the British on the frontier supported by the forces in Tobruk.

The second action taken by Wavell came in mid-June after some strong prompting from Churchill to do something about lifting the siege of Tobruk and to go on the offensive against Rommel. With a recently arrived shipment of tanks to give him numerical superiority in armour, Wavell moved across the frontier below Fort Capuzzo to take the German frontier positions in the rear as a prelude to using his two divisions in a move towards Tobruk. This was an ambitious plan in the light of German strength, together with Italian forces which were also available, and the poor state of preparedness in the British armoured units. This action, known to the British as Operation Battleaxe and to the Germans as the Sollum Battle, was also over in a couple of days and resulted in a British withdrawal to their starting position. Halfaya Pass, with its garrison under *Hauptmann* Bach, had been cut off but was not taken.

This battle was notable for the success of the 88mm guns used in a ground attack role against tanks (especially the heavily armoured Matilda tanks), the effective co-operation of the *Afrikakorps* and the *Luftwaffe*, the command deficiencies of the British system with the field commander stationed behind the front and hours away from important decisions (and conversely the superiority of Rommel's practice of putting himself in the forefront of the fighting). There was also the efficiency of the German battlefield tank recovery and repair crews who rescued and restored many tanks so that they could be used again in the fighting; the poor discipline of the British radio operators who gave the German intercept readers much valuable information; the deadly effectiveness of the German anti-tank guns that worked in close co-operation with their own tanks (the British were unaware of this for some time, and blamed the hits against their tanks on the German Panzers); the smooth and quick combinations that the Germans could achieve in the field between their various units. Lastly it established the ascendency of Rommel as a master of the desert battlefield. Rommel had hoped for a complete victory, but the main part of the attacking British force escaped.

Then followed a period of *Sitzkrieg*. For the next five months, Rommel had to build up his strength and make preparations for a carefully planned attack on Tobruk. At the same time General Auchinleck (Wavell had been removed by Churchill as a sign of his displeasure at the failure of Operation Battleaxe) started rebuilding the now retitled 8th Army before again attacking Cyrenaica to relieve Tobruk. Rommel realized the importance of the frontier area and he started improving its defences with minefields. He also had the novel idea of setting in concrete the turrets of some of the Matilda tanks that had been captured during the fighting of May and June. These were emplaced above Halfaya Pass, on the Bardia side, with a wide field of fire.

Supplies were a problem for both sides: for the Germans and Italians because of the attacks on their convoys by aircraft and submarines from Malta; for the British because of the long distance they had to cover around the Cape of Good Hope. On balance the British lines were more secure, for the Germans had no ULTRA to reveal the British convoys and after 22 June Germany was fully committed to the invasion of the Soviet Union. The *Luftwaffe* squadrons which had been transferred from Sicily to Russia made Malta a more serious threat to the Axis convoys too. Some reinforcements did arrive for Rommel, but they were not large enough to tip the balance – a few batteries of artillery to help in reducing

The fatigue of battle, half-smiles for the camera, but the eyes are distant – back at El Agheila again in December 1941. (ECPA)

Tobruk and a couple of battalions of infantry and various sub-units to fill out a new division being raised in Africa from the collection of unmotorized and replacement units which came to be known as the *Afrika* (for special purposes) Division and later as the 90th Light Division.

In October, the 5th Light Division was upgraded to a full Panzer division, but this did not mean Rommel was being reinforced. Units were shuffled around between the 5th Light and the 15th Panzer – 5th Light lost one of its machine gun battalions to 15th Panzer which transferred one of its motorized infantry regiments to the new 21st Panzer. In terms of the size of the Panzer divisions then fighting in Russia, each of

Reinforcements for the Afrikakorps *to make good the losses of the battles in November and December 1941, passing through the Brenner Pass in early 1942. (Author's collection)*

Mines played an important role in the fighting, whether used offensively to screen tanks and anti-tank guns, or defensively. Here a Pioniere *soldier lifts a British mine using the blade of his bayonet to probe the sand. (This photo was taken on 29 June 1942 near Tobruk.) (Author's collection)*

the two Panzer divisions of the *Afrikakorps* had one enlarged regiment of motorized infantry instead of the two regiments common to the divisions in Europe.

Only around the Tobruk perimeter was there any action, and this took place on a very localized scale, with both besieging and besieged troops cooped up in hot and uncomfortable immobility during the day and facing the danger of a quick and deadly skirmish by night. As the Tobruk perimeter stood astride the coastal road, the Via Balbia, Rommel had a new road built that detoured south of the fortress. Known as the Axis highway or the *Achsenstrasse*, it was constructed with great pride by Italian engineering units.

Rommel personally led a raid into Egypt in the middle of September which was codenamed Operation Summer Night's Dream (*Sommernachtstraum*), to stir up the British a little and to gather some information and any available loot. The results of this foray were sparse. The absence of any sign of an impending British offensive gave Rommel a false feeling of security and he proceeded with his own plans to capture Tobruk.

However much Rommel was unaware of British

intentions, they were not in the dark about his plans, and the British offensive (codenamed Operation Crusader) was timed to start only a few days before Rommel's attack on Tobruk. The British plan was to sweep through the desert and up towards the area between Tobruk and the frontier positions, isolating the garrisons around Bardia and Halfaya. At the same time, the German armour was to be drawn out and destroyed. ULTRA gave the British not only the starting time for Rommel's attack on Tobruk, but also provided them with an accurate assessment of Axis armoured strength. In numbers, the British had superiority and the decision was made to divide the tanks in order to protect and open paths for the infantry. Though opposed by the tank commanders, it was considered a safe policy as the British had 736 tanks – plus reserves which increased this number to nearly a thousand – while Rommel had only 240 plus 150 Italian tanks.

Operation Crusader (known to the Germans as the Winter Battle) opened on the night of 17/18 November 1941, when an enormous stream of Allied tanks and other vehicles poured into eastern Cyrenaica. The Germans were totally unaware of what was happening as their reconnaissance had been misled, and as the 8th

The élite of assault troops, Panzer Pioniere, *line up prior to an attack. They are heavily armed with machine guns and sacks of grenades. (ECPA)*

Army moved forward a severe rainstorm concealed their presence until the afternoon of the next day. But the British plan to draw the Axis tanks out early in the offensive failed, and the initiative very soon passed to the *Afrikakorps*, which was further helped by the British decision to split their tank forces. The early engagements saw the hapless British fighting a stronger German armoured force and they were steadily worn down. After every engagement the British foolishly presented the *Afrikakorps* with the chance to recover their salvageable tanks by withdrawing to 'laager' – form a defended camp – for the night. The German tank recovery units worked flat out through the nights (and even in the day during the battle) repairing whichever tanks could be quickly made battleworthy and towing away to their mobile workshops those that could be repaired.

Three weeks of very confused fighting followed in which no one was ever sure for too long which side controlled particular areas of desert. As the battle went on, increasing numbers of transport vehicles were captured by both sides, and places such as field hospitals that could not easily or quickly be moved during the flowing tide of battle changed hands many times – sometimes more than once in a single day. Prisoners would be taken only to be released by their own side hours or days later. At night the sky was full of coloured flares as the scattered troops tried to make contact with

A German prisoner captured by the 2/32 Battalion of the Australian 9th Division inside their sector of the Tobruk perimeter. (Australian War Memorial)

their units, or merely to let friendly troops know that their side had occupied one small square of desert sand.

Firm information about the course of battle was scarce because air reconnaissance was unreliable but by the fourth day a focal point emerged. This was the area above the small desert airfield at Sidi Rezegh where a tomb had been erected to honour an Arab martyr. North of this was the track known as the Trigh Capuzzo, an inland route from Tobruk to the border area around Fort Capuzzo. The main supply dumps used by the *Afrikakorps* were sited just north of the Trigh Capuzzo and luckily for Rommel the British did not move out to molest the transport columns that daily travelled back and forth replenishing the German forces east of Tobruk and north of Sidi Rezegh. Some of the bitterest fighting in this campaign took place around Sidi Rezegh involving the greater part of the 2nd New Zealand

Part of Rommel's 'Devil's Garden' at El Alamein: two Pioniere *soldiers are priming the deadly anti-personnel Schuh mines before scattering them through the fields of heavier anti-vehicle mines. (ECPA)*

Division and elements of the 90th Light Division, and the flat stony ground was contested constantly as the battle surged back and forth. Only a few days before, the 90th Light Division had been besieging Tobruk but it now had to turn around to defend the rear and to prevent a connection between the New Zealanders and the garrison in Tobruk.

Strangely, it took Rommel nearly four days to accept the magnitude of the British offensive and that he would have to give up his own plans for an attack against Tobruk. When he accepted it, he ordered the *Afrikakorps* commander, General Crüwell, to take the two Panzer divisions north to Sidi Rezegh to remove the threat of a link between the Tobruk garrison and the enemy force outside. A great battle now developed. Both the Germans and the British lost heavily in the fighting around Belhamed and El Duda, areas relatively close to Sidi Rezegh which were vital to the British if they were to effect a corridor into Tobruk. Then, having turned the enemy aside from Sidi Rezegh, Rommel had the further satisfaction of knowing the British were starting to falter.

After ravaging the greater part of a British tank brigade on 22 November, Crüwell then led one of the most bizarre attacks of the campaign. Germans traditionally honour their dead on the last Sunday before Advent, known as *Totensonntag* (Sunday of the Dead). On this day, the 23rd, General Crüwell led the *Afrikakorps* (both Panzer regiments together with the lorried infantry from the 15th Panzer Division and

various anti-tank and Flak units) and the Armoured Regiment from the Italian *Ariete* Division in a line-abreast charge against the British force outside Tobruk. What could have been a disaster for the *Afrikakorps* instead resulted in the destruction of two of the 8th Army divisions as fighting forces, the 7th Armoured Division and the 1st South African Division. As the extended line of the *Afrikakorps* raced across the desert, many commanders standing in their staff cars were killed or wounded, and the British guns took their toll of the advancing tanks and the following vehicles. But once the German tanks had passed through the British front a terrible carnage was inflicted on the exposed British rear and wild chaos ensued as men and vehicles tried to escape under the fire of German guns. This was truly a 'Sunday of the dead'.

Rommel, who had been out of touch with his main forces for two days (the entire *Afrikakorps* headquarters had been overrun near Sidi Rezegh the day before), now decided that victory was within his grasp if he could unhinge the British position with a strongly delivered blow that would shake their morale. He therefore collected the *Afrikakorps* and led it eastwards towards the frontier, away from what remained of the main striking force of the 8th Army and into an area that had

So desperate was the supply situation after Rommel was stopped at El Alamein that teams of gliders, like this Gotha 242, were used to fly cargoes of fuel and ammunition from Greece and Crete to airfields in Libya and Egypt. (Author's collection)

General Georg Stumme, Rommel's replacement in September 1942, inspecting installations in Tobruk Harbour. (ECPA)

been relatively quiet. This famous 'dash to the wire' – the long line of coiled barbed wire that the Italians had strung along the frontier to keep the rebellious desert tribes inside Libya – was meant to be the victorious culmination of everything that had gone before. It was a gamble, and it might have paid off had the 8th Army been aware of what Rommel was doing sooner and reacted with the same amount of force that Rommel had committed to the action. Rommel was searching for his enemy's jugular vein, the supply dumps and rear headquarters and the lines of communication that ran between these areas and the front. But the British did not withdraw from Cyrenaica and Rommel, instead of throttling the 8th Army lifeline, became distracted by a number of minor skirmishes around the frontier positions. While he was thus occupied, the British moved to recapture all the valuable ground gained by the *Afrikakorps* prior to Rommel's strike towards the wire. With the situation outside Tobruk now critical and an advance by the British inside Tobruk to link up with the NZ division imminent, the decision was made by the young *Afrikakorps* operations officer, Lt Col. Siegfried Westphal, to recall one Panzer division from the frontier to save the situation.

The crisis in the battle had now been reached, and when on 24 November Auchinleck himself took command and relieved a jittery General Cunningham, Rommel could no longer expect success by knocking the British off balance. Rommel, who did not know of the change in command, was now faced by an 8th Army that had been given a new strength of purpose and which firmly intended to remain where it was and to fight it out to the end. Rommel stayed on the frontier for a further two days before returning westwards to hammer the New Zealanders at Sidi Rezegh again and break their tenuous link with the Tobruk garrison. But

Flare signal codes

One enduring memory of all troops who took part in the battles in North Africa, especially the fluid and quick-moving fighting in the open desert in 1941, was the steady stream of flares that lit up the night sky after the opposing sides had lost contact in the darkness. The German Army made more use of flares than either the Italian or Allied Armies.

A booklet written in German and Italian was widely distributed among the Axis forces listing the basic conditions under which flare signals were to be used, and containing a list of the current allocation of colours. This updated list was issued as an appendix to the booklet in the form of a colour chart which could be glued inside the covers of the booklet. This allocation of colours was usually changed on a weekly basis. The three-part list of colour combinations reproduced here was the one current on 23 October 1942, the day of the opening of the final 8th Army offensive at El Alamein.

The first listing contains four signals intended as a means of identifying one's own unit to friendly units:

Orange-yellow: We are friendly troops
Orange-yellow + red: We are surrounded, cut off – the enemy is behind us
Orange-yellow + green: Repeat the move to attack (this is a command)
Green: We are moving forward – we are attacking – we are going into action in the same direction.

The basic colour in this set of signals was orange-yellow, with the extra colour green, and the signals were ones that could be used to communicate with friendly units in the same area.

The second lot of signals were ones that would have been used in an emergency when under enemy attack:

Red: The enemy is attacking us
Red + green: The enemy is attacking us from the right (going around us and penetrating)
Red + white: The enemy is attacking us from the left (going around us and penetrating)

The basic colour in this set of colours is, of course, red.

The third and last group of signals was intended for use by Panzer units, and used violet as the basic colour.

Violet: Enemy tanks in front of us
Violet + red: Enemy tanks behind us
Violet + green: Enemy tanks to the right of us
Violet + white: Enemy tanks to the left of us
Violet + orange-yellow: Commence combat, move forward, our own tanks are advancing

The section of the booklet dealing with instructions for the use of flares mentions such items as the need to ensure that at least 2,000-metre clear vision is present before sending up a flare, the importance of spacing sets of flare signals (at least thirty seconds between groups of signal pairs) in order to make the signals easier to read, the need to use signals only under clear orders, and the necessity of repeating the set of signal flares to make sure that they would have been properly understood and seen by other units in the area.

The last instruction in the booklet was an order to ensure at all costs that the colour codes did not fall into enemy hands.

For obvious reasons, the same colour signals were used by both the German and Italian Armies.

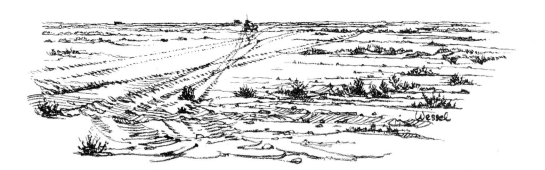

German strength was now ebbing, and on 4 December the eastern half of the ring around Tobruk was abandoned and Rommel retreated to a position running south from Gazala. Unwilling to be outflanked in the open desert to the south, Rommel ordered a retreat to Agedabia and then to El Agheila. The British followed slowly, and suffered a couple of sharp ripostes from Rommel to remind them that even though the *Afrikakorps* was retreating, it was not a beaten army.

In the Winter Battle the *Afrikakorps* lost its two

An Australian soldier stands triumphantly on the Minaret at Tel El Eisa, a feature bitterly fought over in the El Alamein battles. (Author's collection)

Panzer divisional commanders, von Ravenstein captured by the New Zealanders, and Neumann-Silkow who was wounded on 6 December by artillery fire and died in hospital at Derna two days later.

Access to all the high-level messages between Berlin and Rommel's headquarters in Africa that the British enjoyed through ULTRA did not weigh heavily on the outcome of the fighting during 1941. This was because in a running and quickly changing battle Rommel's communications were invariably long out of date by the time they reached the 8th Army. In any case Rommel was not beyond concealing his real plans from Berlin or making his intentions ambiguous to give him more tactical freedom. Only when the fighting became static did the advantage swing to the British. But this was not the pattern of the fighting in 1941. On the other hand, Rommel received more immediate and worthwhile intelligence from the British radio operators' casual disregard of discipline in the field. On balance, this was of greater use to him than were the intercepts of his radio contact with Berlin to the British.

1942

This year was to see the fortunes of Rommel and the *Afrikakorps* rise to full flood, then the ebb to a defeat that was the beginning of the end.

The year started with the German and Italian garrisons at Halfaya and Bardia cut off and under attack which resulted in their surrender. The valiant Major Bach led a spirited defence at Halfaya but there was no hope for such an isolated position so far from Rommel's main position at El Agheila. Rommel lost nearly 14,000 men (4,030 of whom were German) in the two abandoned positions on the Egyptian frontier. Nevertheless, conditions were turning in Rommel's favour. The entry of Japan into the war in the Far East had diverted British reinforcements away from North Africa and his own supply situation was improving. With winter conditions in Russia restricting air operations on the Eastern Front, the *Luftwaffe* was able to transfer a sizeable force of bombers to Sicily and they set about neutralizing Malta's capability to strike against the Axis supply convoys across the Mediterranean. With his supply line from Europe more secure, Rommel started to receive replacements for both men and arms lost in the Winter Battle, and, most importantly, new tanks.

The redoubtable Major Georg Briel (left), on 23 October 1942, the day of the opening of the final British offensive at El Alamein. (ECPA)

Medical problems

Except in the very heaviest battles, such as the fighting in the Alamein Line prior to the Allied breakthrough in October–November 1942, the attacks against the Tobruk perimeter in April–May 1941, the heaviest engagements in Libya in November–December 1941 and the end fighting in Tunisia in 1943, the largest single cause of manpower losses was sickness. During the late summer of 1942, when the *Afrikakorps* was dug in before the Alamein line, the number of troops being repatriated to Europe because of sickness exceeded the number that could be sent in as replacements, and these statistics include two entirely new formations which had arrived as reinforcements, the 164th Light Division and the Paratroop Ramcke Brigade.

The following extracts taken from the monthly report compiled for Rommel by the Chief Medical Officer of the *Afrikakorps*, Major General Bayer, give an illuminating – though not, of course, complete – insight into the health problems that plagued not just the *Afrikakorps* but all who fought in the desert. The first section contains extracts from reports made between September and November 1941. The second is a larger extract from a report submitted in January 1942 and deals in some detail with the nature of illnesses related to living and fighting in the desert, and the operation of the *Afrikakorps* medical services.

The most unhealthy periods for the *Afrikakorps* were the times when they were forced to engage in static warfare, and the worst of these was during the time spent in the Alamein line in 1942. Conditions in Tunisia were kinder, at least from the health angle, because of the different climate and the proximity to areas of settlement, whether farms and villages or the large city of Tunis with all its services.

Contracted extracts from *Afrikakorps* medical report Sept–Dec 1941

Sept 1941

The diphtheria epidemic which began in Aug has spread further. 416 new cases were reported in Sept.

The incidence of jaundice also increased. Sores which will not heal have also been on the increase. The incidence of bowel diseases has dropped somewhat.

On the whole, the health of *Afrikakorps* has taken an unfavourable turn. The number of new cases is continually mounting.

Oct 1941

The health of the troops in *Afrikakorps* has taken a still less favourable turn. Certainly the number of diphtheria

The field lavatory – walking off into the desert with a shovel was a necessary precaution against infectious diseases. (Author's collection)

cases has not increased, but there has been a big increase noted in jaundice and bowel diseases. The number of sick within the Corps over a period of 10 days varied between 2,550 and 3,000. In the three 10-day periods of the month 724, 715 and 854 men were admitted to hospital. There is always an average of 2,500 men under treatment by their own unit MOs (Medical Officers). At the beginning of the month there were 1,000 sick in the Corps medical installations, and since 6 Oct there has been 1,300 on the average. The highest number was 1,486 on 25 Oct.

Corps statistics for Oct:

With Units:
On 1 Oct: 2,088
Admitted during Oct: 8,441
Transferred to hospital: 2,159
Discharged fit: 5,424
Under treatment on 31 Oct: 2,515
Afrikakorps Installations: (Bardia–Derna):
Patients on 1 Oct: 1,071
Admissions during Oct: 2,733
Transferred to PzGp hospital or Europe: 1,500
Discharged fit: 927
Died: 30
Patients on 31 Oct: 1,347

From the above figures it can be seen that out of about 9,000 sick from the Corps for the month, 2,733 were sent to hospital. 927 of these were discharged fit. 1,500 have left the Corps, 1,220 by air to Europe and 280 via PzGp hospitals by hospital ship to Europe.

Nov 1941
The health of *Afrikakorps* leaves much to be desired. The incidence of diphtheria and jaundice is on the wane, but that of bowel diseases is constantly increasing. The Corps' medical centres are continuously crammed to bursting point – between 1,342 and 1,487 cases.

Extracts from Panzer Gruppe Afrika Chief Medical Officer's reports January 1942

From Aug to Oct 1941 only a few of the German troops were in contact with the enemy, in the form of mixed formations in the fortified line between Sollum and Sidi Omar. *Afrikakorps*, with 15 and 21 PzDivs, was in an assembly area between Tobruk and Bardia. *Afrika Div* (later 90LtDiv) was being formed platoon by platoon from unmotorized troops, who were being brought across the Mediterranean with the greatest difficulty. By the middle of Nov the division consisted of the following formations: 155InfRegt, 361*Afrika* Regt

Wounded German troops captured during the El Alamein Battle in October/November 1942. (Imperial War Museum)

(composed partly of ex-members of the Foreign Legion), a battalion of 255 InfRegt and one of 347InfRegt, 900 EngrBn and 605ATkUnit. These formations were very scantily equipped in consequence of the shocking supply difficulties and the torpedoing of so many supply ships. It had no medical services. This caused an extra heavy load on *Afrikakorps*' and PzGp's medical services, which were insufficient even for their own troops. All efforts to bring medical services over from Italy (where they were in readiness) were in vain, because more urgent supplies were given priority by PzGpHQ. Even the supply of medical stores was fraught with the greatest difficulty. It seemed as if ships carrying them were fated always to be lost. The most vital and urgent supplies were flown over from Athens.

The captains of hospital ships at first firmly refused to bring over medical supplies, but later agreed to bring over small quantities of supplies certified as indispensable. We were particularly grateful for the invaluable help given by the 12th Army Chief MO, who sent over large quantities of urgently needed equipment by any means he could. His co-operation was of the utmost value during the critical period of the English offensive.

Our relations with the Italian medical people were always marked by excellent co-operation and mutual support. The Italians had more medical services than we did, and were always most willing to place material at our disposal to relieve shortages. We also tried to help them when we could. The treatment of PWs (prisoners of war) was left to the Italians in general although of course we gave them the initial attention when more convenient. Although the surgery in the

Italian hospitals was excellent, wounded English PWs invariably asked not to be handed over to the Italians. They were as a rule agreeably surprised with the treatment they received in German dressing stations, and full of praise for it.

The general health of the troops deteriorated up to Nov, as the length of their stay in Africa increased. There were four diseases in particular which caused an unusually high sickness rate from July on – dysentery, jaundice, diphtheria and sores on the skin. The worst of all were the bowel diseases. Unfortunately they were at first not regarded as dysentery. The diarrhoea which affected almost every soldier was regarded as an 'African sickness' caused by the climate, and was as a rule treated within the units. Not until chronic cases began to show signs of dangerous weakness did we investigate and discover amoebic dysentery.

The shortage of medical services and

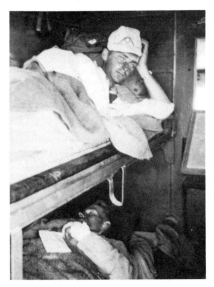

Wounded German troops wait in an ambulance for evacuation from the battlefield to a field hospital. The man in the top bunk stares into the camera with eyes dulled by shock and fatigue. The photo was taken somewhere in Cyrenaica during Operation Crusader. (Author's collection)

A wounded German medical orderly having an ankle wound dressed by a New Zealand medical orderly south of Sidi Rezegh, late November 1941. (Author's collection)

their primitiveness was a great disadvantage in dealing with bowel diseases, which need above all good living conditions and careful treatment. The lack of beds and transport meant that most of those suffering from them had to remain with their units in the desert, quartered in bivouac tents with insufficient food and care. It is not surprising, therefore, that many of them got into such a state that they could not be evacuated without great danger. Several deaths were certainly due to this.

At the end of July a diphtheria epidemic broke out in 21PzDiv, and spread to 15PzDiv in Aug. This has now died down.

Jaundice occurred in all formations to about the same extent. It began to increase in Aug and reached its maximum incidence in Oct. About 5,000 men (10–12% of the total strength) had it, while among the Italians only 3–4% were affected. (Immunity gained by many of the Italians in childhood?)

There were a few cases of recurrence of infectious diseases, caused probably by ticks in the dugouts in Tobruk pos-itions. There were a few cases of typhus and paratyphus – in July there was even a small epidemic of it in a field hospital in Benghazi.

From captured English MOs we learnt that jaundice was also widespread among the enemy, particularly the English. Diarrhoea was also bad. Amoebic dysentery was rare and diphtheria did not occur to the same extent as with us.

Statements of all PWs agreed that the enemy was much better fed than our men and had warmer clothing.

Lice were negligible during the warm weather, but increased more and more during the winter. The main reasons for this were:

(1) the use of captured English blankets,
(2) the occupation of old Italian positions, particularly in the Tobruk front,

(3) inadequate personal hygiene due to the lack of water, soap and washing materials.

The soap supply for several months was lost on a torpedoed ship. In many units the men had only the clothes they wore. This made it almost impossible to keep bodies and clothes clean, even without the added hindrance of active operations.

There was no danger of infestation with lice by the Arab population, because even the simplest soldier instinctively avoided any connection with them. Anyone who had once been literally covered from head to foot with fleas after visiting an Arab tent or cave was always careful to dodge it a second time.

In mid-Nov the medical services were disposed as follows:

Hospitals in Tripoli.
Special hospital for diphtheria and jaundice in Apollonia.

200	Forward Hospital in Derna.
36	Fd Hosp in Derna.
2/592	Medical Company Medical Dressing Station (MDS) at the 'White House'.
2/200	Med Coy MDS at Mrassas.
2/33	Med Coy MDS at El Adem.
1/33	Med Coy MDS north of the Via Balbia 42km east of Tobruk.
1/200	Med Coy MDS south of Via Balbia 37km west of Bardia and Advance Dressing Station in Bardia.
531	Amb Park in Derna.

These dispositions were fairly well suited to the altered conditions after the beginning of the English attack, and at first were not changed. The MDS at El Adem was particularly valuable. The fact that it was within shell range of Tobruk was accepted in view of its advantageous situation. Until the withdrawal from Tobruk it was the main surgical centre. It also took most of the

wounded from *Afrika* Div, which was involved in heavy fighting on two fronts and had the heaviest casualties of all. Many of the wounded from the Pz divisions also came there, and up to 5 Dec a total of 1,372 wounded and 371 sick were admitted. The MDSs 42km east of Tobruk and 37km west of Bardia received wounded mainly from the Pz divisions when they were operating in the Bardia–Sidi Omar–Bir el Gubi–Axis track area.

On 22 Nov 1/200 MDS had to withdraw west in a hurry in the face of an English armoured attack, leaving behind all its equipment and all seriously wounded, with the necessary medical personnel to look after them. The personnel went mainly to Mrassas. The wounded were taken to El Adem or 1/33 MDS. The latter was cut off on 24 Nov when the enemy pushed up to the Via Balbia from south of Gambut.

A limited amount of supplies got through to it, and a limited number of wounded were evacuated from it, by convoys. The last to get away were 103 lightly wounded, who were evacuated to El Adem on 3 Dec. 400 wounded had to stay behind. On 4 Dec they fell into English hands together with the entire company.

The dressing station at Bardia became very important for the 6,000 Germans cut off in Bardia and in the Halfaya–Sidi Omar positions. Communications between Bardia and the Halfaya positions were maintained by sea via Lower Sollum at night, and wounded and sick were evacuated by this means. Supplies were brought in by air and submarine. Shortly before the surrender of Bardia on 2 Jan all wounded and sick except for a few who could not be moved were sent to Italy.

2/200 and 2/592 MDS took the overflow from 2/33 MDS. The MDS at the 'White House' also acted as a CCS (Casualty Clearing Station).

The *Luftwaffe* co-operated nobly, and the Chief Corps MO organized all the transport from the forward stations well, so that evacuation presented no serious difficulties despite the shortage of transport. Serious cases were evacuated by two medical Junkers aircraft, which flew between Gazala and Derna 6 times a day.

German wounded POWs at a New Zealand Forward Dressing Station in Libya, November 1941. (Alexander Turnbull Library – NZ National Archives)

Transport aircraft also took wounded to Derna or direct to Athens, and the rest of the wounded were evacuated on supply transport or buses borrowed from the rear-line formations.

The evacuation to Greece was completely successful. In the first three weeks after the opening of the English offensive an average of 150 wounded and sick were flown daily from Derna airfield. The aircraft arrived from Greece in varying numbers and at varying hours, unannounced, and had to unload and load at the airfield in the shortest possible time because of the danger of air attack. This caused great difficulties, particularly since the 8km from the hospital to the airfield included a steep zigzag up the escarpment, which was often attacked from the air.

Between 18 Nov and 14 Dec a total of 4,058 sick and wounded went through Derna. Urgent representations to the Italian Navy led to the arrival of hospital ships in Derna on 6 and 15 Dec. The latter took away the last of the wounded only a matter of hours before Derna was evacuated.

Operations of the medical services with the fighting troops during the tank battles of the first two weeks deserves special mention. Each Pz division had only one light platoon (1/33 and 1/200) available for mobile operations. 21 PzDiv also had most of its ambulances, while 15PzDiv's ambulances were for the most part split up among the MDSs and had to look after *Afrika* Div as well. This arrangement was due to the plan of attack on Tobruk, by which 15PzDiv was to have been used to a very limited extent at first.

15PzDiv's mobile light platoon followed it into the blue on 19 Nov. On 20 Nov its store truck was knocked out by enemy action. 70 wounded were assembled in 9 vehicles and the platoon commander tried to get them through to 1/33 MDS. The column was chased by the enemy and finally on 24 Nov stumbled into an enemy camp and was captured, although the commander managed to escape with the trucks at the tail of the column. Many unit ambulances were also captured, but they were replaced very soon by captured vehicles. To avoid further losses the divisional MO directed that wounded should be sent back only with the supply convoys, and that empty ambulances were to go forward the same way. This order, however, was often impossible to carry out owing to difficulties arising from the movements of the Pz divisions.

21PzDiv's light platoon operated much more successfully. Its company commander had had previous experience in the desert, and was very skilful in overcoming difficulties. Until 23 Nov the platoon went with its division, collected and dressed the wounded, and evacuated them to the MDSs adroitly dodging the enemy. At night the division laagered, and work could be done under this protection; on the night 23–24 Nov the platoon supported *Afrika* Div at Sidi Rezegh. This division had particularly heavy casualties that day. When the division pushed over the Egyptian frontier the platoon lost touch with it and was pushed north by an enemy force. On the night 25–26 Nov a convoy carrying wounded was sent off to the MDS east of Tobruk. It reached its objective, although it passed right through the enemy lines on the way.

On 26 Nov the platoon contacted its division again and stayed with it thereafter. On 30 Nov it treated the German wounded found in an English MDS, which was in our hands for a short time.

The experiences of the light platoons in a mobile role lead to the following conclusions:

Care of wounded in the desert is very different from that in the usual type of warfare. The divisions are fighting widely separated and often in wild confusion with enemy armoured columns. This makes it impossible to establish MDSs or other fixed medical stations on the battlefield, or to send unprotected vehicles from or to fighting units. It makes it necessary to:

(a) establish medical stations at the divisional supply centres,
(b) form a mobile platoon with as many ambulances as possible and allot it to the fighting formations,
(c) evacuate wounded in co-operation with the divisional administrative staff with supply convoys (supply columns concentrated under unified direction and protected by tanks).

Care of the wounded in *Afrika* Div was particularly difficult, because the division did not have its own medical services and communications were too bad to permit it to keep in touch with the Pz divisions' medical people. In any case, 15PzDiv could not spare enough ambulances. The division helped as best it could by establishing vehicle posts on the Axis track, using vehicles of DivHQ and 900EngrBn. Later it formed an ambulance platoon from captured vehicles.

On 4 Dec the MDS at El Adem was moved back to 60km east of Derna. The night before the relief it was attacked from the air with bombs and cannon for an hour. The MDS at the 'White House' suffered a similar attack four days later. As the enemy had previously respected medical installations, it was assumed that this was a reprisal. A possible reason for this was the fact that a few days earlier German guns had been sited beside an English MDS which had been temporarily in our hands, and had given rise to a very destructive English bombardment of their own MDS. Probably also troop concentrations and HQ in the immediate vicinity of the MDSs concerned had contributed to the attacks. This could not always be avoided.

On 7 Dec the MDSs at Mrassas and the 'White House' were moved back. The MDS 60km east of Derna was also moved on 11 Dec.

By the middle of January Rommel was able to contemplate further offensive action and, when he learnt through his intelligence services of the weakness in the British line in front of El Agheila, launched an attack on 21 January which was reminiscent of his advance over the same ground the year before. He sent the Italian divisions north to Benghazi and then led the *Afrikakorps* inland via Antelat and Msus to Mechili. The British were unable to hold him and they retreated to a line running south from Gazala. But Rommel had now reached the limit of his strength and the two sides dug in at a point that was nearly mid-way between the respective supply bases: Tripoli for the Axis army and the Nile Delta for the British.

The following months were to be a race by both sides to build up enough strength to attack. The race was won by Rommel though strategic considerations were in the long run working against him. With the battle to subdue Russia still hanging in the balance, he could not look forward to reinforcements and the time was approaching when the might of the United States would be brought to bear in Africa. His supplies would continue to arrive only for as long as the *Luftwaffe* was operating in strength against Malta. The island was the key to securing certainty of supply and in February Rommel agreed with Kesselring's insistence that Malta had to be captured before Rommel could move forward in Cyrenaica. Plans were set in motion for an airborne assault on Malta, a joint operation by Italian and German paratroops.

However, by mid-April the threat posed by the British build-up at Gazala had to be reckoned with. Rommel proposed a 'spoiling' attack to dislodge the British and to capture Tobruk before the *Luftwaffe's* invasion of Malta. Both the High Command and Kesselring agreed, as an advance by Rommel to Tobruk would put the RAF in Cyrenaica out of range of Malta and so would deny the island any land-based air support.

The attack launched by Rommel on 26 May 1942 was carefully planned, but almost from the beginning things started to go badly for the Axis forces. Rommel's plan to take the *Afrikakorps* around the southern end of the British line would have benefitted from his being able to capture the southernmost point in this long line of fortified positions. This was the old Italian desert fort of Bir Hacheim, which the Italians were to attack, just sixty-five kilometres south-west of Tobruk. Rommel's first sweep took him up behind the British line and fierce battles with the 8th Army's armour followed. While the Bir Hacheim fortress was in enemy hands

A captured British 25 pdr gun used by the Germans at El Alamein, abandoned after being caught in an Allied air attack. The power of ground strafing is evident in the wreckage of this gun and its equipment trailer. (Author's collection)

Rommel's line of supply was blocked, apart from what could be squeezed through the minefields and boxes (an area surrounded by thick minefields and enclosing a strong artillery force with infantry dug in) of the deep British defensive line. The British armour had been strengthened by numbers of the American-made General Grant tank. This was armed with a 75mm gun which, although not having full 360° traverse, did at least mean that the British tank crews could engage the Panzers from greater range. Despite decisions to keep 8th Army's armour concentrated, old habits now reasserted themselves and Rommel's Panzers were able to take on the British armoured units one by one. But the early successes did not last and the full weight of the British armoured strength became concentrated around one of their boxes, called the 'Cauldron' by the Germans.

The plan had not worked. The Italians had failed to take Bir Hacheim or to find a gap between the British boxes through which to feed supplies to Rommel's forces behind the line. Attacks by the RAF were taking their toll, and as fuel ran low Rommel began to lose his mobility. By the end of May the situation was looking desperate for the Germans, and supplies ran so low that Rommel himself went through the British minefields to guide a convoy carrying fuel, water and ammunition.

If the 8th Army could have found the means and the will to exert maximum pressure against an *Afrikakorps*

One of the many bridges on the coastal road destroyed by the retreating Germans to slow the British advance after the retreat from El Alamein. (Author's collection)

starved of supplies, the german forces could have been brought to their knees. Fortunately for Rommel, British generalship was weak and nothing was seriously done to hamper the Germans' desperate efforts to smash an opening in the British line at the point of the 'Cauldron' facing the British 150th Brigade. Almost at its last gasp the weary *Afrikakorps* overwhelmed an equally exhausted British 150th Brigade, and the crisis had passed. At this point Rommel left the *Afrikakorps* still in combat with the disorganized British forces outside the 'Cauldron' and moved southwards to tackle the Free French defenders of Bir Hacheim. This was one of the toughest battles fought in Africa. The Free French put up an epic stand against almost constant attack from the *Luftwaffe*, the 90th Light Division and the Italian *Ariete* Armoured Division, holding their small fortress for nine days. In the meanwhile, the British had frittered away their armoured strength in a number of poorly co-ordinated attacks against the *Afrikakorps* to the north.

By the middle of June the *Afrikakorps* was able to

shift the focus of the battle away from the 'Cauldron' and nearer to the area south of Tobruk. At this point the British started to withdraw from the entire Gazala line. Some units went back inside the Tobruk perimeter while others escaped into the desert further south and made for the frontier. Rommel would have liked to fling the *Afrikakorps* out in a great encircling manoeuvre to make a trap for the fleeing 8th Army, but his troops had reached the limits of their physical reserves. In diaries picked up later by New Zealanders at El Alamein that belonged to German soldiers who fought through the Gazala battles there were entries showing the men had fought for days on end with only brief spells of sleep. One such daily entry read simply 'no sleep again'. Under these conditions it was not surprising that troops who had been under almost constant battle strain for up to three weeks, on reduced rations and fatigued from lack of sleep, were incapable of an energetic attack against the fleeing enemy. Even Rommel's call to fight was not enough to rouse them, for a few days at least.

Again Tobruk beckoned to Rommel, its capture being part of the original agreed plan. Quickly preparations were put in train for another attack and Rommel made ready to follow the plan he had worked out for the previous November. As his artillery batteries took up their positions they found to their amazement that the British in some places had not removed German ammunition supplies built up the previous year, and this became an important factor in the speed with which Rommel was able to mount his assault on Tobruk. By 18 June Tobruk was again besieged, three short days after the first German troops had reached the Axis Highway. The assault was to begin on the 20th; Rommel was giving the mainly South African garrison no time to dig in. With a tremendous air attack delivered by the *Luftwaffe* to soften up the defences, the assault was launched with a storm of artillery from German and Italian guns. This time, in contrast to 1941, Rommel knew just what lay ahead of him, and the pioneers bridged the first anti-tank ditches for the waiting tanks and lorry-borne infantry which stormed ahead and into the fortress. Not least in the minds of the attacking troops was the vision of a mountain of loot inside Tobruk, especially such items as succulent tinned fruit and tasty bully beef which the Germans were denied in their own diet.

The plan had worked, and early the next morning a very elated Rommel accepted the surrender of the garrison commander, the South African General Klopper. The prize had been won, but an even more tempting prize lay ahead, the Nile Delta, and within a few hours of taking Tobruk Rommel issued an order to prepare the *Afrikakorps* to move off towards Egypt. Such an order was contrary to the commitment he had made earlier to stop at Tobruk until Malta could be taken. But, eager to pursue the disorganized columns of ragged British survivors from the Gazala battles who were straggling into Egypt, he was afraid he might never again have a chance like the one before him now. Confident that Hitler would give him the authorization he asked for, Rommel went ahead with his decision to follow the 8th Army and strike it down as soon as his troops could bring it to bay.

Although he did not know it, Rommel was heading down a road of no return. The supplies he captured in Tobruk were enough to take him into Egypt, but not enough to cover his needs if there was much mobile fighting. As he moved into Egypt so the *Luftwaffe* squadrons would have to go forward with him, taking them far out of range of Malta. While the Axis Forces were behind the Gazala line the *Luftwaffe* units on African soil could both support the *Afrikakorps* and attack Malta (and the convoys that supplied the island). With the drive to the Caucasus already under way in Russia, the strong *Luftwaffe* presence in Sicily had been

A light 20mm Flak gun deployed against ground targets as Rommel pulls his men back into the Buerat position in late December 1942 behind a thin blocking screen. (Author's collection)

withdrawn to support this offensive, and the Italian Air Force and Navy were not strong enough to repeat the performance of the *Luftwaffe* the previous spring which had neutralized Malta as a base for attacks against Axis convoys.

Rommel certainly never entertained the idea that he would be tied down inside a narrow corridor of land for an extended period of time and forced to fight a battle of attrition. If he worried at all about supplies, he must have been confident that he could capture enough fuel and food to keep his divisions moving. This was the most important thing – to keep moving at any cost – and it had to be done with maximum speed as soon as possible. Hitler had backed Rommel's request for permission to advance into Egypt, and had shown his pleasure with the performance of his favourite general by creating him a Field Marshal, at 50 the youngest in the German Army, but could offer no support apart from assigning to *Panzerarmee Afrika* the resources that had been earmarked for the now-postponed invasion of Malta. The die was cast, and using petrol and the many vehicles captured in Tobruk and loaded with loot, the German troops crossed into Egypt on 23 June heading for the next battle.

Auchinleck was not without reserves and he had rushed the New Zealand Division from Palestine to occupy a blocking position at Mersa Matruh, together with British armour and some Indian troops. This force was in fact much stronger than the advancing German

February 1943 and Rommel has arrived in Tunisia with the remnants of his Army. (ECPA)

columns pushed on by Rommel. The 21st Panzer Division, for example, when it reached Mersa Matruh on 27 June, was less than a thousand strong, and its Panzer Regiment 5 had only 23 tanks. More were following up, but the pendulum effect was now working against the Germans. The 90th Light Division, which took up a blocking position on the eastern side astride the coast road, was not much stronger, while the total British strength inside Matruh was in the order of 20,000, with more units outside. But again the British command was poor where it counted most – in sound tactics and a willingness to counter Rommel's moves. For instance, because of confused communications and misunderstood intentions on all sides, British armour abandoned the desert below Matruh. This allowed an unimpeded encirclement of the Mersa Matruh position by the leading elements of the *Afrikakorps*. And once again Rommel was able to stampede the jittery and confused 8th Army Command, for though Auchinleck had taken over personal control, and the New Zea-

landers had a competent General in Freyberg, communications remained jumbled and contradictory, and the 8th Army as a whole was at sixes and sevens.

On the night of 27/28 June the bulk of the New Zealand Division broke out across the open desert which took it directly through an area near Minqar Qaim held by III Battalion of the 104th Motorized Infantry Regiment of the 21st Panzer Division. What followed was an incident that was to incense Rommel and gave rise to charges in the German press that the New Zealanders were gangsters fighting an uncivilized war.

The New Zealand break-out steamrollered over the unsuspecting Germany infantry, most of whom were partly undressed and lying asleep beside their vehicles, or in shallow trenches under their overcoats. These men were cut down by automatic gunfire from everything that the New Zealanders could bring to bear. The New Zealanders' attack then rolled right over the Regimental Field Hospital which lay behind the first line of German vehicles and trenches. Most of the wounded and sick in the hospital – a better description of it would be a Field Dressing Station or a Casualty Clearing Centre – were killed. But what caused real resentment among the Germans was when the following waves of New Zealanders blasted their way through the already devastated hospital. Undoubtedly, they did this because they had no means of knowing who was dead and who was merely pretending to be, but the bayonet was used to 'clear' out a path eastwards. Many Germans who tried to surrender were shot down for the New Zealanders' orders had been, in essence, 'kill or be killed'. The dead and wounded in the 104 Regimental Field Hospital were treated no differently, and it was this which so angered the Germans when next morning they inspected the scene of the previous night's slaughter. Among the dead in the remains of the tents and vehicles of the field hospital were badly mutilated bodies, including at least two which had been decapitated.

Later Rommel spoke to the New Zealand Brigadier Clifton, after he had been captured, questioning him about the events of that night at Minqar Qaim. Clifton was able to convince Rommel that in the confusion the mutilation of the German dead had been a result of the following waves attacking everyone in their path on the assumption that they were still alive. Though this engagement was not a significant one in the balance of the whole campaign, it rates mention because it was the one engagement when the Germans accused the 8th Army of a deliberate breach of the rules of warfare and the German press reported it as an atrocity and a massacre. New Zealand accounts of this engagement claim that their advancing columns were unaware of the field hospital, and Rommel accepted Brigadier Clifton's explanation that in the night and 'fog of war' his men did not realize either that they were overrunning a field hospital or that many of the Germans attacked were already dead.

Rommel took another impressive bag of prisoners from what remained at Mersa Matruh after the New Zealand break-out, and fuel, vehicles and a number of tanks found in a repair workshop. Ahead of Rommel there was now only the unevaluated line at El Alamein, a narrow neck of desert running between the coast and the impenetrable marshy sand of the Qattara Depression. This was the best position for defence along the entire North African coast. As long as the line itself could be held, it could not be attacked from the rear – the Qattara Depression meant that it was impossible to outflank from the open space to the south.

On the morning of 30 June 1942, a line of vehicles – half-track troop carriers, a few trucks and some mobile anti-tank guns – under command of the redoubtable *Hauptmann* Briel, came up against the first minefield in the El Alamein line, and British artillery fire came down near them. The Battle of El Alamein had begun – it was to last four hard months.

When the 90th Light Division made ready for the initial assault against the Alamein positions (at this time it did not warrant the name of a 'line' as the defences were far from complete and there were gaps between the prepared boxes), Rommel was committing a division in name only, the effective strength being well under 2,000 men. Coming face to face with the minefields and artillery of the Alamein positions in their early morning attack the Division faltered and broke ranks, one of the few occasions that a German unit in Africa did not carry out an order to press home an assault. The sheer exhaustion of these men was such that even Rommel's appearance was not enough to inspire them to resume the attack, and under continuing British shellfire they dug in.

The two weak Panzer divisions attacking further south did have some initial success but they too were stopped on this first day of the battle. The next day, the 90th Light Division again attacked on the axis of the coastal road but made only small headway, so

A graphic photo taken shortly after a successful tank attack by 21PzDiv on 15 February 1943 against American units near Sidi Bou Zid in western Tunisia. The wounded company leader discusses a follow-up with his section officers. The Leutnant *on the right is wearing a set of American Tanker's overalls. (Charles Hinz)*

In the Tunisian dusk a 7.62cm anti-tank gun, with its crew in a half-tracked prime mover, move back to new positions on 17 March 1943. (Author's collection)

Rommel had to move the *Afrikakorps'* Panzer divisions north in support (the original intention had been to have the Panzers advance around the south and swing north behind the British facing the 90th Light Division).

In the light of the weakness of Rommel's forces, this plan was too ambitious. The British were able to block the Panzers' move northwards though Rommel was still pressing forward, however weakly, by the end of the second day. The third day again saw some small gains by the Germans and the Italians who were now arriving in support (notably the *Ariete* Armoured Division), but the increasing tempo of air attack by the RAF (which not only interfered with Rommel's battlefield dispositions but was destroying a significant part of his supply columns) and stiffening opposition from the 8th Army continued to block Rommel's attempts to get behind the British positions. His army was exhausted and incapable of doing what he asked of them, and so on the morning of 4 July Rommel ordered a stop to all offensive operations. He called his armour back to rest and regroup while the front was taken over by infantry, mainly Italians recently arrived in the line.

Auchinleck, however, was not prepared to let Rommel get his second wind and on the night of 9/10 July he launched a strong attack against the northern sector of the Axis line held by the Italian *Sabratha* Division, which collapsed under the cold hard steel of the bayonets of the Australian 9th Division. Everything that the Germans could scrape together was thrown into the breach in an attempt to seal the dangerous hole in the line. During the next 24 hours fierce and confused fighting followed which extended further south. In the north the crisis continued to develop and throughout 11 July Rommel desperately shuffled his meagre forces to try to restore the line, but the Australians kept up their attack and captured the feature known as Tel El Eisa, north-west of Alamein on the coastal road.

The defensive fighting forced on Rommel ate into his small reserves of fuel and ammunition and caused him to abandon his plans for an attack on the southern edge of the British line. Although he was managing to hold the continuing attacks against his positions, it was a close run thing and his successes had as much to do with faulty British tactics and lack of co-ordination as it had with the Germans' ability to beat back British pressure. For six days and nights he had to counter attacks along the low prominence known as Ruweisat Ridge which crossed the front parallel to the coast 15 kilometres south of the coastal road, while strong fighting continued around Tel El Eisa which was still held by the Australians. Further British action against a shallow depression known as El Mrier continued to keep Rommel fighting on the defensive, and such was the attrition in front-line strength that on 22 July he reported to the Italian High Command in Rome that if British pressure was maintained he could not guarantee that the front could be held. The loss of manpower, especially in the infantry units, and the intermittent supplies which just barely covered his daily requirements, were pushing Rommel to the edge of his endurance. Fortunately for the *Panzerarmee*, the British were also running out of strength.

By the end of July the fighting faded and both sides settled down to a period of consolidation and reinforcement. The first battle of Alamein had ended with the final issue still in doubt, but the fortunes of war were now running against the Axis. In the all-important field of intelligence the British were clear winners. Not only was ULTRA providing the 8th Army with daily summaries of all intercepted radio traffic between North Africa and Berlin or Rome, which gave detailed information on Axis strength, intentions and dispositions, but during the night attack by the Australians against Tel El Eisa Rommel had lost his most reliable source of information when the *Panzerarmee*'s signals interception unit was overrun and completely wiped out. This highly experienced and efficient unit, *Nachr-Fern-Aufkl-Kp 621* commanded by *Hauptmann* Alfred Seebohm, had become expert at reading British radio traffic. Every indiscretion, nuance in particular kinds of signals, individual peculiarities of certain operators, significance in sequence of commands, every whisper holding a hint of something important, the daily menu of field commands that are a part of running the organization of a large army, all the idle chatter interspersed with official communications – all of this was picked up by Seebohm and his team, then evaluated for Rommel.

The destruction of Seebohm's unit was not an incidental part of the Australian attack against Tel El Eisa. The British knew Seebohm's location and one Australian battalion was given specific orders to locate and destroy it. The Italian infantry in the front line had not been much help in holding the Australians back, and Seebohm's men were overwhelmed by a superior force.

Just as important as the information Seebohm and his men gathered, was the interception and decoding of all the messages sent by the US Military Attaché in Cairo to Washington. The Germans had come into possession of this code late in 1941 and since then Rommel had been receiving daily reports from Seebohm of everything of importance in this privileged inter-Allied appreciation of British military strengths and weaknesses in the Eastern Mediterranean. The American Military Attaché, Colonel Fellers, passed on to Washington a constant stream of reports on British reinforcements, plans, morale, tactics – everything in fact that could be of interest to his military masters in Washington and, of course, to Rommel.

There were some very nasty surprises for British intelligence when they digested the fruits of the Australian raid on Seebohm's unit. The extent of their own looseness in radio discipline was exposed, as was the fact that Seebohm had been reading the radio signals between Fellers and Washington. Now these two open windows in the British High Command were closed to Rommel, and he was not to get another look through them. Although a similar unit to the one commanded by the dead Seebohm was immediately flown out from Germany, it did not have the rich experience of Seebohm and his men and had to learn from scratch how to operate in Africa. The British, now armed with the knowledge of their earlier weakness, took steps to block both sources. From this time British radio traffic was controlled and better disciplined, and their security services monitored it to ensure that it remained so. Rommel now had to fight without accurate intelligence about British plans, and, worse, his inexperienced signals interception unit could not cope with British deception which, as a result, succeeded in feeding him misleading information.

* * *

During August Rommel's position improved somewhat after the pressure of the 8th Army's attacks slackened and then stopped. In response to his calls for German infantry, a new Division, the 164th Light, was now in place (its regiments had been arriving in July and were pitched into the fighting as soon as they became

The edelweiss in Africa – members of Gebirgsjäger *Regiment 756 captured by the Green Howards in Tunisia, April 1943. Note the unit's insignia on the arm of soldier on left. (Imperial War Museum)*

available) and a tough brigade of German paratroops led by their equally tough commander, General Bernard Hermann Ramcke, had been fed into the line. This unit had been originally earmarked for the invasion of Malta, now postponed indefinitely. Replacements for the casualties of the earlier fighting and the many sick were also arriving. The most common route for these new arrivals was by air from Greece and Crete, and the *Luftwaffe* was also bringing across as much as it could of badly needed stocks of fuel. To augment the carrying capacity of the overworked fleet of Ju52s, the *Luftwaffe* employed scores of transport gliders loaded up with supplies and towed behind bombers at near sea level.

Without the drain of constant fighting, the stocks of ammunition and all the other material the army needed were built up. Large complexes of dumps were constructed in pits blasted out of the stony ground and covered with large sheets of camouflage netting, and as protection against any further attacks extensive minefields were laid along the length of the line.

Rommel's health began to fail during August, but he went ahead with plans for the attack which was scheduled for the end of the month, when there would be a full moon, against the southern part of the British line. Though weak – in the vital area of tanks alone the British had a superiority of over three to one, and there was barely enough fuel for two days' operations – Rommel knew that this was his last chance to get through the British line and reach the Nile Delta. The attack, launched in the late hours of 30 August, was intended to take the *Afrikakorps* into British territory just south of the Alam Halfa Ridge, after which they would wheel northwards to take the 8th Army in the rear.

Forewarned by ULTRA, Auchinleck's successor, General Bernard Montgomery, was waiting. The British had been preparing for over a month for this German attack. It was slow to start because of unexpected minefields, and so as to accelerate its progress Rommel, after some initial uncharacteristic hesitation, ordered his forces to move its axis of advance closer to the Alam Halfa Ridge. This took the *Afrikakorps* into the jaws of the British trap which had been so carefully laid. From the northern side of the ridge, British armour in 'hull down' positions, dug in anti-tank guns and artillery poured a deadly rain of fire into the German columns, while the RAF mounted continuous attacks on the German supply convoys destroying many loads of precious fuel, ammunition and water.

When the leading German tanks and infantry tried again and failed to reach the crest of the ridge on the morning of 2 September, Rommel decided to call the attack off and to retreat back to a line he could hold. In spite of heavy losses, and the unprecedented scale of attacks by the RAF, German morale was still high and there was surprise among the *Afrikakorps* when the news of Rommel's decision reached them. It was Rommel's morale that was cracking, under the cumulative effects of his ill health and his instinctive aversion to being forced into a battle where he had to attack a strongly entrenched enemy head on. Some historians claim that if Rommel had persisted he would have eventually broken out and if this had happened then Montgomery would have been no match for the *Afrikakorps* in a fast-moving, fluid battle at which it excelled. But this view assumes a healthy and confident Rommel, not the sick and unusually vacillating commander of September 1942. While Montgomery may not have been a leader in the Rommel mould, he was a master at fighting the 'set piece' battle where allocation of men and weapons were under the firm hold of a plan of action worked out well beforehand.

Rommel left for his spell of sick leave on 23 September, four days after his replacement, General Georg Stumme, arrived from his previous command in Russia. Before he left, Rommel ordered Stumme to continue strengthening the lines of minefields and booby traps and the string of defended posts extending over two kilometres to the rear manned by infantry and anti-tank units. Along with the captured British minefields that had been incorporated into the Axis system, a total of nearly half a million mines had been planted in Rommel's 'devil's gardens' by the time of Montgomery's attack.

On the night of 23 October, when a storm of 8th Army artillery descended on the Axis lines, a great Allied steamroller was about to start its slow and deadly advance. Qualitative and quantitative superiority had now irreversibly passed to the Allies. Only in generalship would the Germans retain superiority, though on balance even this advantage was neutralized by ULTRA.

Rommel returned on the afternoon of 25 October, two days after the start of Montgomery's offensive. Stumme had been killed the day before, but the *Panzerarmee* was holding the line and the British were still trying to infiltrate their infantry through the 'devil's gardens'. The morale of the *Panzerarmee* was high and it rose even higher when all units received the signal sent out on his first night back: 'I have taken command of the army again. Rommel.'

The main thrust of Montgomery's attack seemed to

A collection point for surrendering German troops, on a main road near Enfidaville. This photo was taken on 13 May 1943. (NZ National Archives – Alexander Turnbull Library)

be in the north and Rommel moved his reserves, the precious Panzers, into the battle. So began the process of steady erosion of Rommel's scarce reserves of tanks, manpower and the all-important fuel – and this is how Montgomery fought the battle. He had more men and tanks, unlimited supplies of fuel, superiority in the air and he was prepared to draw on these heavily to break the Axis line. Excluding the three hundred Italian tanks, Montgomery had a superiority over Rommel in armour of four to one, and nearly half of the British armour was the new American Sherman tank carrying a 75mm gun (in comparison, only thirty of the German tanks were armed with the long 75mm gun). The battle dragged on through October, more and more of Rommel's strength being consumed by the unrelenting British pressure and the sheer weight of their material superiority. If it had not been for ULTRA which faithfully reported the dangerously low levels of front-line strength Rommel was just able to maintain, the battle might well have been called off. After five

days the British had still not broken the German defences and British casualties were already over 10,000. Montgomery's qualities as a commander were starting to reveal themselves. With his overwhelming superiority in men and weapons, and with ULTRA to reassure him that the *Panzerarmee* was weakening to the point of collapse, Montgomery persisted.

In a running battle out in the open desert, Rommel was not too seriously disadvantaged by the British use of ULTRA. But in a static position like the Alamein line where details of every attack, including its planning, order of battle and proposed timing, had to be communicated to Berlin, ULTRA was of great advantage to the British. Henceforth, everything of importance that Rommel had to say to his superiors would be known to the British commander facing him within twelve hours or less. At all times the 8th Army had a complete picture of the army facing them.

The following is an extract covering a 24-hour period from the war diary of the German-Italian Panzer Army, as it was relayed on a daily basis to the German Supreme Command (*Oberkommando der Wehrmacht*) in Berlin. It is given in full to show the importance of ULTRA in weighing the balance against Rommel's Army. The passage reproduced here is the summary for 28 October 1942, transmitted to Berlin from Africa during the night of 28/29 October 1942. The signal would have been intercepted and decoded by the intelligence staff at Bletchley Park, and a digest of it been in Montgomery's hands before noon on 29 October. The value of such information during the course of a battle can be readily seen in its content and area of reference.

The appendix numbers referred to in the text indicated the specific diaries and reports from which the summary was compiled, details of which were transmitted separately (though not necessarily with the priority accorded to the daily summaries). The fuel 'consumption units' mentioned are a standard German Army term for the amount of fuel required to move a formation with all its vehicles for 100 kilometres.

The passage as reproduced is not the text of an ULTRA intercept; it was seized in Germany after the war with other records of the OKW relating to the North African campaigns. This translation is on file in the New Zealand National Archives in Wellington, under File 'DA 438.2/1', and the original can be found on File '34375/1–2' in the German Military Document Section, U.S. Defense Department, Washington D.C.

28 OCT 42

1. Events
During the night the enemy made his main point of attack more obvious by continuing his air and ground attacks almost exclusively in the northern sector.

NTR in the southern and central sectors except normal artillery and reconnaissance activity. Our own situation was unchanged. (*Appendix 66.*)

In the northern sector the enemy renewed his tank and infantry attacks from the gap between Minefields J and L and from Minefield K. He succeeded in making a few breaches in our positions, which were cleared partly by immediate counter-attacks and partly by counter-attacks by reserves. One enemy group which had penetrated along the boundary between two battalions was surrounded and destroyed in the early morning. About 300 prisoners were taken, and many

tanks and weapons destroyed. To restore the position on the front of II and III Bns 61Regt (Trento Div) west of Minefield K, a successful counter-attack was mounted in the early morning by 164LtDiv; this restored the liaison between II Bn 433Regt and II Bn 382 Regt. (*Appendix 67.*)

The reorganization ordered in 90LtDiv and Trieste Div was completed during the night. The divisions were now in defensive positions in their new areas.

Quiet night in the rear Army areas.

During the morning the enemy renewed his tank attacks from the area between Minefields J and L. Three successive attacks were beaten off by counter attacks by *Afrikakorps*. The German armoured units suffered considerable losses from the heavy enemy anti-tank and tank defensive fire. The enemy tanks, firing from hull-down positions at over 2,000 yards range, simply out-shot our tanks.

In the late afternoon strong forces of 90 Lt Div, supported by Stukas, attacked Point 28 again. The attack was again unsuccessful, being stopped by heavy defensive fire.

Situation at 2000 hours:

No unusual enemy activity during the day in the southern and central sectors. The number of enemy tanks at the two points of attack in the southern sector – 6 km north of Himeimat and near Deir el Munassib – had noticeably decreased. A slackening in artillery fire led to the conclusion that some enemy batteries had moved. The impression was gained that the extraordinary amount of movement on the front, observed and reported by 10 Corps, did not indicate preparations for attack, but were of a purely defensive character.

In the northern sector we succeeded during the day in warding off several enemy attacks after extremely heavy fighting. The present main defence line was held. West of Minefield K the line was strengthened by the entry into the second line of a newly arrived battalion of Trento Div. Another battalion of Trento Div, formed from stragglers of 62InfRegt, was placed in a supporting position astride the coast road. 90LtDiv, organized for defence into three battle groups, was in its old area.

Army reserve – Trieste Div, 580 Recce Unit and Army Battle Gp immediately west and south of Sidi Abd el Rahman.

No change in the Mersa Matruh–Siwa–Sollum–Tobruk rear areas.

(Situation map and daily reports *Appendix 68.*)

At 2200 hours, after terrific artillery preparation, the enemy launched expected attack in the northern sector. The main weight of the attack came in against the left flank of 155GrenRegt and the right of 125GrenRegt. At midnight the situation was still confused.

Afrikakorps was ordered to be prepared to counter-attack early on the 29th with all available tanks if the enemy broke through. 580RecceUnit was brought up to the vicinity of Pt 31 SE of Sidi Abd el Rahman to guard against a possible enemy advance along the coast road.

Today's fighting, again with very heavy artillery and air support and of a most bitter nature, cost both sides heavily in men and equipment. The enemy lost 37 tanks, bringing the total since the 23rd to 293. 510 prisoners had been taken to date. Our own missing now totalled 1,994 Germans and 1,660 Italians. According to reports most of our prisoners were wounded. The number of available tanks had dropped further; in particular, the hitherto almost intact 21PzDiv had considerable losses.

Available tanks:
15PzDiv	– 21 MK III and IV	
21PzDiv	– 45 Mk III and IV	
Littorio		
Armd Div	– 33 M	
Ariete		
Armd Div	– 129 M	
Trieste		
Mot Div	– 34 M	

In vehicles and by foot the surrendering German Army moving towards Allied lines on 13 May 1943. (NZ National Archives – Alexander Turnbull Library)

Air situation: The enemy's air activity, still increasing in comparison with previous days, was again directed against the front-line troops in the northern sector. One division was attacked three times in fifteen minutes by 18 heavy bombers. During the day 11 heavy bombing attacks were carried out on 21PzDiv's area. In the southern sector the enemy's so-called 'tank busters' (single-engined fighters with 4cm cannon) attacked our armoured reconnaissance troops at various times. 33 Recce Unit reported that during the last six days it had lost 18 armoured cars through enemy fighter action. (*Appendix 68/1.*)

Our own Air Force, as on previous days, supported the defence by bold raids with all available forces; but it was much too weak numerically to bring any relief to the troops, who were suffering severely under the vast English air superiority. Army therefore requested the C-in-C South to reinforce the air strength, especially with fighters. (*Appendix 69.*)

German troops' supply situation: The petrol flown over on the 26th and 27th (187 tons and 204 tons) made a total of 0.6 consumption units. This supply did not give the Army scope to carry out successful counter-attacks with mobile forces against the heavy enemy day and night attacks. The petrol supply, which now amounted to 1.3 consumption units, would necessarily sink to a minimum in a very short time. This would mean that the Army would be immobilized, and would be cut to pieces little by little by the enemy's vastly superior air and artillery power. (*Appendix 70.*)

It appeared from the Italian Supreme Command's sea transport programme, received by radio the previous day, that the majority of tankers were to go to Benghazi. (*Appendix 71.*) This would mean that no relief from the very serious petrol shortage would be obtained until seven days after the arrival of the first tanker at Benghazi. Considering the great superiority of the enemy, ready to break through with fully motorized forces, it was unthinkable that the Army's motorized formations should for so long be in no condition to carry out mobile operations on a larger scale.

The certainty of tankers being lost on the way to

Tobruk was, in the Army's opinion, only to be expected if – as in the case of the *Proserpina* – convoys were without fighter protection in the danger area. The captain of *Proserpina* had stated that his ship was protected against submarines by destroyers, but that there was not a single fighter over the ship. In consequence she was helplessly exposed to the heavy British bomber and torpedo bomber attacks, in spite of gallant defence, during which the ship's AA guns shot down eight aircraft. (*Appendix 72.*) With strong fighter protection ships could even reach Tobruk harbour, as was proved by the arrival of the tanker *Alfredo*. The German GOC Rome was therefore requested to arrange with the Supreme Command for the majority of tankers to be escorted to Tobruk. Army also requested the destroyers and auxiliary cruisers to come nearer the front line to Mersa Matruh, because the scanty convoy space allowed insufficient supplies to be brought up from Tobruk and Benghazi. (*Appendix 73.*)

Army advised further that the total of 400 tons of ammunition which it was proposed to send over by 4 November was not nearly sufficient, and bore no resemblance whatever to the present needs – even with the utmost economy about 500 tons of ammunition were fired daily. GOC Rome advised that on 30 October ten submarines would be sent from Sicily to Mersa Matruh and Tobruk with about 200 tons of ammunition in short supply. (*Appendix 74.*)

Appreciation and Intentions:

Air reconnaissance reported about 16,000 MT in the area west of a line from Alem el Qata to Burg el Arab. 10,000 of these were north of a line from Ruweisat to El Bzeiwiyn. Ground reconnaissance and the enemy's behaviour confirmed the impression that the enemy had moved fairly strong forces from the southern to the northern sector. Army therefore decided to withdraw more German mobile forces from the southern sector and place them behind the northern. During the day these orders were given in this connection:

(a) *Afrikakorps* was to return the mobile reserve group of 21PzDiv, at present in the southern sector, to the division immediately. (*Appendix 75.*)

(b) 20 Corps was to assume complete control of the defence of the southern sector. For this purpose 10 Corps was attached to it. (*Appendix 76.*) Battle groups of *Ariete* Div with *Afrikakorps* in the northern sector would return to the Corps. (*Appendix 75.*) In view of the petrol situation the Corps, because of the movement and changes of position among its tanks, was to take precedence over 10 Corps for the purpose of building up supplies and of strengthening the motorized formations

behind the front. (*Appendix 77.*) Nizza Recce Unit – on the way to El Daba at midday – was placed under command of 20 Corps again and instructed to release 3 Recce Unit from command. Nizza Recce Unit was due to arrive early on the 29th. (*Appendix 78.*)

(c) After reverting from command of Nizza Recce Unit, 33 Recce Unit was to move early on 30 October to the area 5km SW of Sidi Abd el Rahman and come under Army command. (*Appendix 78/2.*)

It appeared from a captured operation order that the enemy was trying to break through our line and reach the Tel el Aqqaqir area with 30 British Corps (51 British Div, 2 NZ Div and 9 Aust Div), and then to exploit the breach with 10 British Corps (1 and 10 British Armd Divs) and thrust NW to the coast road. (*Appendix 79.*) The forming up of strong armoured forces in Minefield J after midday led the Army to expect the enemy to attempt a decisive breakthrough on the night 28/29 October. Army ordered all formations to prepare to meet this attack. The Army artillery commander was instructed to lay on the greatest possible concentration of army and anti-aircraft artillery fire on the enemy when he advanced from his forming-up place in Minefield J, and thus to destroy the attempt. Further orders to all troops were:

(a) to open machine gun fire at long range on enemy attacking formations and attacks recognized as such. (*Appendix 80.*)

(b) instead of harassing fire, which for the most part involved unnecessary ammunition expenditure, to open fire on the enemy at sight with short, concentrated salvoes. (*Appendix 81.*)

The Army was certain that the impending enemy attack could only be beaten off by the greatest possible effort by all arms. The army commander instructed all commanders: 'This battle is a life and death struggle. I therefore demand that every officer and man put forward his utmost effort.' (*Appendix 82.*)

2. Interim and daily report to GHQ. (*Appendix 83.*)

But as comprehensive as the overall view of Axis strategy and tactics given through ULTRA was, the 8th Army was not able to pinpoint accurately every enemy front-line position. Axis dispositions in the actual front – where units were placed, the location of minefields, siting of anti-tank guns, preparations for battle made by battalion and company commanders – had to be determined if possible by the time-tested methods of reconnaissance and interrogation of prisoners.

So it was that while ULTRA gave the Allied commanders an inside view of command level plans and orders, the rank and file of the Allied armies felt no immediate or apparent benefits inside the confines of front-line contact.

Montgomery's decision to shift the main point of pressure to the south on the night of 1/2 November was again very costly to the 8th Army, but German strength was now fast running out and the Italian divisions that had not already been cut to pieces were starting to show signs of breaking. By the end of October Rommel was considering a withdrawal to a line at Fuka, though this thinking was not relayed to Berlin with the result that Montgomery had no knowledge of it through ULTRA.

Fuel did not present a problem to Rommel as a retreat used much less petrol than an advance (a withdrawal is usually done in a straight line towards bases holding stocks of fuel, while an advance normally incorporates all the zigzag manoeuvres of fighting at high speed, while taking the advance further and further from the points of supply). However, there was an acute shortage of vehicles in which to transport Rommel's Army and this made his plan no simple matter.

In fact, Rommel had furtively been taking steps to prepare a new line at Fuka since the beginning of November, as he rightly anticipated that Hitler would not easily countenance a withdrawal. After a serious penetration by the 8th Army, he ordered the retreat during the night of 2/3 November at the same time sending an appreciation of the situation to Hitler with a postscript-like ending saying he intended to pull his Army back. Hitler had already sensed the pessimism in Rommel's reports – which must have been like sweet music to Montgomery when he read them by courtesy of ULTRA – and what followed was a signals mix-up between Rommel and Hitler. Rommel's nightly transmission to Hitler's headquarters was not brought to the Führer's attention by the signals duty officer because he thought it was just a normal situation report, and he missed the significant last part of the message. As a result, Hitler did not sight the signal until the next morning. In the meantime, Rommel had received a signal from Hitler exhorting the *Panzerarmee* to continue the fight – which was meant to stiffen Rommel's resolve. This message ended with the sentence: 'To your troops therefore you can offer only one path, the path that leads to Victory or Death – Adolf Hitler.'

When Rommel received this message he interpreted it as a reply to his message of the previous night – and stopping his plan to withdraw. That the British also made this interpretation of Hitler's signal is borne out by the slackening of the 8th Army's efforts from this time. Rommel dared not disobey what he took to be

Hitler's order to stand and continue the fight in the present position, so he modified his order to retreat to include only a few units already on the move.

Hitler's order probably contributed to the preservation of what remained of the *Afrikakorps* as it slowed any British exploitation of a German withdrawal for two days, though, given Montgomery's reluctance to try his hand in rapid outflanking strokes against Rommel, this is by no means certain. Then Kesselring persuaded Rommel to disregard Hitler's signal as a binding order to stand still, and the general withdrawal of the *Panzerarmee* from the Alamein position began on the afternoon of 4 November. That night a signal was received from Hitler authorizing the retreat.

However, Rommel's countermanding of his earlier order to withdraw meant that when the full retreat was put into effect on 4 November, the unmotorized Italians on the central and southern sectors of the front, and also the unmotorized Ramcke Brigade, were not able to disengage in time to escape.

Three days after Rommel moved westwards with the units he had been able to salvage from the El Alamein line, the Americans and British landed in force in Morocco and Algeria. The conditions for the end phase of the North African campaign had arrived: Rommel's Army was between the powerful jaws of two Allied Armies whose single aim was to defeat the Axis in Africa. Early in 1943 the two jaws would meet, and in May they would close tight, even though Rommel himself and a small handful of officers and soldiers would escape.

Ahead of Rommel in November 1942 was a long retreat, a fighting retreat that was a succession of small skirmishes ahead of an enormous 8th Army that had to repair destroyed bridges, and defuse the thousands of skilfully laid mines and booby traps that the retreating German pioneers had placed everywhere. (Wartime Allied propaganda claimed that the Germans had booby-trapped their own dead, but this was not done, and would not have been done by German troops to their own comrades.) The retreat was noteworthy for the timidity of Montgomery in taking chances that could have cut off the line of retreat of the remnants of the *Panzerarmee*, Rommel's reluctance to stand and fight anywhere but on the Tunisian border, his determination to save his 'Africans' so they could be transferred back to Europe, and the continuing high morale of his Army.

The retreat was a stern test of their training and discipline, under conditions that must have made things seem black at times even to the most optimistic. The only bright spot to relieve the otherwise dismal outlook

The Commander of the 164th Light Division, Major General Freiherr von Liebenstein, surrenders his division to General Freyberg of New Zealand, commanding British 10th Corps, on 13 May 1943. (Author's collection)

following the retreat from the Alamein line was the amazing appearance of Ramcke and a large number of his paratroopers who, after all, managed to escape from their position in the line. After first marching westwards into the desert Ramcke and his men had captured a British supply column and, staying well south of the coastal road, had reached the *Panzerarmee* on 7 November.

Rommel halted briefly at El Agheila, at Buerat, and at Homs before moving back from Tripoli on 22 January. He arrived in the old line of French fortifications inside the Tunisian frontier, known as the Mareth Line, in early February 1943, exactly two years after the first German units had arrived in Libya.

The Allies lost a golden opportunity to strangle Rommel while he was still in Libya, and to seize Tunisia by putting the limit of their advance too far to the west in their planning for Operation Torch (the codename

for the landings in November 1942). The Allied planners had been apprehensive of the *Luftwaffe* operating against their spearheads in Tunisia before their own air forces could become established, and there was also the possibility that Allied shipping losses could even put a landing in Tunisia at risk. In the race to occupy and hold Tunisia, the Germans were close winners. Within two days of the Allied landings, German troops had arrived in Tunis and were building a bridgehead which was soon to be expanded and held by a new army command in Africa, the 5th Panzer Army.

Hitler has been criticized for not sending all, or a part, of the forces he sent to Tunisia, to Rommel at El Alamein. This claim ignores the impossibility of supplying even the forces Rommel had at Alamein without doubling the size of his army there, and this assumes that some way could have been found to move such a force to Egypt. The conditions for reinforcing the Tunisian bridgehead only occurred because of the Allied landings – for the first month the *Luftwaffe* was able to control the short sea route from Sicily to Tunis and Bizerta (any other route would have been impossible to protect). The forces sent to Tunisia became available because they were no longer needed in Europe as a reserve against a possible Allied landing on the European continent.

Exactly the same conditions that had prompted Hitler to send German troops to Africa in the first place had appeared again, for Allied possession of the North African coastline posed a threat to Italy that could bring about its collapse. Despatching troops from Europe was a strategic move to defend Germany itself rather than a matter of just sending reinforcements to Africa. At Alamein the security of Germany was not immediately at stake; at Tunis in November and December 1942 it was, in the same way as the battles in the Soviet Union were central to the ultimate security of Germany. There is no comparison between reinforcements which might have gone to Rommel at Alamein and the force which Hitler sent to Tunisia at the end of 1942. Rommel could not even receive enough supplies for the army he had at Alamein, while an army in Tunisia could be adequately supplied, in the opening stages of the campaign at least, and it made sense to fight the enemy in Africa rather than have to defend the entire length of the Axis-controlled European Mediterranean seaboard.

1943

With Rommel's arrival in Tunisia in mid-February, the last stage of the North African war had commenced.

He had outpaced the pursuing 8th Army all the way from Alamein. On the one occasion when Montgomery did manage to manoeuvre a blocking force behind Rommel's line of retreat at Nofilia in mid-December 1942, it was too late and too weak, and the Panzers easily smashed a line through the leading elements of the 5th New Zealand Brigade that had cut the road. After failing to trap Rommel in Egypt or Libya, the overcautious Allies then gave the Germans time to establish a strong bridgehead in Tunisia by landing too far back along the North African coast. With more foresight, and stronger Allied generalship, the Axis Forces could have been captured by the end of 1942, and indeed the Tunisian campaign might never have had to take place at all.

The two Axis armies in Tunisia in the middle of February 1943 were under the command of Field Marshal Kesselring, with the 5th Panzer Army under *Generaloberst* von Arnim and the 1st Italian Army (previously *Panzerarmee Afrika*, Rommel's old command) still under Rommel. Realistically, there should have been one ground commander in Tunisia to co-ordinate the operations of the two armies, but Rommel was under a cloud as Hitler kept postponing his recall from Africa. Kesselring therefore acted as a *de facto* ground forces commander, but he had the responsibility of overseeing everything to do with the German presence in the Mediterranean and also had to cope with the intrigue and infighting taking place in Rome. So his attention, to the detriment of the front in Tunisia, was divided.

Although by February the supply situation of the Axis armies in Tunisia was quickly deteriorating – a situation with which Rommel was all too familiar – good interior lines of communication gave the Axis forces the chance of combining against any one point in the Allied lines. The first joint action started on 14 February with an attack by the 10th Panzer Division, supported by the 21st Panzer, against American units at Sidi Bou Zid with the Americans suffering a clear defeat. Rommel's attack, one day later, directed through Gafsa at Feriana, was equally successful, and the American and French forces retreated. Rommel was for a time the Rommel of old and demanded that he be given command of the three Panzer divisions (the 15th had been in Rommel's attack through Gafsa) in order to exploit quickly the American retreat and concentrate against Tebessa inside Algeria. But von Arnim's more conservative plan, to drive in a northerly direction, had Kesselring's support and Rommel was left with his 15th Panzer to use as a means of following up his success at Feriana. In an effort to change von Arnim's mind and to

demonstrate the tactical logic of his own plan, Rommel pushed the 15th Panzer northwards towards Kasserine Pass which brought him closer to the 5th Panzer Army, enabling the two armies to work in conjunction. Rommel thought that a strong single thrust deep into the Allied rear through the mountain passes would unhinge the entire front line, but von Arnim was obstinate and refused to see Rommel's viewpoint.

The basic difference between the two plans was that von Arnim wanted to push north towards Le Kef, behind the then Allied line but keeping the extent of his advance a narrow one. Rommel, on the other hand, was all for a strong attack that would take his advance firstly through Tebessa and then deep enough into Algeria to give his Panzers a chance to savage the rear base areas, bringing about a general Allied withdrawal from their entire north-south line inside Tunisia. Rommel's plan also had the advantage of taking the Panzer divisions away from the Allied reserves and into an area where there would be enough captured supplies to feed the advance of the Panzer divisions.

After a delay of nearly two days, which gave the Allies time to prepare for the coming battle, a compromise was decided upon. The unified command asked for by Rommel was granted, under his leadership, but the order for the advance was ambiguous. Rommel interpreted it to mean he was to drive northwards, but the order placing von Arnim under Rommel's command had not been explicit enough to curb von Arnim who did not think he was required to co-operate completely with Rommel. This was the background to the battle of Kasserine Pass, where Rommel's Panzers, reinforced by those elements of the 10th Panzer Division, which von Arnim had grudgingly relinquished, forced a passage through the pass. The green American troops were routed, but the attack was not followed up quickly enough by the 10th Panzer Division, and Rommel blamed its commander, General von Broich, for this failure (von Broich had not served under Rommel before and did not know him in the way the old desert commanders did).

The 10th Panzer Division could probably have captured the next objective, Thala, had it been quicker off the mark, but it was held back by the arrival of British reserves. Although Kesselring finally gave Rommel the unfettered command he wanted, it was too late for him to follow the plans he had in mind ten days earlier, and Allied resistance continued to stiffen.

Rommel's attention was drawn instead to the projected plan for an attack against the 8th Army, now deployed in front of the Mareth Line, at Medinine. In

A historic photo – the last minutes of the existence of the Afrikakorps. Field Marshal Messe, the Italian who commanded the 1st Italian Army – the remnants of the 'old' German and Italian formations – stands surrounded by Italian and German officers. Minutes after this photo was taken, and Messe had thanked the men who had served under him, the official surrender took place and there were no longer any Axis military units in existence in Africa. (NZ National Archives – Alexander Turnbull Library)

the earlier battles, ULTRA had proved of limited use as the fighting overtook the currency of the signals being fed into Allied headquarters during the advances through Gafsa and Feriana and beyond. At Medinine it was to be a different story. ULTRA gave Montgomery the exact place and time and strength of the impending attack, and he prepared accordingly to meet it. Meanwhile, further north, von Arnim's pet project, Operation Blockhead (*Ochsenkopf*) came to nought, which infuriated Rommel who had not been consulted about it.

The final plans for the attack at Medinine were left to General Messe, the Italian who had assumed command of the 1st Italian Army on 23 February. His plan meant that the three Panzer divisions, with the 90th Light Division in support, were obliged to advance against well-concealed lines of British anti-tank guns, including large numbers of the new and deadly 17pdr guns. Over a third of the tanks used in the attack were lost (52 out of a strength of 150), and the infantry suffered heavy casualties as well. That evening Messe proposed calling off the attack and Rommel, after inspecting the front for himself, agreed.

Rommel's days in Africa were now numbered, and his ideas for a withdrawal from the south to a line in the north through Enfidaville (being shorter, Rommel argued it would be easier to defend), earned a rebuke from Hitler, who dismissed his appreciation of the situation in Tunisia. Rommel left Africa for good on 9 March. Defeat was now only two months away.

A series of delaying actions followed, with the German troops in Africa buying time for Hitler in Europe – the longer the front held in Africa the more impossible it would be for the Anglo-American Armies to launch a cross-Channel invasion against mainland Europe that year. Supplies were only trickling into Tunisia through the Allied blockade between Italy and Tunisia, and when the 8th Army launched its attack northwards on the night of 25/26 March, the 1st Italian Army was hard pressed to hold itself together as it was pushed back to El Hamma. Once again Montgomery failed to advance his armour to cut off the retreat, and though many Italians were captured, the German formations extricated themselves. Concurrently with the British advance from the south, the Americans were making headway further north against the 10th Panzer Division.

The attack by Montgomery against the next line, at Wadi Akarit, came on 6 April. Once again the experienced anti-tank guns and rearguard units prevented the British from overwhelming the retreating German units, and by the middle of the month they were establishing themselves in the last natural obstacle in front of Tunis, a ring of steep rocky hills which was the same line, through Enfidaville, that Rommel had requested earlier and had been refused. They were to prove very expensive for the Allies to attack in the last weeks of the campaign.

In the north, the Americans and British continued to make headway against the 5th Panzer Army, now commanded by General Gustav von Vaerst after von Arnim succeeded Rommel as overall commander of the ground forces. One location in particular was bitterly disputed throughout the first four months of the year: a strategically sited hill known to the Allies as Longstop Hill and to the Germans as Christmas Hill. This feature was defended tenaciously by the 756th Alpine Regiment, which had been included in the 334th Infantry Division for just such a purpose. This regiment had been hurriedly put together from available drafts in southern Germany in November 1942, but it fought with all the élan and toughness of many of the older and well-established units in the German Army.

On 6 May, the Allied Command launched a powerful attack from the south-west towards Tunis, and under the full weight of the Allied onslaught the Tunisian front was split open. Bizerta fell on 7 May to the Americans and Tunis a day later to the British. Only in the south around Enfidaville did the German and Italian line hold as the 8th Army tried in vain to negotiate the steep hills slashed by deep wadis.

The last message sent to Germany from the German command in Africa was composed by General Hans Cramer, the last commander of the *Afrikakorps*. It read: 'Ammunition expended. Arms and equipment destroyed. In accordance with orders received the *Afrikakorps* has fought itself to the condition where it can fight no more. The German *Afrikakorps* must rise again. Heia Safari*. Cramer, General Commanding.'

This message was not strictly true. Much equipment and ammunition remained, but the command organization had largely broken down after the Allied thrust to Tunis and Bizerta, and the Axis front had been fragmented. The will to fight had not been lost by the German troops, but there was no possibility of a coherent front any longer, and the individual German soldier was not a fanatic who would take to the hills with his rifle or pistol and try to fight a lonely guerrilla war.

The last surrenders took place on 12/13 May, and they involved most of the 'old' units of Rommel's army of the desert campaigns which had opposed the 8th Army on the southern part of the front. The famous 90th Light Division asked in its communication with 8th Army HQ if the New Zealand Division could accept its surrender. Across the lines of battle the enemies had a firm sense of the identity of their opponents, and the 90th Light Division's request reflected a familiarity and a respect for its old enemy. At noon on 13 May the headquarters of the 1st Italian Army surrendered to General Freyberg of the 2nd New Zealand Division, and all military authority in Africa passed to the Allies.

The wartime figure for the number of Axis troops that surrendered in Tunisia was a quarter of a million, supposedly 150,000 Germans and 100,000 Italians. This figure was too high, though the Allies took as their guide the ration returns provided by the command of *Heeresgruppe Afrika* (Army Group Africa). The real figure for the German total is nearer 125,000, of which the greater part was made up of support troops, not front-line units. A few units, close enough to the coast to find fishing boats and other small ships, did try to cross the sea to Sicily, but most of these fell victim to the watchful Allied air forces. The number who managed to make this hazardous crossing successfully did not exceed 700. In the two years and three months of the German participation in the North African war, 18,594 German soldiers were officially recorded as being killed, and a further 3,400 were posted as missing.

What had been intended as a relatively small force sent to prevent an Italian collapse in early 1941 had in the end absorbed a very large part of Germany's military strength.

After the surrender, the Afrikakorps *behind barbed wire. Only the uniforms were unchanged. (ECPA)*

---

* This was the warcry of the *Afrikakorps*. It comes from Swahili and roughly translated means 'let's go get 'em', or 'tallyho'.

German Army and Luftwaffe Uniforms and Equipment

German Army Tropical Uniform

Introduction

With the entry of Italy into the war in June 1940, the possibility of German military involvement in the Mediterranean theatre became a reality and within weeks the German High Command took the first steps towards creating a tropical uniform. Though Hitler's offer to Mussolini of a Panzer division was declined, preparations nevertheless went ahead to equip a Panzer division with tropical uniform and equipment suitable for North Africa.

The design work for the new tropical uniform was handed to the Tropical Institute of the University of Hamburg. What evolved, from advice prepared by the staff of the Institute, reflected characteristics of both traditional German military uniform and practical considerations stemming from the harsh extremes of climate found in Libya. The uniform was stylish and in the main well liked by the German troops who had to wear it, and it allowed a combination of items to be worn to satisfy all conditions with little modification in the field.

By the end of 1940, production of the tropical uniform was in top gear, so much so that stocks available early in 1941 were sufficient to equip both divisions sent to Libya, and items dated '1940' were still being issued from stores held in North Africa at the end of 1941.

The Feldgendarmerie *gorget worn by a* Hauptfeldwebel *of the Field Police. (ECPA)*

Note on the manufacture of Afrikakorps uniforms

When the first contracts for the supply of tropical uniforms were awarded by the German Army Clothing Department, most suppliers were in Berlin, or nearby, though a few were in Silesia.

The specifications for the items of uniform were very exact and there was negligible difference in detail between various manufacturers. However, the uniforms made in 1940 had a wider range of colours in their cotton twill material. They ranged from a deep chocolate brown through a full spectrum of greens and olives to a light sandy colour. Uniforms made after 1940 show much more uniformity in colour when the cotton mills were able to supply a closer approximation of the drab olive green specified by the Army.

Troops sent to Africa in the 5th Light Division appear to have all worn the German style of the tropical shirt and use of the modified French Army shirt (see page 142) is not apparent in photos until later in 1941. Unmodified French shirts were issued in small numbers in 1941, mostly to officers who would wear the shirt beneath their tunics where rank insignia was not needed.

Unused material cut from the tunic pattern was used in the making of shoulder straps, twill on the outer edges and drill (from the reinforcing patches) on the inside part of the tongue of the shoulder strap. For this reason tunics and shoulder straps arriving in batches from the one factory were usually a perfect colour match.

A relatively large number of manufacturers were used to supply the tropical tunics and trousers in the early period, but only six manufactured the field cap in 1940. However, by the end of 1942 the number of different manufacturers' stamps seen in field caps had grown to nearly twenty, and a still larger number were making the caps in 1943. The quality of field caps varied, the most significant differences being in the care with which the insignia was applied and the symmetry of the cap's appearance, which showed the pattern had been carefully cut out.

German military clothing was usually well marked by the manufacturer showing size numbers, maker's name and city or place of manufacture and a date which was normally preceded by a letter indicating which *Wehrkreis* depot had processed the issue of the item. This was taken from the first letter of the city where the *Wehrkreis* main depot was located and there was therefore much duplication, e.g. 'B' could be either Breslau or Berlin, 'S' could be Stuttgart or Stettin, and so on. However, this system was not used often in marking field caps. After early 1943 the manufacturers' stamp was replaced with an RB number (RB = *Reichsbetriebs* = State Manufacturing), which acted as a code to conceal details of industrial production from Allied Intelligence, making the manufacturers hard to trace.

The stamps on the tropical tunic were found over the wound dressing pocket, or behind the flap that covered the front line of metal buttons. Trousers and shorts and breeches were stamped inside the waist band.

One type of maker's stamp which appeared in field caps before the introduction of the RB number indicated that they had been made by a co-operative of small tailoring firms. In wartime Germany the work available for small tailoring firms was curtailed because the civilian demand for clothes declined and much of the stocks of material were reserved for military use. It was obviously beyond a small tailoring firm to tender alone for an order to manufacture military uniforms, so the co-operatives were formed to allow a number of these firms to contract an order to supply uniforms on a large scale. These co-operative maker's stamps were usually seen on caps, as few small tailoring businesses had the large industrial sewing machines or the staff to make larger and heavier items like tunics or trousers. Their standard of finish of field caps – and of tunics, etc., in the smaller number of cases where they were also made – was usually high. The co-operatives were established in regions like Hesse, Saxony, Central Germany, Silesia, or in the larger cities like Berlin, Vienna and Breslau. They assigned a number to each member which was displayed somewhere inside the maker's stamp, and numbers as high as sixty have been seen. The name used by the co-operatives was either *Landes – Lief. – Genossenschaft* or the acronym LAGO.

As well as using idle capacity in the large number of small private tailoring firms, the *Wehrmacht* also made use of the clothing industries in occupied countries. As with the uniform items made by the co-operatives, the quality of work done by firms in the occupied countries was generally very high which indicates the importance of these orders to the economies and populations of those countries, and of their dependence on the German *Wehrmacht* for their livelihood. French factories made a large proportion of the army tropical shirts, trousers and breeches, while Dutch firms in Amsterdam and Rotterdam made many tropical items of uniform for the *Luftwaffe*. Many of the privately purchased items used by officers were made by tailors in Italy which explains why these pieces sometimes show a cloth type not seen in German-made uniforms, and in some instances display non-standard insignia that was obviously made up by the tailors, when the German officer ordering the uniform was unable to supply German insignia.

Waffenfarben – Arm of Service Colours

This traditional feature of German military uniform during World War II served to identify a soldier's unit in terms of military function by a system of colour piping worn on the uniform. It indicated which arm of the service a soldier was part of: e.g. Infantry, Artillery, etc. The colour appropriate to that arm therefore would be worn by all men serving inside a basic tactical unit. For Infantry and Artillery this was normally a regiment. For other arms – such as Signals or Reconnaissance – it was a smaller-sized unit known as an *Abteilung*, roughly of battalion strength.

The only exceptions to this rule were medical personnel who wore their own dark blue *Waffenfarbe* regardless of which unit they happened to be part of, and specialists with officer rank (*Sonderführer*) who were attached as interpreters, etc. *Sonderführer* wore blue-grey *Waffenfarbe* with distinctive thin black/white/red chevrons on the officer rank shoulder strap braid.

However, the *Waffenfarbe* did not always indicate a soldier's special training and employment. An anti-tank gunner serving in a Reconnaissance unit would wear the gold-yellow or copper-brown of Reconnaissance, not the pink piping worn by anti-tank units. Similarly a motorcyclist serving inside a Panzer Regiment or a Motorized Infantry Regiment would wear the colour assigned to these regiments, not the grass-green (or, later, copper-brown) which identified Motorcycle Battalions. While an armoured car crew would normally wear the colour for Reconnaissance, they would wear the lemon-yellow of a Signals *Abteilung* if part of a Signals unit which also used armoured cars.

For its 1941 uniforms the *Afrikakorps* had the *Waffenfarbe* as an edging on the shoulder straps and in the soutache, an inverted 'V' of braid worn on the field cap above the cockade.

The German Army in North Africa was not always able to follow rigidly the regulations laid down for use of *Waffenfarbe*. Some colours were in a process of change or re-allocation, and available supplies, often erratic and insufficient, did not always match the current official colours. The soutache on the field cap was stitched in place and could not be switched from cap to cap. If a soldier could not get a cap in his head size with the correct soutache colour he often had to take a cap with another colour. In some cases battalion or company tailors modified large-size caps with the correct soutache by gathering in the rear seam to make a smaller cap. The problem of shortages of caps in some soutache colours appeared in late 1941 and became acute in 1942, and photos taken over this period show that some

The smiles of these two soldiers about to pull on their high canvas and leather boots makes light of the unpopularity of this difficult-to-lace footwear. (Author's collection)

soldiers elected to wear caps with the wrong soutache colour – but this may also have indicated that they had transferred from another unit with a different colour.

The problem of outfitting troops with their correct *Waffenfarbe* was initially not as acute with the field tunic or shirt as these had removable shoulder straps, though with increasing supply shortages, eventually there were difficulties with the issue of shoulder straps too. The shoulder straps worn on the tunic and shirt were identical, being made in the factories manufacturing tunics using offcuts of tunic twill material, but they were not actually fitted until a soldier was in the field. The shoulder straps were issued separately by unit quartermasters. However, many batches simply failed to arrive in Africa, or were not supplied in sufficient quantities. To help remedy these shortages, many troops in Africa either used the brown woollen shoulder straps from their tropical overcoat for their tunic and shirt, or made use of the dark green woollen shoulder straps they had kept from their Continental issue tunics.

Soldiers wearing Continental shoulder straps were a minority in 1941, but by mid and late 1942 it was just as common to see non-regulation shoulder straps being worn as the proper tropical ones. So critical was the shortage that by 1942 army tailors were producing field-made ones from damaged tunics, old shirts and hessian material, with folded strips of coloured cloth serving as *Waffenfarbe* piping.

These difficulties did not arise in the case of officer

A Schütze *(Private) from InfRgt115 (mot) wears the black leather Continental type Y-straps. Soldier on left shows a back view of the complete set of field equipment carried on the Y-straps and the waist belt. (Author's collection)*

stamps in field caps to show that the gold-yellow soutache was still being applied to caps made in early 1942, despite its official replacement by copper-brown.

For the various shades of green, the picture is even more confusing. The colour worn by rifle regiments (*Schützenregimenter*) in the 1940 Panzer Divisions was a light green (*hellgrün*), a colour also used by other specialized infantry (*Jäger* Battalions and *Gebirgsjäger* Regiments). This light green was actually a medium green, slightly darker than the softer grass-green (*wiesengrün*) worn by members of motorcycle battalions in 1941. It was not an easy matter to tell them apart – there were some slight manufacturer variations in shade and the braid sometimes faded under the drastic bleaching suffered by uniforms. The confusion really began in 1941 when a new green was being introduced, reseda-green (*resedagrün*), or lime-green, a light green with a distinct yellowish tinge – this colour braid even exists on field caps with a 1940 maker's stamp. The new colour was intended for use by the motorized infantry regiments (renamed in 1942 as Armoured Infantry, (*Panzergrenadiere*)). But although the colour itself was continued, the name reseda-green was discontinued from early 1942 in favour of the by then unused grass-green, motorcycle battalions having switched to copper-brown. The three shades of combat green were well mixed in the motorized formations in 1941, although the new official green with a yellow tint (lime-green) was predominant in the motorized infantry regiments of the two Panzer divisions by the time of the fighting during November and December 1941.

An order dated 15 September 1941 stated that the motorcycle battalions in Panzer and motorized infantry divisions were henceforth to wear a copper-brown *Waffenfarbe* instead of grass-green. To what extent this was followed in Africa is not known, but it would have been impossible to issue every soldier in the 15th Motorcycle Battalion with new caps and shoulder straps – supplies simply did not exist. That some issue of the new colour did take place in 1941 is evident from the caps and shoulder straps with copper-brown piping picked up as souvenirs by 8th Army troops in November and December 1941. The same colour was worn by the reconnaissance units too, but it is likely that initially only new arrivals into the motorcycle battalion were issued with the new colour, and that existing stocks of caps and shoulder straps with grass-green braid were issued to the motorized infantry. This would have supplemented the scarce stocks of caps and shoulder straps carrying the lime-green colour, and would further explain the mixture of greens worn by the motorized

shoulder straps as there were no special officer tropical variations. The standard dull silver-grey braid officer shoulder strap was the same for all theatres of war. Officers in Africa seem to have had a good supply of their own personal shoulder straps.

The changes in colour allocation implemented between 1940 and 1942 affected *Waffenfarben* worn by motorized infantry regiments, reconnaissance units, and motorcycle battalions. Among these troops the old and newer colours became mixed and were worn at the same time. Gold-yellow, the colour of the old cavalry formations, was used by reconnaissance units in pre-war Panzer and light divisions, but by late 1941 this was being replaced by copper-brown. This was not always easy to distinguish from the red worn by artillery and *Luftwaffe* Flak troops, just as the brighter gold-yellow faded under sunlight to a lighter shade, making it hard to tell apart from the paler lemon-yellow used by signals units. The change from gold-yellow to copper-brown for the reconnaissance units was not a clean-cut one and there is evidence from manufacturers' date infantry around this time.

White *Waffenfarbe*, not a common colour in the *Afrikakorps* in 1941, was officially assigned to infantry (non-motorized) regiments, Army anti-aircraft battalions, and to machine gun battalions. Although the 5th Light Division as it was constituted did contain two machine gun battalions, these units arrived in Africa wearing the light green (*hellgrün*) *Waffenfarbe*. This was due to the decision taken in 1940 to manufacture a tropical uniform for a Panzer division, along with ancillary troops, *not* for a Light Division as was ultimately sent at short notice to Africa in February 1941.

The Panzer divisions did not include machine gun battalions in their order of battle. Instead, the machine gun component was organized as companies which were an integral part of the motorized infantry or rifle battalions, unlike the Light Division, which had the machine gun battalions as self-contained units. So members of the two machine gun battalions in the 5th Light Division were issued with the readily available caps and shoulder straps bearing the light green *Waffenfarbe*, which had been intended for use by the rifle regiments of a Panzer division. The available number of uniforms carrying the white piping was only sufficient to equip the anti-aircraft units, who also wore this colour. (Army anti-aircraft units were differentiated from their *Luftwaffe* counterparts by the prefix *Fla*, which stood for *Flugabwehr*, while the *Luftwaffe* acronym FLAK stood for *Flugabwehrartilleriekanone*.) Later in 1941 the two machine gun battalions were incorporated into the rifle regiments of the two Panzer divisions, and so their light green *Waffenfarbe* became their correct colour after all.

In 1941 the small number of caps and shoulder straps that were manufactured with white *Waffenfarbe* were issued firstly to the Army anti-aircraft units, e.g. *Heeres Fla. Bataillone 606*, etc., (white was originally assigned because their early anti-aircraft weapons, in 1935/36, were machine guns). Later in 1941, a small number of white-piped caps and shoulder straps were issued to some of the various unattached and non-motorized infantry drafts who were eventually absorbed into the 90th Light Division.

This reorganization in late 1941 – the incorporation of non-motorized infantry into new motorized infantry regiments – called for a general issue of caps and shoulder straps with green piping. Photos taken of infantry in the 164th Light Division arriving from Crete in July 1942 show that many in this previously part-motorized division were wearing white *Waffenfarbe* they had been issued with on the island.

By the middle of 1942, the high incidence of troops transferring between units, brought about by the chronic shortages in many units, meant that from this time the *Waffenfarbe* carried on a soldier's cap or shoulder straps was no longer a reliable guide to his parent unit. By the time of the El Alamein battles of October–November 1942, 8th Army Intelligence had decided that in the majority of cases they could no longer identify a German soldier's unit by the colour of his *Waffenfarbe* alone. This may have been too drastic an assessment as many individual soldiers did try to find the appropriate *Waffenfarbe* if Army clothing stores could not supply the right colour. This involved using Continental shoulder straps, tailor-made items put together in the field, and exchanging shoulder straps with their comrades to suit their current unit.

From late July 1942 the soutache braid was discontinued as a feature of the field cap, and all caps made after this date no longer had the distinctive inverted 'V' of braid stitched over the cockade. This was merely a response to the organizational and supply problems alluded to above and was not intended as a security measure to conceal the unit or service identity of soldiers taken prisoner. However, caps issued to troops and already in use did not necessarily lose their soutache from this time, though supply depots removed the

Infantry from InfRgt115 in the late summer of 1941 showing a range of field equipment: leather Y-straps, flare pistol holster, medical belt pouches, map case, rifle ammunition belt pouches, and camouflaged steel helmets. (Author's collection)

Members of the Gebirgsjäger (*Alpine troops*) *Company in* Sonderverband 288 *display the metal edelweiss on the left side of their field caps, and the woven edelweiss on the right sleeve of the tunic. This photo was taken in June 1942 during the summer offensive. (Werner Kost)*

soutache from all caps held for issue and by the end of 1942 there were very few caps with it.

The use of *Waffenfarben* was an effective way of reinforcing a soldier's sense of identity with his unit, and German troops wore their particular colour with pride. The distribution of colours was, however, based on an older tradition, and the organization of a 1941 Panzer division was quite different from the pre-1936 ones. The new motorized warfare brought with it an 'all-arms' philosophy of integration of function rather than the separation inherent in the system of *Waffen-farben*. The motorized infantry regiments and the motorcycle battalions were given greens as specialized infantry in the tradition of the *Jäger* units. However, it might have been simpler to have introduced new or under-used colours such as brown, or grey, or a system of stripes incorporating two colours.

The following table of *Waffenfarben* lists the colours that would have been in use by the German Army in North Africa between 1941 and 1943. The list is not comprehensive as some formations, such as training schools and divisions using a non-standard traditional colour, did not appear in North Africa.

ARM OF SERVICE COLOURS USED IN NORTH AFRICA, 1941–1943

Armour (*Panzer*)	Pink (*Rosa*)
Anti-tank Units (*Panzer-Jäger-Abteilungen*)	Pink (*Rosa*)
[1] Rifle Regiments – 1940 (*Schützenregimenter*) Panzer Grenadiers – 1942 (*Panzergrenadiere*)	Light green (*hellgrün*) and Reseda-green (lime-green) (*resedagrün*) then grass-green (*wiesengrün*)
Motorcycle Battalions – 1941 (*Kraftradschützen-Bataillone*)	Grass-green (*wiesengrün*)
Motorcycle Battalions – 1941/2	Copper-brown (*kupfer-braun*)
Army Anti-aircraft Battalions (*Heeres-Fla. Bataillone*)	White (*weiss*)
Machine Gun Battalions – 1941 (*Maschinengewehr-Bataillone*)	Light green (not official) (*hellgrün*)
Infantry Regiments (*Infanterie-Regimenter*)	White (*weiss*)
[2] Reconnaissance Units – 1941 (*Aufklärungs-Abteilungen*)	Gold-yellow (*goldgelb*)
Reconnaissance Units – 1941/2	Copper-brown (*kupfer-braun*)
[3] Alpine Regiments (*Gebirgsjäger-Regimenter*)	Light green (*hellgrün*)
Artillery Regiments (*Artillerie-Regimenter*)	Bright red (*hochrot*)
Engineer Battalions (*Pionier-Bataillone*)	Black (*schwarz*)
Signals Units (*Nachrichten-Abteilungen*)	Lemon-yellow (*zitronengelb*)

Motorized Supply & Transport Units (*Fahr-und Kraftfahr-Abteilungen*)	Light blue (*hellblau*)
Medical Units (*Sanitäts-Abteilungen*)	Dark blue (*kornblumenblau*)
Smoke (Projector) Units (*Nebel-Abteilungen*)	Bordeaux red (*bordorot*)
Field Police (*Feldgendarmerie*)	Orange-red (*orangerot*)
Veterinary Service (*Veterinäreinheiten*)	Carmine (*karmesin*)
4 Field Chaplains (*Heeresgeistlichen*)	Violet (*violett*)
General (rank) Officers (*Generale*)	Bright red (*hochrot*)
Propaganda Troops (*Propagandatruppe*)	Light grey (*hellgrau*)
Specialist Officers (*Sonderführer*)	Grey-blue (*grau-blau*)
5 Army Administrative Officers (*Wehrmachtbeamten*)	Dark green (*dunkelgrün*)

NOTES

1. Light green used by rifle regiments early in 1941 was replaced by reseda-green (lime-green) later the same year. This was then renamed grass-green and remained the colour used by the Panzer Grenadiers for the rest of the war.

2. Reconnaissance Unit 33, in the 15th Panzer Division, was taken from Cavalry Regiment 6, another reason for continuing the traditional use of gold-yellow by this unit.

3. Alpine Regiment 756 was part of 334th Inf. Div., sent into Tunisia in December 1942/January 1943.

4. Field Chaplains did not wear shoulder straps on their tunics, and *Waffenfarbe* appeared only on the officer braid collar tabs, and on the cap soutache or piping.

5. Army Administrative Officers carried a metal device of the letters 'HV' (standing for *Heeresverwaltung*) in Gothic script on their shoulder straps, which incorporated a secondary *Waffenfarbe* system denoting their special area of qualification or service.

Unlike the various depot units and pre-war formations which wore devices such as numerals or letters on shoulder straps, tropical shoulder straps were *not* issued in this style. Some officers serving in Africa did wear shoulder straps displaying such unit devices (as did some Continental shoulder straps used personally by other ranks), but this happened only because these were shoulder straps transferred from a Continental uniform.

As far as the distribution of *Waffenfarben* went, the most common colour represented in the German Army in Africa was green, reflecting the large numerical content of the various motorized infantry formations. By and large, the great majority of troops in the DAK managed to display the correct *Waffenfarbe* right through the campaigns in Africa, and if the Army could not supply shoulder straps in the correct *Waffenfarbe* piping then individual soldiers took it upon themselves to acquire some sort of shoulder strap bearing the

The two common styles of tropical shirt: on the left a French Army modified version with button-down collar and three plastic front buttons; and on the right a German design with four fibre front buttons. (Dieter Hellriegel)

proper colour piping. This again is further evidence of the pride taken by the average German soldier in wearing the correct markings for his particular arm of service.

The 15th Panzer Division and later reinforcement drafts were issued with their tropical uniforms in Germany before travelling to Africa. So these men arrived in Africa wearing their correct *Waffenfarbe*. The problems of supply and issue usually arose when men were reissued with new uniforms, or were sent to a unit which did not match the *Waffenfarbe* they had been given in Germany. The serious shortages of supply in this regard were experienced after November 1941 when most of the uniform stores were overrun in Cyrenaica during Operation Crusader, and the month of hard fighting necessitated widespread replacement of uniforms damaged or lost in battle. These losses plus hard wear and tear on uniforms frequently washed in petrol or salt water, meant that many troops had several complete issues of uniform during their service in North Africa.

The Tropical Field Cap

The peaked cloth field cap was the single most distinctive part of the tropical uniform and it quickly became synonymous with the *Afrikakorps*. The German

troops called it simply *Afrikamütze* (African cap).

The cap, manufactured from the same olive cotton twill as the tunic, varied in colour from a light beige through various shades of olive-khaki to a dark chocolate brown. These colour differences were due to variations in shade from different cloth mills.

One distinctive feature of the cap was the red cotton lining, a colour selected by the design team at the Tropical Institute of the University of Hamburg as being best suited to the hot arid climate of North Africa. It was found that this red-coloured lining struck the best balance in trying to minimize the transfer of heat on to the head from the outer surface of the cap while not preventing body heat being passed from the head into the space between the head and the top of the cap. This attention to such fine detail characterized the approach of the German Army towards the design of uniform and field equipment in World War II.

The peak on the cap was wide and joined the body of the cap above the ears of the wearer. It evolved from the style of field cap worn by the Austro-Hungarian

General Crüwell, right, wearing the officers' dress field service cap and the general's grade overcoat with red felt facings on the lapels and gilt metal buttons. (ECPA)

Army in World War I, and the false seam around the sides of the cap, with a pronounced scallop running across the front, showed these origins. A similar style of woollen cap was worn by German Alpine troops.

The cap insignia consisted of the German Army eagle and swastika in its tropical colours of light blue woven on a tan background, and below the eagle was a woven cockade of the black, white and red national colours on a tan diamond patch. Until July 1942 the cap also carried a coloured braid soutache stitched either side of the cockade. As mentioned earlier, the colour of the soutache indicated the arm of service of the soldier wearing the cap, but supply problems made this a difficult regulation to enforce.

A design change was introduced in early 1942 when a sweatband made of an ersatz leather material was incorporated. Field use had shown that the lower edge of the cap suffered from heavy perspiration and grime.

Photos of German troops in Africa invariably show a predominance of caps faded to a near white colour by the sun and frequent washing. But this was not always the result of long service in the desert. New arrivals stood out with their new darker-coloured caps and many deliberately bleached their caps to effect the appearance of old hands. One common method used to accelerate the bleaching was to dissolve anti-gas tablets in water – or any available liquid masquerading as water – in which the caps were washed.

A second style of tropical field cap used in Africa over the same period did not have a peak. The side panels were not stitched down and it had only one metal ventilation eyelet each side, instead of the two eyelets found on the peaked cap. German Army slang for this cap was *Schiffchen*, or little ship, and it closely followed the style of the M38 German Army woollen Continental field cap. It was widely issued in Africa though it found most favour with tank crews and others who fought from vehicles, as the more common peaked cap could catch on a doorway or hatch and be knocked down over the eyes.

Tropical field caps worn by officers were distinguished by a length of metal cording stitched around the crown and along the front scalloped seam. For generals this metal cording was gold coloured, and for all other officers the colour was silver. Many officers, overly conscious of their rank, removed the standard issue tropical insignia and replaced it with the silver wire eagle and/or the raised cockade from their Continental officer field caps, further enhancing its appearance.

The tropical field cap, especially the peaked variety, was immensely popular with German troops in Africa. Some manufacturers – such as the firm of 'Silesian Cap Factory, Frankenstein' – were more popular than others because they bleached more easily to the bone-white colour that was so fashionable.

After the surrender of German forces in Africa in 1943 the *Afrikamütze* continued to be worn for the rest of the war by units serving in warm areas such as Crete, and in the Balkans and Italy in the summer months.

The Tropical Sun Helmet

This headgear followed the accepted lines of a military topee, even down to retaining the top ventilation cap with a screw thread to receive a traditional spike. The pith helmet, or *Tropenhelm* to give it its German title, was a wide-brimmed lightweight sun helmet made of compressed cork and covered with panels of olive-coloured cloth. The lining was the same red cotton as for the field cap. The edge of the brim was stitched in leather and the helmet carried an olive or grey leather chinstrap. Insignia on the helmet were two light stamped metal shields – on the right side embodying the black/white/red national colours, and a silver-on-black Army eagle on the left.

The helmet was issued to all troops in Africa from beginning to end but was not popular. Unlike the cloth field cap, it was bulky and difficult to pack and carry around when not being worn. In a war of rapid movement it was one of the first things to be 'misplaced'.

The German Army Command retained a naïve faith in this piece of tropical clothing, and in 1942 German troops were still being enjoined to wear the sun helmet between the hours of 0800 and 1600 to ward off sunstroke. The helmet was also liked by the propaganda photographers as an effective and attractive item to illustrate photos intended for Germany. Parades of newly arrived troops, held for propaganda purposes in Tripoli, invariably show the sun helmet being worn.

The helmet had no rank distinctions, and the same helmet was worn by other ranks and officers. A second variety produced from the end of 1942 onwards had an external covering of olive brown felt, but this style did not see service in Africa.

Supplies of the sun helmet were not adequate to equip the members of the 5th Light Division in February 1941 and so stocks of Dutch sun helmets were used. These were smaller than the German-designed helmet, and had a decorative pleated cloth wound round

it (a pugaree) with four metal ventilation eyelets on each side. This helmet was widely distributed among men of 5th Panzer Regiment, and some were issued later to members of 33rd Panzer Artillery Regiment in the 15th Panzer Division. The normal lightweight metal Army eagle and tricolour shields were worn on it.

The Tropical Field Tunic

This important piece of uniform was made from a high-quality olive-coloured ribbed cotton twill material, and featured two patch-style pleated breast pockets and two larger box-style pleated pockets on the hips. All external buttons were the usual pebbled metal style, painted olive green on the outer surface. The tunic was open necked with a large collar and the tunic flared slightly from the waist down. Apart from the buttons stitched on the shoulder seams to secure the shoulder straps, buttons were removable being held in place by small 'S' configuration spring steel clips. Inside, the tunic was reinforced around the armpits, behind the side-seams,

Issue of new tunics and trousers early in 1942 after Rommel had advanced to Gazala. (ECPA)

Uniform variations: Major Bach, left, wears a tailor-made tunic with a turn-back cuff; the Medical Officer in the centre has a Continental woollen officer field cap and officer silver bullion breast eagle; and the Leutnant *standing to the right wears an other rank belt and British canvas gaiters. (ECPA)*

farbe or any rank variation. The breast eagle and swastika, woven in blue thread on a tan background, was worn above the right breast pocket with the lower part of the wreath-enclosed swastika stitched over the top of the pocket flap. This position, lower than for Continental tunics, was necessary to expose the eagle beyond the area covered by the open collar.

Identical tunics were issued to both officers and other ranks. It was the responsibility of officers to provide their own shoulder straps. These should have been the current removable variety but they too were in short supply and some officers had to use the 'sew-in' style cut from their Continental tunics. This necessitated opening the shoulder seam and stitching the flat ends back in. Naturally officer shoulder straps attached in this manner could not be removed and they suffered accordingly when the tunic was washed, and quickly became faded. The addition of Continental officer collar tabs and a silver wire officer eagle in lieu of the standard all-ranks tropical insignia was at the discretion of officers, provided this insignia was available.

The quality of tunics remained consistently high throughout the period of the African fighting, and only two minor variations were introduced towards the end. In late 1942 a new tunic was produced which did not feature pleats on the pockets, and in early 1943 another style appeared which did away with the pointed or scalloped pocket flaps of the two earlier styles. These modifications served to make slightly easier the manufacture of tunics which were being made increasingly by semi-skilled workers in a now badly overworked clothing industry.

Army Tropical Shirts

The tropical shirt was intended for wear either beneath the tunic or without the tunic and for this purpose it carried removable shoulder straps. It was made from a light olive or khaki cotton drill material and was so long it reached down to below the level of the buttocks.

Two distinct types were used, one being of German design and the other a modified French Army tropical shirt. The basic French pattern was distinguished from the German by a button-down collar (two small brown plastic buttons on the collar points and one in the mid-rear line of the collar), larger pockets, a three-button front and only one button per cuff. Large stocks of these French Army shirts had been captured after the fall of France and they were used to augment supplies of German shirts right up until the end of 1942. The modification entailed sewing loops on the shoulders along with detachable pebbled metal buttons to take shoulder

and behind the top corners of the pockets. The sleeves were cuffless but could be adjusted by buttoning up on the two small composite fibre buttons inside a reinforced concealed flap. Inside the right lower front flap there was a pocket designed to hold a supply of field surgical bandages. To help support the weight of equipment worn on the waist belt the tunic had metal belt hooks on each side supported by cloth straps which were stitched inside the tunic below the armpits where the tunic cloth was reinforced.

Standard insignia consisted of shoulder straps held by sewn loops on the shoulder edges and pebbled metal buttons. A special tropical variation of the collar tabs, a feature of all German military uniforms, were stitched on to the collar ends. These consisted of elongated woven patches that flared at both ends and contained three gold-coloured stripes on a light blue-grey background. Unlike the Continental variety of collar tabs, those worn on the tropical tunic did not show *Waffen-*

Lunch break for two members of a 105mm howitzer gun crew. Plainly visible are two individual modifications to the trouser cuffs with string and lace drawcords. (ECPA)

straps, and substituting removable pebbled metal buttons on the breast pockets for the small plastic buttons. For shirts obtained directly from French clothing factories the modifications went further and some of these shirts were produced embodying features of German as well as French design. After stocks of French-cut shirts had been exhausted, the French factories went over to making the German design and a large proportion of the shirts used by the German Army in Africa were of French manufacture.

The standard German design was also a pullover type. This had two pleated breast pockets with the flaps secured by pebbled metal buttons on detachable 'S' clips, loops and similar removable buttons on the shoulders, and it buttoned down the front with four small composite fibre buttons. The cuffs were fastened with two of the same small fibre buttons.

This item wore out more quickly than any other part of the uniform, and to prolong its life the battalion or company tailors turned the collar and patched areas that had been torn. There was no special shoulder strap made specifically for the shirt and they were issued with the same style of shoulder strap worn on the tunic. A tie made of the same cotton drill material as the shirt was issued, but this was only worn on formal occasions and the shirt was normally worn open-necked, either with the tunic or on its own.

Tropical Breeches, Trousers and Shorts

These standard items of uniform were made from the same heavy olive-coloured ribbed twill material as the field tunic. Some breeches (but not trousers or shorts) also were made of a corduroy material.

A design innovation in all three items was a concealed integral belt which fastened on a claw buckle. The belt was a length of canvas or reinforced twill contained in a waist seam that ran around the back and buckled above the fly, the end of the tightened belt being tucked into a loop on the left.

Standard features were two side slit pockets, one rear hip pocket fastened by a dished-out steel button, and a small fob pocket on the right side front. Buttons were provided inside the waistband for braces, though these were rarely worn as there was no need for them. But the style of trousers worn in the Continental uniform at this time did not have any means of support other

Combat dress for an Engineer group: hessian covers over steel helmets, stick grenades pushed through belts and straps, MP38/40 leather and canvas magazine pouches, and canvas Y-straps to support the weight of ammunition and equipment carried on the waist belt. (ECPA)

This Oberleutnant *of the* Feldgendarmerie *directing traffic below Halfaya wears two cufftitles.* AFRIKAKORPS *on his right sleeve and his uniform* Feldgendarmerie *title on the left sleeve. (ECPA)*

than braces, which meant that the tunic and any equipment had to be removed to drop the trousers – a time-consuming business and possibly dangerous if under fire.

To minimize the incidence of leg infections only trousers or breeches could be worn on the front line, with shorts reserved for non-combat areas. Trousers were by far the most popular with the troops, as the breeches had to be worn with the high canvas and leather boots. The preferred combination of trousers and low boots resulted in a sensible modification followed by the majority of troops: the hem on each trouser leg was opened and a length of string or tape was threaded through allowing the trouser bottoms to be pulled tight over the ankles. This gave the characteristic bloused look so common in photos, but it was not a regulation issue feature and all trousers had to be modified by the soldiers themselves.

Another style of breeches – issued in small numbers and favoured by officers – was made from a brushed cotton material and featured a side lace-up arrangement on the outer calf instead of the usual leg end tape ties common on the other styles.

Tropical Woollen Overcoat

Unlike other items of tropical uniform, the overcoat (greatcoat) was not manufactured in a light olive or khaki colour. Chocolate-brown was the predominant shade but many were made from a lighter brown or dark tan woollen material.

The coat followed the design of the contemporary Continental woollen overcoat, though in the tropical version the collar was the same colour as the rest of the coat. It was a long garment, flared from the waist, double-breasted and buttoned with two parallel rows of six olive-green pebbled metal buttons. A two-piece waist belt at the back was adjusted by two pebbled metal buttons and there were two small tabs below it that could be buttoned down to pull the waist in further. To make movement easier, the skirt at the back buttoned from the waist down and there was an inverted pleat from neck to hem.

The coat had an angled slit pocket on each side covered by rounded flaps, and a large inside breast pocket. The collar could be turned up and held closed with a metal hook and loop at the base of the collar, and a woollen tab that fastened to a button under the opposite collar. A small piece of reinforced double thickness woollen material was issued with the coat which could be buttoned in place across the upturned collar to improve insulation by covering the join between the two collar edges. The coat was lined, from the waist up and inside the sleeves, with a layer either of synthetic silk or cotton twill material. The sleeves had deep turn-back cuffs which were stitched in place.

The coat was normally worn long, with the lower edge which was unhemmed coming to a point just above the ankles. It had sewn buttons and loops to take shoulder straps (for other ranks in the same brown woollen material as the overcoat); the garment was identical for officers and lower ranks. The only rank distinction was that accorded to General rank officers, who wore a coat with a red felt facing on the top edges of the area exposed when the collar was open, and it had gold-coloured pebbled metal buttons.

The tropical overcoat was a well-designed and essential piece of uniform as desert nights were cold, and not only in winter. Photos of German POWs taken in Africa invariably show them in possession of their overcoats. Whatever else may have been lost in the turmoil of battle, most evidently made the effort to hold on to this garment.

Tropical Motorcyclist's Coat

Although its nomenclature may indicate that this specially designed coat was issued only to motorcyclists, it saw quite widespread use beyond this arm of service. Many vehicle drivers also wore it and it was a popular acquisition by officers who often preferred it to the heavier woollen overcoat. In design it was identical to the rubberized canvas coat issued to motorcyclists in Europe, but the tropical variety was manufactured from the same heavy olive cotton twill as the tunic.

It was worn very long – and there was a practical reason for this. The rear part of the skirt buttoned vertically to the waist and the two lower flaps in this arrangement could then be buttoned around the

Awards worn on the field tunic: Major Frey who commanded the Supply and Transport Column in 15PzDiv: AFRIKAKORPS *cufftitle, Iron Cross 1st and 2nd Class (with bars for awards in both World Wars), and War Merit Cross with swords. (ECPA)*

wearer's legs. There were two large side pockets covered with button-down flaps and another angled slit pocket on the chest. The coat was double-breasted, with an attached waist belt made of the same material as the coat; shoulder straps were worn on sewn loops and the buttons were pebbled metal.

Tropical Woollen Sweater

This simple knitted pullover made of a chocolate-coloured woollen yarn was standard issue. Two styles were worn, one with a rollneck collar and the other with a short open collar. Both styles saw wide use and as with other tropical uniform (except the field cap) there was no distinction between officer and other ranks issue.

Cost of personal items

One paper that was picked up at El Alamein sheds interesting light on the amount of clothing and other items of a personal nature that were privately purchased as part of the kit of an NCO. Officers were required to buy all items of their uniform and personal belongings, and were given an allowance to cover this expense. No such extra payment, however, was accorded to other ranks (enlisted personnel), but as this paper shows the German Army was prepared to reimburse such material when it was lost in action.

The paper detailing the claim was headed *Antrag* (proposal) and was written out by an *Unteroffizier* (Senior Corporal) Karl Schmidtkronz, in *Nachrichten Kompanie 200* (Signals Company 200, in 21st Panzer Div.): 'During my leave when I was attached to my former unit, Signals Company 713, I was posted to the island of Crete. My belongings along with all the others of my company were loaded on the steamer *Ythaka* for transportation to Crete. This ship was torpedoed on 10.11.41 by an enemy submarine south of the island of Milos and was sunk.'

The list of missing items:

Item		Purchase Price RM	Estimated Current Value RM
1	set pyjamas	15.–	8.–
1	tracksuit	20.–	12.–
10	handkerchiefs	4.–	2.–
2	polo shirts	8.–	6.–
2	athletic singlets	6.–	4.–
3	underpants, short	12.–	8.–
2	Turkish bath towels	8.–	6.–
1	pullover	20.–	15.–
1	bathing trunks	4.–	2.50
1	athletic shorts	3.–	2.–
1	sports tights	6.–	3.–
1	pair slippers	8.–	4.–
4	pair socks	12.–	8.–
1	pair trouser suspenders	2.50	1.50
1	pair leather gloves	12.–	8.–
1	tropical trousers	7.–	5.–
1	travel accessory box	10.–	8.–
1	compass (Byzard)	6.–	5.–
8	rolls of film	8.–	8.–
	tobacco	10.–	10.–
1	sewing kit	3.–	3.–
1	writing case and contents	5.–	5.–
1	suitcase	20.–	20.–
		209.50	154.00

Troops being re-issued with new tropical pith helmets in early 1942 after the end of the fighting in Cyrenaica from November 41–January 42. (ECPA)

This paper has all the trappings of an insurance claim, with one and half pages of solemn statements alleging the total honesty of all details. A footnote to it is a declaration by his Company Commander, an *Oberleutnant*, that the foregoing claim is verified and complies with conditions as laid down under the OKW (Supreme Command) order relating to the loss of private possessions – OKW Az. 2 f 32 Beih. 1 – WV (III a) Nr. 9527/39 v. 21.2.40.

The *Oberleutnant* added that the claim did not exceed the RM500 limit, and that he was recommending that the 154 Reichsmarks be paid.

Tropical Boots

German troops in Africa were issued with two types of special tropical boots, one that reached up to just below the knee and the other being ankle height. Normal issue was one pair of each type. Both styles were made of a combination of leather and canvas, a design decided on by the Tropical Institute of the University of Hamburg. The use of canvas in those parts of the boots where most flexing occurred was meant to extend the life of the boots, as leather, it was thought, would dry out and crack easily in the hot and dry climate of North Africa. A heavy leather was used on the sole and the parts enclosing the sides of the feet – this was thought to be better able to survive the dehydrating atmosphere of the desert.

Both low and high styles of boot laced up the front on a combination of eyelets and hooks. The high boots had a patch of leather stitched over the inner ankle, both to support the canvas above and to prevent it gathering in ripples around the ankle. The high boots were really quite sensible as the canvas enclosing the calf offered protection against the sharp camel thorn and other low plants that easily scratched the legs producing sores that quickly turned septic. The German troops, however, preferred the ankle boots because it was time-consuming and a bother to lace up the high boots properly. Many troops converted their high lace-up tropical boots to ankle height by simply cutting off the canvas above the ankle.

The original style of boot, as designed and first manufactured in 1940, had a large area of canvas between the leather toecap and the seam at the lower edge of the laces, but the piece covering the instep area proved to be a design weakness. The seam joining the two areas was not placed for comfort and weakened with hard wear. To remedy this problem, a second style of boot was introduced in the middle of 1941 which extended the lower edge of the laces further on to the instep, with reinforced stitching along the seam to stop any separation. In this style, the arrangement of lower laces and the corresponding smaller area of canvas over the instep followed the original design of the ankle boot. It also allowed a better fit as the laces could be used to adjust the flexible instep area of the boot to a foot's individual contours.

But this modification was not good enough and the pattern was superseded at the end of 1941 by a third and final style which did away with the area of canvas over the instep and had an enlarged leather toecap flush with the lower edge of the laces. This last style, which did not see wide use until late in 1942, was slightly

A Leutnant en route to Tunisia photographed in southern Italy, January 1943. He is wearing a late-pattern officer field cap with no soutache, a tunic with pleatless pockets and scalloped pocket flaps, and the special tropical officer belt with a circular buckle. (Author's collection)

shorter than the two previous models of high boot.

The ankle boots also underwent a design change at the time that the third style of high boot was introduced. They remained the same height, but the canvas was also removed from the instep area and was replaced by a larger leather toecap.

Footwear was always in short supply, and it was common to see other than standard issue tropical canvas and leather boots being worn by German troops in Africa. Some higher-ranking officers, emulating Rommel, wore the high leather riding-style boots, and the standard Continental black leather laced ankle-height boots also saw much service. The special climbing boots issued to Alpine troops were also seen in Africa though not in large numbers (some troops from the 164th Light Division arrived in Africa from Crete wearing these boots). Other common footwear were canvas sandshoes (plimsolls) and leather sandals worn in rear areas, and captured British or American boots.

While the majority of Army tropical boots used an olive-green canvas, a small number were made with a tan-coloured canvas. In all cases, the colour of leather was a light brown. Unlike the Continental-issue boots, most tropical boots did not have large hobnails on the sole. The most common type of sole reinforcement consisted of a large number of small soft metal-headed nails which either flattened with use or fell away to expose a smaller head which was flush with the sole.

Sundry Uniform

Other regular uniform articles issued were a pair of olive woollen gloves and several pairs of olive or grey woollen socks.

There was also a special tropical waist belt made of heavy olive canvas web instead of the leather found in the Continental style. There was a rank distinction for these belts. Other ranks wore it with a standard rectangular metal buckle bearing the Army eagle inside a wreath bearing the legend *Gott Mit Uns*. Officers had a different design of canvas web with a circular buckle featuring the Army eagle inside a wreath of oak leaves. Many officers, however, preferred to wear the standard Continental leather belt for officers, which had a plain, open, pebbled metal claw buckle.

Uniform Variations

Not every German serviceman in North Africa wore the same basic uniform. The *Luftwaffe* had their own uniform, and some Army officers purchased privately-tailored uniforms. This was common practice in Europe, but not in Africa. Tailors in Germany did not normally carry stocks of olive twill material and so tailor-made officer uniforms did not appear until late in 1941 and then only in small numbers – the most notable seen in Africa was of course the one worn by Rommel. When they did appear, tailor-made officer uniforms were generally more elaborate, with turn-back cuffs, wider lapels, fancier scallops on the pocket flaps, etc., with Continental wire bullion officer insignia professionally attached.

Very few examples of privately tailored officer field caps are known to exist. The standard issue officer field cap was made by only a few manufacturers, and the quality of these caps was uniformly high. No manufacturers produced exclusively a line of officer caps. The number of officers who bothered to replace the standard issue tropical insignia on their field caps with more impressive-looking Continental insignia was not high for, unlike the tunic, officer caps already had the distinctive silver cording.

With ankle boots, two kinds of leggings were sometimes encountered – olive canvas gaiters, or cloth leg tapes (puttees) which were usually used with breeches.

The Italian *Sahariana* tropical tunic was also worn by German officers, as was the Italian Army tropical shirt which was used by all ranks when German shirts were scarce. Mention has already been made of British shirts and footwear, and British Army trousers were also used, especially after mid-1942.

No examples are known of British tunics being worn, partly because the German tunic proved so durable, and also because it was considered necessary to retain the 'German' appearance of the uniform with German caps and tunics.

Although regulations specifically prohibited the use of tunic breast eagles on the tropical shirt, many Germans flagrantly disobeyed this order and displayed a variety of breast eagles on their shirts. Ironically, officers appear to have been the worst offenders in this respect.

German troops seem to have had an affection for displaying their insignia in non-regulation ways. Some ranks transferred the lightweight metal shield showing an Army eagle from the sun helmet to the side panel of their cloth field caps.

After the order was issued in late July 1942 to discontinue the soutache on the field cap, it should have disappeared. But it continued to be worn, at least until the end of the Alamein battle. That this order was largely ignored reflects the pride felt by the average German soldier in displaying his arm of service identification.

Tank crews serving in Europe had the distinction of wearing a special black woollen uniform, and the black woollen sidecap with pink soutache from this uniform was retained by many Panzer crews in Africa. The cap was worn extensively in the first years of the campaign, though its appearance was not common after mid-1942.

On more formal occasions some German officers wore their Continental dress caps, the *Schirmmütze*, in combination with their tropical uniform. Rommel usually wore this style of cap, with a pair of lightweight British goggles. Other generals and higher-ranking officers also affected this style of dress.

The old style of peaked field cap for officers was also worn in Africa, though in small numbers. Overall, the tropical peaked field cap was the most popular headwear among officers, and its attractive appearance together with its light weight and ease of storage made this a sensible choice.

Another item of uniform more commonly seen in Europe than in North Africa was the leather overcoat privately purchased and worn by some officers. These expensive brown or black leather coats were made in the same style as the standard issue woollen overcoat, double-breasted, and bearing shoulder straps on the shoulder seams.

Desert Camouflage

The German Army in North Africa had no official policy of modifying standard tropical uniform or per-

Men of Machine Gun Battalion 8 in June 1942 wearing green Waffenfarbe on their tropical field caps. The man in the centre at the rear, however, is wearing a Continental woollen M38 cap with the original white Waffenfarbe for this unit. (Author's collection)

The Dutch pith helmet with distinctive wide pugaree worn here by a soldier of 15PzDiv filling a jerry can from a well at Point 165, west of Bardia in the summer of 1941. (Author's collection)

A tank crew in 1941. Note the black woollen Panzer sidecaps worn by the soldier at left, and the Leutnant with goggles over his cap. (ECPA)

The 'Free Arab Legion' in Tunisia, 1943. Behind the German NCO, the Arab troops are wearing French Army uniforms with German steel helmets and an armband bearing the legend 'In the Service of the German Armed Forces'. (ECPA)

A mortar crew in a pit near the Tobruk perimeter in the summer of 1941 wear steel helmets that have been coated with a light-coloured paint which originally was issued for camouflaging vehicles. (NZ National Archives – Alexander Turnbull Library)

sonal equipment for camouflage purposes. However, many individual soldiers took it upon themselves to camouflage metal surfaces which could reflect the sun's rays and so give away their position. The most common piece of equipment to be given some sort of desert camouflage was the field-green steel helmet.

The first step taken to make the helmet blend in with the colour of the desert landscape was to paint it, usually with paint available for camouflaging vehicles. As this was often mixed with old sump oil or Italian paints, there was a marked range of colour tones. Predominant colours were pale yellow, mustard-beige or orange-tan. The standard of finish varied, depending on how much care a soldier took and how the paint was applied. Only a few took the trouble to mask the insignia – the eagle

and tricolour shields – on the helmet. It was easier and more effective to simply paint over the entire surface and sometimes inside the rim below the liner as well.

Another easy way to improve the camouflaged appearance of the helmet was to sprinkle sand over the wet paint. It was then indistinguishable from the surrounding desert, and the combination of thick paint and a layer of sand also meant the helmet was less likely to show chips and knocks. In Tunisia greater use was made of dark tan paints which gave some helmets a mottled appearance when these were painted over the original colour.

A third method of camouflaging the steel helmet involved covering it either with layers of hessian material or the canvas used for sandbags. An oval piece of material was cut and placed over the helmet with a drawcord securing the lower edge inside the rim of the helmet. This system was widely used by the Sappers (*Pioniere*) as the fabric covers not only effectively camouflaged the appearance but also helped muffle sound if the helmet hit another object or the ground.

Other items of personal equipment that received painted camouflage treatment were bayonet scabbards, mess-tins, gasmask canisters and the metal drinking cups on water canteens. Other pieces of metal equipment, such as spare barrel holders and drum magazines for machine guns, metal ammunition containers, the tubes on the 'scissor-scope' optical instruments and metal parts on binoculars were also painted, though this was nowhere near as common as camouflaging the steel helmet. It is wrongly assumed today that any German World War II equipment bearing beige-coloured paint must be 'tropical' but in 1943 the German Army introduced a standard beige-coloured base camouflage for vehicles and equipment. This paint was applied in the factories, not in the field, and saw service in *all* theatres of war, though very little was in use by the end of the fighting in Africa in May 1943.

Tropical Army Uniform Insignia

The tropical uniform carried the same combinations of insignia as were worn on the Continental uniform, but there were special tropical versions of this basic insignia.

The eagle and swastika displayed on field caps and tunics was woven in a light blue thread on a tan base outline. Earlier examples were woven in a heavier thread which gave the detail in the eagle more relief while later ones, appearing from late 1942, were made with a thinner synthetic thread that had a flatter appearance.

The cockade worn on the field cap incorporated the German national colours of black, white and red and

was woven on a tan diamond backing. Later examples of the cockade used a synthetic thread as opposed to the earlier style woven in a cotton thread.

Other rank shoulder straps were made from the same olive twill material used for tunics and field caps. The *Waffenfarbe* on the shoulder straps was either a woollen or a synthetic material. Initially the woollen piping was more common but as the campaign progressed the silk-like synthetic piping gradually replaced it. The underside of the upper part of the shoulder strap was a chocolate-brown woollen material until 1943 when field grey or blue-grey was used. The shoulder straps worn on the tropical overcoat were made in the chocolate-brown colour of the overcoat.

The tropical NCO braid (tresse) which was stitched around the outer edge of the tunic collar, and on the edges of the NCO shoulder straps, was a deep gold or a lighter gold-tan colour woven in a distinctive zigzag diamond pattern. The same braid was worn on the sleeve chevrons for junior NCO ranks (*Gefreiter*, etc.).

Two prisoners captured at El Alamein. The one on the right wears a Continental woollen M38 field cap with white soutache. (Imperial War Museum)

The rank carried by those on the first rung above an ordinary private (*Oberschütze*, etc.) was indicated by a four-pointed starburst embroidered on a circular patch of twill or brown woollen material. In 1941 this insignia was in a light olive-grey thread which contrasted poorly with the olive-green uniform when the cotton twill faded. In 1942 the colour of the starburst was changed to a light blue. There are also examples of this insignia in existence with the starburst embroidered in black thread but their exact period of use has not been established.

Trade specialist patches were embroidered, for tunics, in yellow thread on round patches of ribbed twill material, or on the chocolate-brown wool of the overcoat. These sleeve badges indicated a qualification in some branch of training, such as weapon maintenance, radio operator, medical specialization or farrier. The individual qualification area was indicated by a symbol or a stylized letter. For men who had qualified as signallers, but who did not serve in a signals unit where the *Waffenfarbe* alone would indicate this overall specialization, the insignia was a zigzag arrow or *Blitz* embroidered in their own particular *Waffenfarbe*. The trade specialist patch was worn on the lower right sleeve of the tunic while the signaller's *Blitz* was carried on the left arm of the tunic midway between shoulder and elbow.

The edelweiss alpine flower insignia indicating mountain troops was worn in Africa by the company of these troops in *Sonderverband 288* and was later worn by members of Alpine Regiment 756 in Tunisia. No tropical variation of this insignia was produced for use in North Africa, and the standard Continental woven style on a dark green backing was worn.

Members of all Panzer regiments in Africa adopted the practice of wearing silvered metal skulls on their tunic lapels. The skulls were obtained from the Continental Panzer collar patches worn on the special black tank uniform. In Africa the skulls were either attached by pushing the prongs through the lapel cloth, or by stitching.

Another metal badge, the traditional (i.e. Imperial) Prussian eagle, was worn in Africa by some members of Reconnaissance Unit 33 which had been drawn from Cavalry Regiment 6. This small eagle was mounted on a pin, and was displayed on the field cap between the eagle and the cockade, and on the pith helmet on the centre front panel.

Field Chaplains wore a small embroidered gothic cross on their field caps; for the tropical officer field cap it was stitched in place above the cockade and below the swastika.

Army Field Police (*Feldgendarmerie*) in North Africa wore the standard Continental gorget – a flat curved metal plate – on the chest suspended by a chain around the neck. The eagle and swastika and the word *Feld-*

The high leather and canvas boots, worn with breeches by a group of men from InfRgt104 in late summer 1941. (Author's collection)

gendarmerie were in a luminous yellowish paint finish against a dull-grey background.

The most exotic insignia worn in Africa by German troops was that adopted by *Sonderverband 288*. Designed as a unit tactical emblem, it incorporated an oval laurel wreath with the two sides of the wreath joined together by a swastika at the bottom and enclosing a typical desert palm tree beside a rising sun. After *Sonderverband 288* arrived in Libya in late 1941, a bronze badge in this design with a pin on the back was produced in the field and was worn by members of the unit on the left breast pocket of the tunic in the style of an assault badge. This was unofficially accepted by the DAK command, which followed the German Army's traditional encouragement for reinforcing a soldier's sense of identity with his unit. However, it was not until late 1942 that the Army officially sanctioned this insignia with the issue of a woven insignia patch to be worn on the tunic sleeve. This was in an off-white thread for the insignia detail, on a dark green oval backing (for tunics) or on a woollen base (for the overcoat). After its introduction some confusion surrounded its correct place on the uniform and evidence indicates it was worn on either sleeve, though by 1943 it was commonly worn on the right sleeve above the elbow.

As well as the various items of uniform insignia covered above, many German troops elected to wear their decorations on the field tunic. For these medals,

Men of InfRgt115 packing up tents and bedding. They wear the drill work suits issued for general fatigue duties out of the front-line area. This photo was taken late summer 1941. (Author's collection)

award badges and ribbons, there were no special tropical variations. The most common example was the ribbon for the Iron Cross, second class, which was stitched in place through the top, or second from top, buttonhole. On formal parades marksman lanyards were also worn by those qualified to display them, but they were rarely seen.

Photographs are misleading in trying to determine to what extent awards and decorations were worn. Most photos have an element of posing or some prior knowledge of a photo being taken, and therefore soldiers would have been more likely to dress for the occasion.

In the case of photos taken by official Army photographers, conscious selection was certainly exercised – a soldier, for example, wearing evidence of his courage and service would have made a more interesting subject than another soldier wearing an unadorned tunic. The photos available from official sources today that most clearly show details of uniforms are often ones taken at formal events staged for the presentation of medals, or for an inspection, and these show a higher incidence of medals and awards being worn than was normally the case.

A young Panzer Obergefreiter wears metal skull badges on his tunic lapels to indicate he is a tank crewman. He wears Continental rank chevrons, and one twill shoulder strap and a brown woollen tropical overcoat shoulder strap, reflecting the current shortages of insignia. (Charles Hinz)

Cufftitles

The cufftitle was an important element of German military uniform and the award of such a title recognized either that a soldier belonged to a body of troops with special status, or that the troops were to be awarded it in the sense of a campaign decoration.

The AFRIKAKORPS cufftitle falls into the first of these two categories. The official order announcing its award to German troops in North Africa was not promulgated until July 1941. When issued, it applied to all German troops stationed there, not only those members of the two divisions which made up the *Afrikakorps*. The only qualification was that a soldier had to have served for at least two months in Africa.

Either because this award was anticipated, or because supplies of the official cufftitle were slow to arrive, a so-called 'first pattern' cufftitle was made up either in

Tripoli, or in Italy. This was not unlike that worn by the SS, with greyish-white block letters embroidered on a black woollen band of material. It appeared in two styles, one with plain letters on a black background, the other similar but with silver trim on the top and bottom edges. This difference would normally indicate a distinction between officers and other ranks, but both styles were issued to all ranks.

After the official cufftitle had been issued, it was decided to recall the first version but some German troops managed to retain them. In some cases these non-regulation cufftitles were still being issued in early 1942. So rare had they become by then that the few German soldiers who were given them were not aware of the reasons for their different style.

The standard cufftitle was a band of dark green material carrying the legend AFRIKAKORPS in block silver letters edged top and bottom with silver trim, and this was edged again with a thin strip of light tan material. The title was meant to be sewn flat down on the sleeve of the tunic or overcoat but many Germans who wore the title turned the outer tan edge in before stitching it on. Only a small minority of troops chose to wear their cufftitles on their tropical uniforms. In a theatre of war where nearly everyone qualified to wear the cufftitle, there was no need to claim identity as a member of the *Afrikakorps* by displaying it. The usual dress in the desert was shirtsleeves and so the tunic was not worn all that often in any case. Also, many men preferred to keep the title as a souvenir or to wear it on their uniform if and when they ever succeeded in getting home leave. (The standard tropical uniform could be worn in Germany during the summer months and for men on leave at other times it was permitted to wear the AFRIKAKORPS cufftitle on a Continental uniform.)

At the end of 1942, the AFRIKAKORPS cufftitle was officially discontinued and from 15 January 1943 was replaced by a new cufftitle which was to have the standing of a campaign decoration and so would be awarded to all military personnel, not just the Army. Known simply as the AFRIKA cufftitle, it was actually an award rather than a part of the uniform and as such was accompanied by an award citation and an entry in the soldier's paybook. Unlike the AFRIKAKORPS cufftitle which was worn on the right lower sleeve, the new AFRIKA title was to be worn on the lower left sleeve. It was made from a soft tan camel hair material with the word AFRIKA in greyish-white capital letters, which was flanked by two similarly embroidered palm trees. The band was edged top and bottom with greyish-white braid, and there were no rank distinctions in style.

The 'Afrika' cufftitle document

Of the approximately 260,000 German troops (soldiers, airmen and sailors) who served in North Africa, just over 100,000 were in Europe at the time of the Axis surrender in Tunisia in May 1943. Of this total of repatriated troops, the greater number had been sent back because of sickness and were, after they had recovered, assigned to other units fighting in Europe. These men, if they qualified in terms of time spent in Africa, were all eligible for the award of the campaign cufftitle AFRIKA.

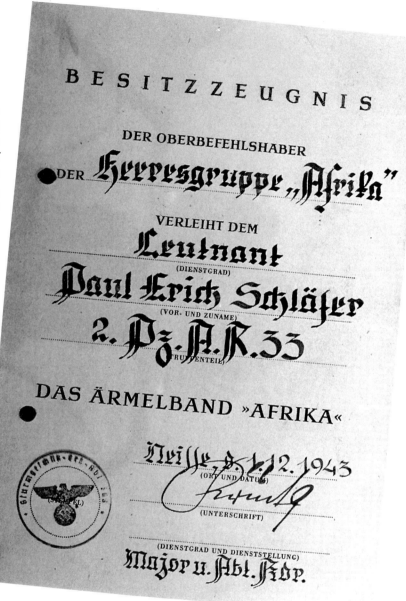

Over the eighteen-month period following the end of the war in Africa these men were tracked down by an office in the OKW and when located were awarded the cufftitle along with the accompanying document. The award was conferred in the name of the last supreme command body in Africa, *Heeresgruppe Afrika* (Army Group Africa). Although it was instituted on 15 January 1943, only a very small number were given out before the end of the campaign in Africa. From photos taken of Rommel after his final return to Europe, it is apparent that he elected not to carry this AFRIKA cufftitle on his uniform, despite being better qualified to do so than most. It could be he felt it unnecessary to display an identity with the *Afrikakorps* and so, out of

Award document for the AFRIKA campaign cufftitle. (Author's collection)

modesty, did not wear the cufftitle. But for all the other men who had served in North Africa, and who fought on in other theatres, the AFRIKA cufftitle was something to be worn on their uniforms with pride.

The olive-coloured cloth-covered tropical pith helmet. (Charles Hinz)

Although the order instituting this cufftitle was dated 15 January 1943, there was not enough time left to organize the manufacture and distribution of it to troops in North Africa before the general surrender in May 1943. It is extremely unlikely that more than a few examples were ever worn in Africa. The earliest known award documents are dated early May 1943 and were to *Luftwaffe* personnel, probably in Italy at this time as the papers are ones bearing a facsimile of Field Marshal Kesselring's signature in his capacity as Supreme Commander Southern Theatre. The eventual recipients of the AFRIKA cufftitle were those troops who had somehow managed to escape the surrender in Tunisia and were serving on other fronts after May 1943. Awards of the AFRIKA cufftitle under the authority of the now defunct Army Group Afrika were made to surviving members of African units up until late 1944.

Because the AFRIKA cufftitle did not appear in Africa

until the final days, those soldiers who had an AFRIKAKORPS cufftitle on their uniform, including Rommel himself, who wore it on his overcoat from the time of his return in October 1942, continued to wear it.

Other cufftitles worn in Africa by German Army troops were for units with special status. FELD-GENDARMERIE ones were worn by all ranks of Military Field Police; PROPAGANDAKOMPANIE were worn by entertainers and by war correspondents, artists and photographers whose job was to report the war in Africa; and FELDPOST by personnel of Army field postal units. All troops entitled to these three cufftitles carried them on the left sleeve; they could wear the AFRIKAKORPS title on their right sleeve as well, and some did.

Arab volunteers attached to German Army units wore an armband above the elbow. This stated simply that the bearer was in the service of the German Armed Forces (*Im Dienst der Deutschen Wehrmacht*) and gave the owner minimum legal status under the Geneva Convention. Those Arabs in Tunisia who were enrolled in the Free Arab Legion were meant to wear a special woven arm patch bearing the legend *Freies Arabien*, but these were only available at the very end of the campaign, and were then issued more as a propaganda exercise. Photos of the Arab volunteers in this unit show them wearing French uniforms, with German steel helmets and the standard auxiliary armband.

Other armbands worn by German troops were the two kinds used by medical personnel: a plain red cross embroidered on a white linen band was worn on the upper left arm of general medical personnel; a plain white armband with the legend *Hilfs = Krankenträger* in black Gothic letters inside a black rectangle, was worn on the upper right tunic sleeve of a stretcher bearer. The red cross armband was officially worn by men in specialist medical service units while the stretcher bearer armband would have been worn by soldiers carrying out this function in their own unit. In practice, however, these regulations were not always adhered to and red cross armbands were also worn by non-medical service stretcher bearers.

A rarely-seen armband was one worn by Army Specialist Officers (*Sonderführer*) acting as interpreters. This was a large embroidered red capital 'D' (standing for *Dolmetscher*/Interpreter) on a green band, worn on the upper left sleeve.

Tropical Field Equipment
There were no new or special items of basic field equipment used by German troops in Africa. As far as design went, the same functional assortment was issued to a

A Field Chaplain – with Rommel standing behind his right shoulder – at a graveside funeral service. He is wearing the officer rank tunic without shoulder straps. This photo illustrates the status given to the tropical pith helmet as a more formal item of headgear than the cloth field cap. (ECPA)

Three members of Motorcycle Battalion 15 wearing the twill tropical version of the long double-breasted protective coat issued to motorcyclists and drivers. (Kerry Foster)

soldier regardless of whether he happened to be fighting in Europe or in the North African desert.

What the German Army did, however, was to issue some of this equipment in a tropical variation which simply meant substituting heavy canvas web material for leather. Production of this tropical issue equipment was not as advanced as the uniform in February 1941, so many standard issue leather Continental items saw service in North Africa.

The only pieces of field equipment to be produced in canvas web were those where the leather straps were felt to be at risk in the arid Libyan climate, i.e. where constant use and flexing could crack the leather. These were the uniform waist belt, the Y-straps that supported

equipment worn on the waist belt and the A-frame assault pack; the bayonet frog, suspension straps on the water canteen cradle, the straps riveted to the A-frame assault pack, the straps on the large canvas rucksack, which was modelled on a similar pack used by Alpine troops, and the multi-pocketed satchel used by engineers. Items such as holsters, the carrying pouch for the entrenching tool, the pouches for clips of ammunition worn on the waist belt, the holster for wire cutters, and the map case, were not produced in a canvas web form.

It is a common mistake today to identify any item of German field equipment from the early years of the war as *Afrikakorps* when it is encountered in canvas. The German Army had already started to introduce canvas web equipment at this stage, such as the MP38/40 magazine pouches. This policy of replacing leather equipment with canvas went on throughout the war.

This rear view of a section of Pioneers lined up before making an attack shows the full array of field gear worn on the canvas A-frame and on the waist belt: mess-tins, rolled shelter quarter with tent pegs, two water bottles per man, breadbag, bayonet, canvas grenade bags, leather carrier for wire cutters, and a spare MG barrel holder. (ECPA)

This was not just related to the production of tropical material for Africa, but was done because canvas was as strong and as efficient as leather. This allowed the rather more scarce leather to be used for items like boots where canvas could not be used on its own.

The waterproof canvas shelter quarter (groundsheet or poncho) issued to German troops in Africa was the standard Continental model in a reversible splinter-pattern camouflage. These soon faded under the desert sun, especially the side with a predominant yellow or beige hue. In 1943, after the German occupation of Tunisia, a shelter quarter was used that was made from a uniform tan cotton material of French manufacture which presumably came from captured French Army stocks. This type of shelter quarter was not a special German pattern intended for use in North Africa.

A very small number of combination canvas and leather pistol holsters were used by officers in Africa, but these were not standard issue. Officers were required to buy their own pistols and holsters, and any canvas/leather holsters in use in Africa were ones privately purchased from factories already using this combination.

Another item of field equipment often wrongly identified by collectors today as being specifically tropical in origin and use is the small folding canvas bag that was rolled up inside the shelter quarter and carried on the A-frame assault pack. This 'implements bag' (used to hold the rifle cleaning kit, a number of tent pole pieces, emergency rations and a length of tent rope) was in use prior to the entry of Italy into the war, and it saw widespread service in Europe as well as in Africa.

German field equipment was well designed and eminently practical. The small cloth bags issued in some number to all German troops are a good example. These 'ditty bags' had a small piece of material sewn in place below the draw cord in different colours – red, yellow, blue, green, white – which enabled a soldier easily to locate and identify one of a number of similar 'ditty bags' in his rucksack, and it was up to him to decide which colour stood for dirty underwear, or clean underwear, or spare food, or souvenirs, or whatever.

The most common entrenching tool issued in 1941 to German troops in Africa was the new 1940 model folding type. The position of the blade in this tool could be adjusted by tightening a knurled ring on a thread against the rear edge of the blade. The three positions available were firstly with the blade extended as a spade, secondly with the blade locked at right angles to the handle making a grubber and lastly folded back against the handle for storage in the pouch. Although the design was sound, in practice sand often clogged the thread which made it impossible to adjust. For this reason the older rigid style of entrenching tool was preferred by troops in the field.

Two items of equipment were peculiar to North Africa, but both saw little actual use in the field. The first of these was a heavy green-coloured felt sleeping bag. This bag was meant to be used in sandy soil by scooping out a shallow depression to lie down in with sand covering the bag for extra insulation. The bag was heavy and bulky and was not popular – after the German retreat at El Alamein a large number of these tropical sleeping bags were found unissued in supply dumps by the advancing 8th Army. Soldiers preferred using blankets, the woollen overcoat and a groundsheet.

The second special item was a canvas web cover for the bolt and breech area of the K98k rifle. This was not regularly used and was among the first to be discarded.

Goggles were standard equipment for all troops and a variety of styles were used from sets of lightweight tinted disposable goggles – which also saw service on the Eastern Front as 'snow goggles' – to more substantial types using rubber or leather frames. Goggles were an essential item of equipment, used more against dust than the glare of the sun, and many troops wore them permanently over their caps just as Rommel did.

Tropical Issue of Uniform and Field Equipment

All uniform and equipment issued to a German soldier were listed in his paybook (*Soldbuch*). From mid-1941 a special sheet was glued in over the pages that showed the issue of uniform and equipment (the books were printed for Continental service) itemizing the pieces of standard gear issued in North Africa.

The following list reproduced from a paybook shows the full range of items printed on this insert. They were issued to a private soldier in Motorized Inf Rgt104 who arrived in Africa in April 1942. The sheet as printed had several empty lines at the end where items not commonly issued – like the canvas satchel issued to engineers, the canvas A-frame assault pack issued to engineers and some infantry, additional clothing, etc. – could be written in.

The weapons issued to a soldier – rifle, bayonet or pistol – were listed separately, with serial numbers, in another section of the paybook.

Item	No. Issued
Feldmütze mit Schirm (peaked field cap)	1
Feldbluse (field tunic)	2
Stiefelhose (breeches)	1
lange Hose (long trousers)	1
kurze Hose (shorts)	1
kurze Unterhose (short underpants)	3
lange Unterhose (long underpants)	
Mantel oliv (overcoat, olive)	1
Schutzmantel für Kraftfahrer (protection coat for driver)	
Hemd mit Kragen oliv (shirt with collar, olive)	3
Hemd aus rohseide (shirt of unbleached linen)	
Unterhemd (netzjacke) (undershirt, mesh singlet)	3
Nachthemden (nightshirts)	2
Halstuch aus rohseide (neckerchief of unbleached linen)	1
Schlips oliv (neck-tie, olive)	1
Fingerhandschuhe oliv (gloves, olive)	1
Unterjacke oliv (sweater, olive (woollen))	1
Socken grau (socks, grey)	4
Überhandschuhe (gauntlets)	
Wadenstrümpfe (half (leg) stockings)	2
Schnürstiefel (lace-up boots)	1
Schnürschuhe mit St. Bl. (lace-up shoes with canvas uppers)	1
Leibbinde (waistband (worn over abdomen))	1
Badehose (swimming trunks)	1
Hosenträger (braces)	1
Tropenhelm (sun helmet)	1
Rucksack (rucksack)	1
Koppeltraggest (belt suspenders (Y-straps))	1
Troppenkoffer (tropical suitcase)	1
Moskitonetz (mosquito net)	1
Schlaffsack (sleeping bag)	
Mückenschleier (mosquito net (head))	1
Aufschiebeschlaufe (belt loop)	
Leibgurt mit Schloss (waistbelt with buckle)	1
Mantelriemen (overcoat (pack) straps)	
Brotbeutel mit Band (breadbag with (shoulder) strap)	1
Feldflasche gross mit Trinkbecher ((water) field canteen, large, with drinking-cup)	1
Feldflasche 31 ((water) field canteen (type) 31)	1
Patronentasche (cartridge pouch)	2
Kochgeschirr (mess-tin(s))	1
Essbesteck (eating utensils)	1
Fettbüchse (fat (lard) container)	1
Meldk.T.m.H. (case for maps and documents)	1
Signalpfeiffe mit Schnur (signal whistle with cord)	
Erkennungsm. mit Schnur (identity tag with cord ('dogtag'))	1
Staub-und Sonnenbrille (dust and sun goggles)	1
Schutzbrille für Kraftfahrer (goggles for driver)	
Waschbecken aus Segeltuch ((hand) washbasin of canvas)	
Satz Reinig-Bürsten (cleaning brushes)	1
Arbeitsanzug (fatigue (work) suit (jacket and trousers))	1
Taschentücher (pocket handkerchiefs)	3
Handtücher (handtowels)	2
Hemden lg. w. (shirts, long white)	
Marschdecke (march (order) blanket)	3
Zeltbahn ((shelter) tent quarter (or groundsheet))	1
Schnürschuhe schwarz (lace-up boots, black)	
Wäschebeutel (washing bag)	
Stahlhelm (steel helmet)	

An Italian officer serving as an interpreter in the German Army wears the distinctive shoulder straps of a Sonderführer, *grey soutache on his officer field cap, Italian campaign and medal ribbons, and an Italian army shirt. (ECPA)*

The affection shown by many German soldiers for adding insignia to their uniform is displayed by this man who has affixed a metal eagle shield, removed from a pith helmet, to the side of his field cap. (ECPA)

Although this list was issued to an infantry soldier, he did not receive either a steel helmet or a canvas A-frame assault pack – both of which were common issue items to infantry in Europe. Printed specifically for tropical issue, it reflects the very different conditions under which the war was fought in the desert, and the expectation that motorized infantry in Africa would not normally find themselves fighting as foot soldiers. It is held by some authors on this subject that the German tropical uniform, as originally intended for field use, was as seen in photos of troops parading in Tripoli in early 1941, and that the later typical informal uniform of a desert soldier, including his peaked field cap, was some sort of modification to this earlier uniform. This is not so. The *Afrikakorps* was never intended to be a 'salon' army, and the sun helmet together with tie, breeches and high boots were more appropriate to a formal parade. When in the desert the troops very soon showed their preference for shirtsleeves, cloth field cap, and shorts if they were out of the front line, a combination

that was not the result of any development in the official style of tropical uniform. The peaked field caps, the shorts, and the low boots were issued from the beginning of the campaign, as was the popular neck scarf (which doubled as a mouth and nose mask against dust).

Finally, not everything carried on a soldier was listed in his paybook as Army issue and when the tropical field tunic was worn its four pockets were invariably well filled with more personal items. This was quite normal as the breadbag – a canvas bag worn on the waist belt which was a traditional item of German military field equipment normally employed to carry a soldier's rations and eating utensils, as well as his more personal belongings – was not worn out of the front line. These items were normally distributed as follows:

Breast pockets:	Paybook, wallet, letters and photos, notebook or pocket diary, pen and pencil.
Hip pockets:	Clean socks and underpants, razor, toothbrush, soap, gloves, goggles, 2 metres of toilet paper, scarf (if not worn), cutlery set, rations (if a breadbag was not worn), cigarettes or tobacco and matches.

The Afrikakorps Ring

Members of the *Afrikakorps* are not likely to have been able to keep very much in the way of personal souvenirs from their time in Africa – for ordinary soldiers maybe some photos, a shoulder strap or a (tunic) cufftitle, a belt buckle and similar small objects. Officers are more likely to have retained a wider range of items because they purchased their uniforms, part of which may have survived the war at their homes. At the time they were in Africa the most common souvenir for all ranks was the *Afrikakorps* ring manufactured by Arab silversmiths in Tripoli and Benghazi.

This ring was designed by an imaginative German officer who, while walking through Tripoli in the spring of 1941, noticed how many troops were patronizing Arab shops that sold rings with various Libyan and Arabic motifs. He had the idea of getting one of these Arab silversmiths to make a special souvenir ring for the DAK. Rings were popular souvenir items among the *Wehrmacht*, usually commemorating some campaign, or a place, or a unit.

The design that this officer came up with featured in the centre the DAK tactical symbol, a swastika superimposed on a stylized palm tree, flanked on either

Note on tropical uniform manufacture

One of the major suppliers of uniform items to the *Luftwaffe* for tropical clothing during 1941 and 1942 was *Wirtschaftsamt Litzmannstadt*, the name under which the Jewish Council in the former Polish city of Lodz operated its commercial enterprises. The Jewish population of this German-established ghetto, like all such Jewish ghettoes, was drawn into the wartime German economy by the need to maintain their very existence. Of all the German uniform material the author has examined, none is superior to the items made by these Jewish workers and delivered to the German *Wehrmacht* through the Economic Bureau (Wirtschaftsamt) of the Litzmannstadt (Lodz) Ghetto Jewish Council. (The Polish city of Lodz was renamed 'Litzmannstadt' by the Germans when it was incorporated into the Reich in 1939.)

Luftwaffe uniforms showed, as did the Army ones, a variety of stamps – size number, manufacturer, year of manufacture and/or uniform designation. And also like the Army ones, the practice of showing the manufacturer's name (and town of manufacture) was discontinued in early 1943 and replaced by a long code, the RB number.

An infantryman, sheltering in a shallow foxhole from the battle evident on the horizon, has essential field gear piled up close at hand: rifle, breadbag, water bottle, gas mask canister serving as a container for extra food and/or ammunition, mess-tins, MP40 (obscured) and a canvas MP38/40 magazine pouch. (ECPA)

German customers. With a number of silversmiths engaged in the same pursuit it was inevitable that variations would occur. One style had the central DAK emblem and the letters/date set in gold against either a bright silver or dark unpolished silver setting. This type of ring was more expensive and too costly for ordinary soldiers, and so there were cheaper and less elaborate examples, more to the price the lower ranks could afford. Some of these cheaper rings with the detail engraved, still in silver, were rather crudely etched. There were even some rings made of steel turned out in field workshops but still following the original design of the first rings.

The rings continued to be made through 1941 into 1942 and some were also made in Tunisia in 1943. Rings made in 1942 and 1943 continued to feature DAK 1941 on the central plate, faithful to the original model. The ring was quite solid and heavy. The very first models weighed 25 grams, but later examples were around 15 grams in weight. This was considered a more comfortable size, and had the added advantage of being cheaper. The rings were usually marked inside by the makers with a figure indicating silver content.

Unteroffizier *Wolfgang Weller in Tunisia in 1943. He has the typical appearance of an old desert campaigner: faded shirt with the collar turned inside out, Continental shoulder straps, and field cap with soutache removed. (Author's collection)*

side by 'DAK' and '1941'. This appeared on the flat upper panel. The shanks featured two designs that fitted well with the romantic image Europeans had of the North African desert – one being the outline of a Bedouin astride a camel and the other a Mosque with a minaret flanked by a palm tree. The very first rings had the DAK emblem and side motifs in silver, set against unpolished silver so that they stood out in a silver against black contrast.

The design soon became well known and the Arab silversmiths were kept busy making rings for their many

Sitting on the edge of his foxhole in the Alamein line, a soldier spoons soup into his mouth and poses for the camera. (ECPA)

Luftwaffe Tropical Uniforms and Equipment

Introduction

The *Luftwaffe* fielded two branches of service in 1941 and 1942 – Flak gunners and paratroops – which fall within the scope of this work as both fought as integral parts of the Army commanded by Rommel in North Africa from 1941 to 1943. The first of these, the Flak units, fought alongside their Army comrades in Africa from the very beginning of the campaign. The second group, the paratroops, first appeared in Africa in July 1942. A third *Luftwaffe* formation which appeared in North Africa was the Hermann Göring Panzer Division, the greater part of which was committed in Tunisia in 1943, and incorporated Paratroop Regiment 5 which had arrived in Tunisia in November/December 1942.

It was practice in the *Wehrmacht* for the *Luftwaffe* to supply Flak units to a field of operations under Army control. These were assigned to higher Army commands (e.g. Corps or Army level), primarily to fill an anti-aircraft role. However, their disposition and function was decided by the Army, though the *Luftwaffe* maintained administrative control as regards supply of uniform, equipment and replacement of personnel. The *Luftwaffe* Flak units sent to North Africa were used by Rommel, whenever possible, in an offensive front-line role. The Flak weapons used in these motorized units ranged from 20mm and 37mm automatic cannon up to the famous 8.8cm guns (88mm Flak) and 105mm calibre guns. Rommel had already used the 88mm guns in an anti-tank role in France while commanding the 7th Panzer Division in 1940, and knew their deadly effect on tanks.

For the three *Luftwaffe* Flak battalions drawn from Flak regiments 33, 18 and 6 assigned to the *Afrikakorps* in early 1941 there was an immediate problem in that the *Luftwaffe* was unable to supply them with tropical uniforms. The need to commit forces for action in North Africa had not been foreseen by the *Luftwaffe* in 1940 and so design work on a special tropical uniform for its personnel did not start until the beginning of 1941. Four months were to elapse before the first tropical uniforms were in use. Instead, the Flak units sent to Libya were issued with the standard olive Army tropical uniform. They were also issued with Army field caps bearing a red soutache, which was their correct *Waffenfarbe*, and Army tunics with red-piped shoulder straps. Both officers and other ranks, anxious to display some feature of uniform identifying them as *Luftwaffe* personnel, replaced the Army tropical collar tabs with the red felt-backed rank collar tabs from the *Luftwaffe*

A Pioneer ready for action. He wears a steel helmet with layers of hessian secured by a rubber band, and carries canvas sacks for stick grenades and canvas MP38/40 magazine pouches. (ECPA)

Continental uniform. Then, in the second half of 1941, all *Luftwaffe* Flak troops were gradually issued with the *Luftwaffe*'s own version of the tropical uniform to replace the Army uniforms.

Even though Germany was well into its second year of war, the peacetime extravagance of maintaining separate logistical organizations for each service continued.

Scarce resources were stretched by continuing the tradition of wearing different uniforms. In Africa at least it would have been cheaper and simpler to outfit the *Luftwaffe* troops with the Army tropical uniform which could have been issued with distinctive *Luftwaffe* insignia and rank badges.

Waffenfarben – Arm of Service Colours

The *Luftwaffe* had its own system of colours to indicate unit and functional identity, although there was some correlation with Army colours, as in Flak artillery. On tropical uniforms the *Waffenfarbe* appeared only on the shoulder straps – and on collar tabs when these Continental items were worn. *Luftwaffe* field caps did not show any indication of branch-of-service colour piping.

Anti-aircraft artillery	Bright red
(*Flak-artillerie*)	(*hochrot*)
Paratroops	Gold-yellow
(*Fallschirmtruppen*)	(*goldgelb*)
Signals units	Gold-brown
(*Luftnachrichtentruppe*)	(*goldbraun*)

For the Hermann Göring Panzer Division, the range of colours was more complex as it contained the same basic organization as an Army Panzer Division, represented by a number of special colours denoting unit roles. The expansion of the Hermann Göring formation from regiment to brigade in 1942, and from brigade to a full division in January 1943 was accompanied by a corresponding expansion in the range of colours worn.

The basic colour assigned to the division was white, tracing its ancestry as an infantry-type unit within the *Luftwaffe*. White appeared on all Continental collar tabs with a secondary colour piped as an edging to indicate a sub-unit identity, but this was only true for the blue-grey, or black for tank crews, uniform worn in Europe. Tropical tunics did not carry collar patches and so the secondary piping shown on shoulder straps was an important feature of this division's officers' uniform. Other ranks uniform carried normal tropical shoulder straps showing only the primary *Waffenfarbe*.

The 1943 arm of service colours as would have been worn in Tunisia are as follows:

Infantry regiments	White
(*Grenadierregimenter*)	(*weiss*)
[1] Rifle regiment	Gold-yellow
(*Jäger-Regiment*)	(*goldgelb*)
Tank regiment	Pink
(*Panzer-Regiment*)	(*rosa*)
Artillery regiment	Bright red
(*Artillerie-Regiment*)	(*hochrot*)

Anti-aircraft regiment	Bright red
(*Flakartillerie-Regiment*)	(*hochrot*)
Reconnaissance unit	Pink
(*Aufklärungs-Abteilung*)	(*rosa*)
Engineer battalion	Black
(*Pionier-Bataillone*)	(*schwarz*)
Signals unit	Gold-brown
(*Nachrichten-Abteilung*)	(*goldbraun*)
[2] Transport and Supply units	Light blue
(*Nachschub-Abteilungen*)	(*hellblau*)
Medical unit	Dark blue
(*Sanitäts-Abteilung*)	(*dunkelblau*)

Notes

1. This regiment was previously Paratroop Regiment 5, under Major Koch, and was the first major German unit to be sent into the Tunisian bridgehead. It was incorporated into the Hermann Göring Division in March 1943 and continued to wear the gold-yellow colour assigned to paratroops (and which was the same as worn by Flight units).

2. Light blue was assigned not only to the motorized transport personnel, but also to the smaller ancillary units within the division such as field police, field kitchen units, base supply staff, etc.

Tropical 'Flyers Cap' (Sidecap)

This was the tropical version of the Continental blue-grey woollen sidecap worn by officers and other ranks. It had a side panel turn-up which dipped at the front to a low point below the *Luftwaffe* eagle embroidered in white cotton on a tan base. As well as the tropical *Luftwaffe* eagle the cap had a cockade of the national colours black, white and red. This cockade was stitched in a circular shape against the outer edge of the black ring in the cockade, giving the cockade a raised appearance. The cap itself was made of a light tan cotton drill material or a light tan linen. The cap carried a rank distinction with officers' versions having a length of silver cording stitched in place above the turn-up edge. Normally these caps had a lining of the same coloured material as the outer cloth, but some officer-style caps were made with a red cotton lining.

The cap was worn by all *Luftwaffe* personnel in Africa but was not a popular item of uniform as it had no peak to shield the eyes. Irrespective of whether this cap was well liked or not, it saw very wide use and was the single most common type of headwear used by the *Luftwaffe* in Africa. A field cap was an essential part of the uniform, and regulations laid down that a cap had to be worn.

Tropical Peaked Cap, with Neckflap

This unique example of headwear was the *Luftwaffe*'s response to the demand by troops in Africa for a field cap that had a peak, or visor. It resembled the normal style of Continental dress peaked cap in shape, having a large oval crown above the usual headband and peak. The neckflap was an innovation in German military headwear and was a feature quite appropriate to conditions in the desert. However, this cap did not see widespread use even though it continued to be produced in small numbers beyond the end of the African campaign. It was expensive to produce and did not have the same success as the Army field cap.

It had a reinforced headband and a stiffened peak which did not fold or crush, so the cap could not be as easily stored in a pocket or breadbag as the Army cap. Therefore, whenever conditions dictated that a steel helmet be worn, there was a real problem as to where it could be put. The inner side of the crown was lined with red cotton, stitched over a circular patch of cellulose which acted as a sweatguard. The outer material was a stiff high-grade cotton twill in a light tan colour. The headband was reinforced and stiff to absorb perspiration. There were two ventilation eyelets either side below the crown, and the first batches of caps delivered had a modification with the small metal eyelets replaced by larger gauze-covered holes. Caps issued after late 1942 reverted to the original small eyelets.

The insignia worn on this cap consisted of a high quality bevo weave* *Luftwaffe* eagle in white thread on a light tan background. The lower insignia was a woven representation of the ornate cockade carried on the Continental *Luftwaffe* dress peaked caps – a central cockade of black, white and red surrounded by an oak leaf wreath inside a pair of straight wings. Before early 1943 the two insignia pieces were hand-stitched around the edges of the outline of the eagle and cockade/wreath. Caps made after this date had the insignia machine sewn in a triangular patch for the eagle and in a rectangular patch for the cockade/wreath.

The neckflap was a simple piece of cloth, hemmed up in a curve around the base and made of the same material as the outer cloth in the cap. It was attached to the base of the headband by three small plastic or dished-out metal buttons stitched equidistant on the sides and rear centre. A tan leather chinstrap was issued with the cap but this was often misplaced as it had to be removed in order to wear the neckflap.

*Bevo weave was the process of making machine-woven insignia using cotton, rayon or artificial silk on a certain type of loom. BEVO is an acronym standing for *Beteiligung Vorstehre*, the main supplier of this type of insignia.

A Luftwaffe *liaison officer assigned to* Sonderverband 288 *in the summer of 1942. He wears a Continental woollen officer sidecap and silver metal eagle mounted on a pin. (Werner Kost)*

Some officers, wishing to create a noticeable officer effect, replaced the tan leather chinstrap with the silvered cords from the Continental officers' cap, and a few even went as far as removing the woven insignia and replacing them with the silver wire badges taken from Continental peaked caps. This was the exception though, and most caps were worn as issued.

This cap was popularly referred to by *Luftwaffe* troops as the 'Hermann Meyer' cap – something large and well ornamented but not overly practical. The 'Hermann Meyer' was derived from a remark made by Hermann Göring earlier in the war that if the British ever managed to bomb German cities his name would be 'Meyer'. (The cap, incidentally, appeared *after* the 1,000-bomber raids on Germany had started.)

Although intended as a universal issue cap, its scarcity meant that most of these caps were issued to officers.

The officers and other ranks who were not issued it were left to their own resources in acquiring a field cap more appropriate to the desert than the tropical sidecap.

Tropical Pith Helmet

Very early in 1941 the *Luftwaffe* obtained a supply of Italian (civilian style) pith helmets which were issued to air squadron personnel serving in Sicily and Libya, but only a few of these found their way to members of the Flak units. This helmet had a tan-coloured cloth covering, and this shade may have had a bearing on the similar colour adopted by the *Luftwaffe* for all its other items of tropical uniform. The helmet was easy to identify as it had two large gauze-covered ventilation eyelets equidistant from the centre on each side, and a brown leather strap crossing the crown below the top screw-base cap. Some helmets had a wide cloth pugaree, others just a narrow strip of doubled cloth running the circumference above the brim. No insignia was worn on the helmet, and the same type was issued to officers and to other ranks.

The standard issue pith helmet appeared in mid-1941 and closely followed the style of the Army helmet, with a few variations. The *Luftwaffe* helmet was a pressed cork shell with panels of orange-beige tan material covering the head and upper surface of the brim. The inside head area was covered in the same red cotton material as the Army helmets, but the brim was narrower, pointed down at a sharper angle and the under surface of the brim was lined with a light green cotton material. The insignia worn on this helmet consisted of a black/white/red metal shield on the left-hand side and a special variation *Luftwaffe* silver metal eagle mounted on the left side (the eagle was turned back to front to show it flying towards the front of the helmet – the normal *Luftwaffe* eagle 'flew' from left to right). A chinstrap in light tan leather was mounted across the front peak.

Tropical Field Tunic

This item of uniform showed quite a number of differences from the Army tunic. The usual colours found in *Luftwaffe* tropical tunics were light orange-tan, and beige-hued tan; both of these colours very quickly faded to a general off-white shade. Six brown pebbled metal buttons down the front fastened the tunic right up to the collar, and a short tab and metal dished-out button under the collar ends allowed the collar to be fastened upright. The two breast pockets were patch style and pleated, while the two large lower hip pockets were in a 'box' style and pleatless. All four pockets carried straight-edged pocket flaps with brown metal buttons. The sleeves carried a false cuff and the ends could be shortened with a concealed buttonhole and two small dished-out metal buttons. No collar tabs were worn on this tunic and the only insignia were shoulder straps, which indicated rank and arm-of-service colour, and a tropical eagle and swastika sewn above the right breast pocket. This was machine sewn around the outside contours of the eagle using a distinctive close zigzag stitch. All metal pebbled buttons worn on the tunic were painted a chocolate-brown. As was common on German field tunics, this tunic had two straps which were stiched inside it to a reinforced section under the armpit to help take the weight of equipment worn on the waist belt. It also had a small pocket inside the right front lower flap to hold field dressings.

It was common for some officers to remove the embroidered eagle on the tunic and to replace it with the silver metal eagle which was worn pinned to the white (European) summer tunic. For other ranks the standard issue shoulder straps were made of the same cotton twill as the tunic, edged with their *Waffenfarbe*.

A rare variation of this tunic, worn by some members of the Ramcke Brigade, appeared in North Africa in 1942. It was modified in that the top pockets were removed and two vertical ammunition bandoliers were stitched in place, covered by a flap held by domed press studs. Tunics so modified were made by the large tunic manufacturer Holz & Binkowsk in Berlin, and were intended to be field tested during the projected airborne assault on Malta. During the Crete landings paratroops were often without ammunition because these supplies were dropped separately in special canisters and usually fell out of reach of the troops on the ground. The inbuilt bandolier arrangement allowed two 25-round sections of machine-gun linked belt ammunition to be carried, with loops and press studs clipping on to the top ends of the metal links. This extra ammunition carried within the tunic would have been additional to that already carried in the paratroop's bandolier. It was evidently hoped this would go some way to solving the problem of ammunition shortages suffered by the paratroops on Crete. However, the airborne attack on Malta was aborted and the Ramcke Brigade was sent instead as a reinforcement for Rommel at El Alamein. A very small number of the modified paratroop tunics went with the Ramcke Brigade to Egypt.

Tropical Shirts

Three styles of shirt were worn in Africa by *Luftwaffe* personnel. The first, which was discontinued in 1941, had all pebbled metal buttons, while later styles had pebbled buttons only on the shoulder seams for the shoulder straps, and plastic or small dished-out metal buttons on pocket flaps, cuffs and the front. These two other styles were different only in the length of sleeve, i.e. short or long. The long sleeves were fastened at the cuff by one small plastic or metal button. The shirts were typically long, reaching down to the upper thigh area, and were made from a light tan cotton drill. Two large pleated patch pockets with scalloped flaps were attached at breast level.

It was recognized that it was necessary to wear a shirt without the tunic in hot weather, and an effort was made to give the shirt some of the characteristics of a tunic (hence the early decision to use all pebbled metal buttons). A tropical *Luftwaffe* eagle was displayed on all shirts, stitched on a triangular patch above the right breast pocket. Special shoulder straps were made for the shirt, using the same light cotton drill material.

In the field of collecting German military uniforms today, *Luftwaffe* tropical shirts are not rare items. The eagle and swastika insignia made the shirt a common souvenir, and meant it would not have been worn post-war by Allied servicemen, at least not with this insignia in place. Army shirts, which did not carry the eagle and swastika, were not common souvenirs, and the few found by Allied servicemen were picked up to be worn. Hence very few of the Army tropical shirts still survive today.

Tropical Trousers and Shorts

The design of the *Luftwaffe* tropical trousers reflects the early experiences of the Army after its arrival in Libya. Like the Army trousers, the *Luftwaffe* design featured an inbuilt waist belt, partly concealed, and in this respect only the buckles were different. The *Luftwaffe* trousers, however, were characterized by being very full and baggy in the legs with a strap arrangement on the ends of the legs to gather them in above the feet. This gave the trousers a bloused effect, and the additional room created inside the trouser legs was a sensible method of making the trousers cooler to wear and less constricting. A large patch pocket closed with a scalloped flap was sewn on to the thigh area of the left leg, another useful feature which recognized that troops needed to carry personal items. It was certainly more comfortable and practical to have these items in a pocket than in, for instance, a breadbag.

The shorts were simply a shortened version of the trousers, with the same arrangements of belt and pockets, but without the large pocket on the leg.

Members of Batterie 5 Flak-Abteilung 1/18 *at Mersa Matruh in the late summer of 1942. The man at the left of this group is wearing an Army* AFRIKAKORPS *cufftitle, while the second from left is wearing red-backed collar tabs from the Continental blue-grey woollen uniform. (Herbert Brandhoff)*

A 20mm Flak gunner in a ground action emplacement, El Alamein, October 1942. Note the steel helmets showing the camouflage finish. (Author's collection)

This Oberleutnant holding sunglasses has a privately purchased peaked field cap bearing a metal pith helmet eagle, and silver cording stitched into the crown seam. The two other peaked caps are Army examples with Luftwaffe insignia added. (ECPA)

The Overcoat

No special version of the woollen overcoat was issued by the *Luftwaffe* to its troops in Africa, and the standard Continental blue-grey woollen type was used. This was similar to the Army overcoat, but had silver pebbled metal buttons and carried, until mid-1942, rank insignia on the collar ends. For the Flak troops in Africa these collar tabs were red felt patches (red because of Flak *Waffenfarbe*) and carried a combination of metal gull wing devices, and silver tresse to indicate NCO rank. However, rank and *Waffenfarbe* were already displayed on the shoulder straps so it was logical to do away with the collar tabs. Overcoats used in the Tunisian campaign did not display collar insignia.

Tropical Driver's Coat

In line with all other *Luftwaffe* tropical uniform, this coat was made in a light tan colour of heavy cotton twill. It was similar in design to the Army version, but the *Luftwaffe* one did not carry shoulder straps, or any other rank insignia.

Footwear

The first Flak units in Africa were issued with Army canvas and leather boots, both high and ankle styles, along with their other items of Army uniform. Even when supplies became available through *Luftwaffe* quartermaster stores the Army footwear continued to be used, with the *Luftwaffe* throughout 1941 issuing either the Army canvas and leather boots, or an all-leather laced ankle boot. Obviously a higher boot would have been impractical with the *Luftwaffe* trousers designed to tighten low down on the ankle.

Nevertheless, in 1942 a high style of canvas and leather boot was manufactured and issued to some *Luftwaffe* personnel, mostly to men in units sent to Tunisia. The reason for this style of high boot was the same as the Army's: to give the lower leg protection against scratches from camel thorn and other abrasive plants. Instead of lacing right up to the top, the laces only extended from the instep to the ankle. From there the calf was covered by a large canvas flap, reinforced with metal strips along the leading edge. The leather strap holding the flap in place was threaded through two openings, also reinforced with metal, in the flap, top and bottom, and buckled on the outside edge at the very top of the boot. One of the criticisms levelled against the Army high boot was the inconvenience of its long lace arrangement. In this respect the *Luftwaffe* design was a definite improvement being so much easier and faster to put on. Its leather was dark tan and the

A Ramcke Brigade Unteroffizier *captured by Australians at El Alamein, wearing Continental shoulder straps, an Army cap with* Luftwaffe *insignia, and a pair of leather paratroop jump boots. (Author's collection)*

canvas parts were either a blue-grey or an olive-tan, and it had a full leather toecap that came over the foot as far as the bottom edge of the laces.

Another design of tropical canvas and leather boot attributed to the *Luftwaffe* was a medium-low style of boot that reached a point just above the ankle. This boot was made of brown leather and tan canvas, and laced up on nine sets of eyelets.

Paratroops sent to North Africa used their all-leather ankle boots (in the pattern current for 1942 with front lacing) or standard issue ankle leather boots.

Steel Helmets

The M35 *Wehrmacht* steel helmet was issued to all Flak troops in its original blue-grey finish, with the mounted through the helmet shell which were hollow to allow ventilation of the space under the helmet shell. This special paratroop helmet was worn by members of the Ramcke Brigade and Paratroop Regiment 5.

Uniform Variations

Many photos of *Luftwaffe* troops in Africa show them wearing Army-style peaked cloth field caps. None of these was standard *Luftwaffe* issue, so it indicates how popular this piece of headgear was. Caps in this style worn by *Luftwaffe* officers were usually privately purchased from military tailors in Germany, Italy or Tripoli. As such they show a wide variation in appearance, depending on how faithfully the tailors were able to copy the Army model. Most caps were purchased without insignia and the officer provided whatever badges he had, usually a metal *Luftwaffe* eagle removed from a pith helmet, together with an embroidered cockade. These privately acquired caps generally did not have ventilation eyelets, and the silver officer cording, if it was present at all, was usually stitched in place only along the crown seam.

The peaked field caps worn by other ranks invariably were Army caps obtained officially or otherwise through Army clothing depots. The usual modification to transform such caps into identifiable *Luftwaffe* headgear involved removing the Army eagle and replacing it with some kind of *Luftwaffe* eagle (from pith helmets, tropical sidecaps, embroidered Continental eagles on a blue woollen base, silver metal eagles from the other rank *Schirmmütze*, etc.). Usually the Army woven cockade was left in place, unless a *Luftwaffe* embroidered cockade was available.

Caps manufactured in the field by company or battalion tailors were also used, and these too displayed a variety of insignia.

The ability of soldiers in the field to provide insignia themselves indicates that they must have travelled with a good personal supply of cloth and metal badges, probably picked up and originally kept as souvenirs. (Many of these unused pieces of insignia were acquired by Allied servicemen through POW searches and kept as souvenirs, too.)

As well as the cloth peaked cap mentioned above, many *Luftwaffe* officers chose to wear their Continental issue *Schirmmütze* in the desert. These caps were not as comfortable or as practical in the North African climate but it does illustrate the importance many officers attached to wearing headgear that was recognized as belonging to an officer. Two styles of the *Schirmmütze* were worn: the summer style with a white cloth top,

A Flak Oberleutnant *wearing Army cap and tunic – only the Continental* Luftwaffe *collar tabs and Flak badge identifies this officer as a member of the* Luftwaffe. *This combination was common among Flak personnel during 1941. (ECPA)*

black/white/red shield on the left side and/or the *Luftwaffe* helmet eagle on the right-hand side. Apart from its colour, and the *Luftwaffe* decals, it was identical to the steel helmet worn by the Army.

The paratroop helmet was an innovation in helmet design, providing a model for all later ones. It was basically a German steel helmet with the flared rim taken away though still retaining the characteristic outline with the lower edge dipping down slightly at the sides and rear. Its steel alloy shell was heavier than its standard *Wehrmacht* counterpart and had a thickly padded layer of rubber above a leather lining perforated by twelve evenly spaced holes to allow air to reach the head of the person wearing it. The distinctive soft blue-coloured chin-strap, arranged with two sets of leather straps in a Y configuration, were anchored by four bolts

The Luftwaffe *tropical trousers, with distinctive thigh pocket, worn by Bernhard Ramcke, standing with Rommel at El Alamein, August 1942. (ECPA)*

The Luftwaffe AFRIKA *cufftitle worn by a paratroop POW captured by the French Army in Tunisia, May 1943. (ECPA)*

and the all-blue woollen variety.

The shortages affecting Rommel's Army applied in equal measure to the *Luftwaffe*, and even the Continental woollen sidecap (*schiffchen*) was worn by officers and other ranks. Among a number of caps picked up from abandoned Flak positions south of Tobruk in late

1941 was a field-grey Army woollen M38 cap that had had its Army insignia removed (eagle, cockade and pink soutache) and replaced with a *Luftwaffe* Continental embroidered eagle and rosette.

As was the case for the Army, the Italian *Sahariana* tunic saw use with some *Luftwaffe* personnel, though it was more popular with flying units in the very early period of the campaign before the *Luftwaffe*'s own tropical uniform was available.

Meeting of minds

During 1971 the late General Siegfried Westphal arrived in New Zealand to attend the Auckland Anzac Day ceremonies, and later toured various New Zealand provincial cities. At one such city General Westphal had just laid a wreath at the War Memorial on behalf of the *Afrikakorps* Veterans Association when a former member of Parachute Regiment 5 marched out from the crowd of onlookers and came to a smart halt in front of the General with a snappy salute and identified himself. Later General Westphal's escort, the President of the Auckland Returned Servicemen's Association, said how the 8th Army had not liked the Paratroops, 'They were bloody tough bastards'. General Westphal smiled and said, 'You know, we in the German Army found the same thing!'

Two significant uniform variations occurred in the Hermann Göring Division. A camouflage smock in the style worn by *Waffen-SS* units in the distinctive SS camouflage colour pattern was issued to some members of the division in Tunisia. This came about because the *Luftwaffe* at that time was unable to obtain supplies of smocks in their own usual splinter pattern camouflage and so resorted to using available SS smocks. Also, a small number of Army Panzer officers were transferred into the division, and they continued to wear their black woollen Army sidecaps, probably wishing to remain identified with their previous units, and it would have set them apart from career *Luftwaffe* officers – though another explanation could be that *Luftwaffe* officer caps simply were not available.

Because they were performing the role of ground infantry, few, if any, Ramcke Brigade paratroops wore their special smocks in Egypt. This garment was, however, much in evidence later in Tunisia with Paratroop Regiment 5. A mixture of styles was used, but the predominant type was the wartime model in a splinter pattern camouflage or a blue-grey colour.

A small number of paratroop smocks made of a pale sand-coloured material were found after the war in a French factory which had supplied the *Wehrmacht* with items of uniform, and it can be assumed that these were part of a batch intended for the Ramcke Brigade which were never issued.

Desert Camouflage

The *Luftwaffe* showed an official interest in camouflage and examples applied to equipment used by *Luftwaffe* troops displayed a great degree of uniformity. Instead of leaving it to the individual soldier to arrange a coat of sand-coloured paint on his helmet, or field equipment, the policy was to ensure every soldier was suitably camouflaged. This practice was organized at battalion or regimental level, and the predominant paint colour used was a beige-yellow.

Specimens of helmets belonging to *Luftwaffe* units not only showed a high conformity in terms of colour shades and quality, but they also had a more professional standard of finish. *Luftwaffe* camouflaging in Africa was more extensive than was practised in the Army. *Luftwaffe* troops also received camouflage cover, usually sprayed on, over leather field equipment like pistol holsters, cartridge pouches, entrenching tool harnesses, and even on the leather Y-straps. As well as the steel helmet, any other metal surfaces such as bayonet scabbards, buckles and metal canteen cups were spray painted. In the case of the Ramcke Brigade, care appears

Uniform of a Luftwaffe *pilot holding the rank of Major. He is wearing the Continental officer peaked cap, a silvered metal breast eagle, and the* Luftwaffe AFRIKA *cufftitle. (ECPA)*

to have been taken not to spray the paratroop helmets too heavily in order to preserve the outline of the *Luftwaffe* eagle insignia. Camouflage paint used in Tunisia was more varied than that used earlier in the desert, and included dark tans and reddish-orange colours. Photos taken of paratroops in Tunisia show that many used mud as an additional layer of camouflage cover on their helmets.

Tropical Insignia

The *Luftwaffe* did not produce the same range of tropical insignia as the Army or, with the exception of the insignia displayed on the 'Hermann Meyer' cap, achieve the standard of appearance that characterized Continental *Luftwaffe* uniform and insignia. The tropical eagle was a plain white embroidered design on a tan base. Braid worn on the NCO tropical shoulder straps and on the sleeve chevrons for senior private ranks was a dull orange-tan colour. This was in short supply and many tropical shoulder straps featured the Continental silver braid, on the tan cloth base.

No special tropical versions of trade qualification patches were produced, and those troops entitled to wear these sleeve badges used the Continental variety which were embroidered in an off-white thread on a blue-grey woollen backing.

The three sets of shoulder straps issued to *Luftwaffe* troops, for the tunic, shirt and overcoat, were made from material similar to the garment they were carried on.

Luftwaffe field police wore the same gorget as the Army (see page 152) and the red cross and stretcher bearer armbands were identical to those used by the Army (see page 156).

The French Army Photographic Archives (ECPA), have a photo which shows a *Luftwaffe* officer wearing a bevo-weave *Sonderverband 288* patch on his sleeve, but this does not indicate official use of this insignia by the *Luftwaffe*. In this isolated instance, it is probable that this man was a *Luftwaffe* liaison officer attached to SV288, or had some other association that 'qualified' him to wear the insignia unofficially.

Cufftitles

It was not until early in 1942 that the *Luftwaffe* introduced its own cufftitle for troops serving in North Africa. It simply bore the legend AFRIKA embroidered on a blue woollen band, in greyish-white cotton for other ranks and in silvered aluminium thread for officers. Supplies of the cufftitles were slow to arrive in Africa (flying units were the first to receive them) and many Flak troops continued to wear the Army AFRIKAKORPS cufftitles they had acquired unofficially. However, the *Luftwaffe* version was in evidence by the time of the El Alamein battles and was worn by those men who had it during the period of fighting in Tunisia in 1943, though by then it had been discontinued officially.

Other cufftitles worn by *Luftwaffe* personnel in North Africa were the KRETA, awarded to those who had participated in the Battle for Crete in May 1941, though very few had received it by the end of the fighting in Africa, and the one worn by members of the Hermann Göring Panzer Division – a blue woollen band with HERMANN GÖRING embroidered in an off-white cotton

thread. Like the earlier AFRIKA cufftitle, there was a difference between the styles issued to other ranks and officers. Other ranks wore the plain band and title, NCOs wore one which had a line of white braid stitched along top and bottom edges, and the officers' version had the title embroidered in ornate silver-aluminium with a similar silvered thread braid edging. In contrast to other *Wehrmacht* units in North Africa, the majority of troops in the Hermann Göring Division did wear their cufftitles.

After January 1943 all *Luftwaffe* personnel with a minimum six months' service in Africa were eligible for the new (campaign award) cufftitle AFRIKA. However, as has been mentioned earlier, it is highly unlikely any of these cufftitles were actually worn in Africa before the end of hostilities there in May 1943.

Field Equipment

The basic range of field equipment issued to *Luftwaffe* troops was similar to that used by the Army. Flak troops used a simpler version of the Y-straps (so-called parade Y-straps) which did not have D rings on the back or the shorter secondary straps to secure the base of the A-frame assault pack. These straightforward leather straps were issued in leather only and no tropical canvas model was manufactured. Flak troops were employed only in conjunction with their artillery weapons and so there was no need for them to carry the array of equipment used by infantry. Being motorized meant that their equipment could be transported on the tractor vehicle towing their gun. Flak troops, however, were expected to defend themselves against ground attack by infantry, and normal weapon issue included rifles and bayonets, and pistols, and it was usual in action to wear bayonets, belt cartridge pouches or pistol holsters. Flak troops were also issued with the standard M35 or M40 model steel helmet.

For paratroops there was a normal issue of basic infantry field equipment, including entrenching tool, canvas grenade bags (the *Luftwaffe* version used by paratroops was in olive canvas with zipper tops and the paired bags were joined by two sets of canvas straps which encircled the chest and went over the shoulders), bayonets and scabbards, pairs of leather cartridge pouches if a rifle was used and canvas web magazine pouches for machine pistols, breadbag in blue or olive-tan canvas, and water canteen. Many Ramcke Brigade paratroops used the special linen ammunition bandolier issued to them which was either blue or in camouflage splinter pattern. This special paratroop ammunition bandolier was also widely used by members of Paratroop

Regiment 5 in Tunisia. The field equipment used in the Hermann Göring Panzer Division was the same as for Army troops.

In 1941 the only waist belt used by the Flak troops appears to have been the usual black leather style with either a silver-aluminium or blue-painted steel buckle. In 1942 a belt appeared made of a blue canvas web with the blue steel buckle. This was followed later in 1942 by a second tropical style made of light tan canvas web and an olive-coloured steel buckle. By 1943 all three belts were being used by *Luftwaffe* units.

Paratroops carried a special utility knife which had a retractable blade that was extended by the force of gravity when it was pointed at the ground. This knife was designed to be used in one hand should the paratrooper be caught up in his parachute harness on landing and have to cut himself free.

Y-straps used by paratroops were the simple leather style without D rings or extra straps. Canvas rucksacks were an item of general issue for all troops and the *Luftwaffe* style was generally similar to the Army one, but made of a blue-grey canvas material.

The early tropical pith helmet, issued to Luftwaffe *personnel in early 1941, which was worn without insignia. (ECPA)*

The Luftwaffe *tropical sidecap (Fliegermütze), worn by a smiling Flak gunner. This photo was taken south of the Tobruk perimeter, late summer 1941. (Author's collection)*

Goggles issued to *Luftwaffe* troops were intended for flight crews, and were generally superior to the models used by the Army. They had optically better glass lenses and adjustable vents to prevent misting inside. Large supplies of British goggles were captured in Libya in 1941/2 and some were re-issued with a *Luftwaffe* eagle ink-stamped inside the leatherette case.

Issue of Tropical Uniform and Equipment

It was not until early 1942 that the *Luftwaffe* had its full array of specialized tropical uniform and other sundry equipment. The following list of items was contained on an insert attached to the paybook of a *Feldwebel* paratrooper who served in the Ramcke Brigade. As will be seen, the range of uniform and other accessories is more comprehensive than the contemporary list of Army tropical items. The numbers shown against the items in this list are those which were issued to this particular paratrooper.

Item	Number
Fallschirmjäger-Dienst (Paratroop Service)	
Fj.-Bluse (paratroop tunic)	
Fj.-Hose (paratroop trousers)	
Fj.-Stiefel (paratroop boots)	
Fj.-Lederhandschuhe mit St. ungef./gef. (paratroop leather gloves with bleached/unbleached canvas)	
Fj.-Knieschützer (paratroop knee pads)	
Fj.-Binden (paratroop tie)	
Fj.-Schleifanzug (paratroop drill uniform)	
Fj.-Stahlhelm (paratroop helmet)	1
Gasmaskentasche (gas mask case)	
Handgranatenbeutel (hand grenade bag)	
Patronentragegurt (ammunition bandolier)	
Bekleidung (clothing)	
Tropenschirmmütze mit Neckenschutz f. Offz. (tropical peaked cap with neckflap for officer)	
Tropenschirmmütze mit Neckensch. f. Uff. u. Mschft. (tropical peaked cap with neckflap for NCO and O/R*)	
Fliegermütze f. Offz. (flyer's cap for officer (*Luftwaffe* sidecap))	
Fliegermütze für Uff. u. Msch. (flyer's cap for NCO and O/R)	1
Tropenrock (tropical tunic)	1
Drillichbluse (drill coat (fatigue))	1
Tropenüberfallhose (tropical assault trousers)*	
Tropenhose lang (tropical trousers, long)	1
Tropenhose kurz (tropical shorts)	1
Drillichhose (drill trousers (fatigue))	1
Mantel graublau (overcoat, grey-blue (woollen))	1
Tropenhemd m. lg. Ärm. (tropical shirt with long sleeves)	3
Tropenunterhemd (tropical singlet)	6

*never manufactured

Item	Number
Tropenhemd m. k. Ärm. (tropical shirt with short sleeves)	3
Unterhose lang (long underpants)	3
Tropenunterhose k., weiss (tropical underpants, short, white)	3
Tropenbinder khakibr. (necktie, khaki-brown)	2
Binder schwarz (necktie, black)	
Tropenstrümpfe P., w. (tropical socks, pair, white)	6
Tropenkniestrümpfe P. (tropical knee socks, pair)	3
Schnürschuhe Paar (lace-up shoes, pair)	1
Schnürstiefel Paar (lace-up boots, pair)	1
Mannschaftsdecken (military blankets)	2
Sporthemd (athletic shirt)	1
Sporthose (athletic shorts)	1
Laufschuhe Paar (running shoes)	
Badehose (swimming trunks)	1
Fingerhandsch. gestr. P. (gloves, reinforced, pair)	1
Schlupfjacke 36. (sweater (woollen))	1
Leibbande (waistband (worn under clothes))	2
Feldhandtuch (field towel)	3
Tropentaschentuch (tropical handkerchief)	
Taschentuch allg. Art (handkerchief, general style)	6
Tropenhosenträger (tropical trouser braces)	1
Tropenschutzmantel f. Kf. (tropical driver's coat)	
Dienstgradabz. f. Gefr. (rank insignia for *Gefreiter*)	
Dienstgradabz. f. Obgfr. (rank insignia for *Obergefreiter*)	
Schulterstücke f. Offz. (shoulder straps for officer)	
Schulterkl. f. Uffz. (shoulder straps for *unteroffizier*)	
Schulterkl. f. Ufeldw. (shoulder straps for *Unterfeldwebel*)	3
Mückenschleier (mosquito net (head))	1
Wettermantel (raincoat)	
Fusslappen (cloth squares for feet (instead of socks)	
Ausrüstung (equipment)	
Tropenhelm (tropical (pith) helmet)	1
Stahlhelm 35 m. Zub. (steel helmet 35 with fittings)	
Tropenleibgurt (tropical waist belt (canvas web))	1
Tropenseitengwhrtsch (tropical bayonet frog)	1
Tropenschloss (tropical (belt) buckle)	1
Trager, f. Patronent. (support straps for cartridge pouches (Y-straps))	1
Ausschiebeschlaufen (belt loop)	1
Zeltbahn 31 (tent sheet (camouflage shelter quarter))	1
Zeltleine (tent guy rope)	1
Zeltstock (tent pole)	1
Zeltpflöcke (tent pegs)	2
Zeltzubehörbeutel (tent implements bag)	1
Tropenmantelriemen (tropical overcoat (canvas roll) straps)	3
Brotbeutel mit Band (breadbag with strap)	1
Tropenfeldfl. m. Zub. (tropical field (water) canteen with attachments)	1
Kochgeschirr (eating utensils (mess-tins))	1
Tropenkochgschirriem (tropical mess-tins strap (canvas))	2
Tropenbesteck (tropical cutlery set (combination knife/fork/spoon))	1

Item	Number
Fettbüchse (edible fat container)	1
Erkenngsm. mit Schn. (identity tag with cord ('dog' tag))	1
Soldbuch (paybook)	1
Tropenkleidersack (tropical clothing bag)	
Tasche z. trpnkldrsck (case for stowing tropical clothing bag)	
Moskitonetz (mosquito net (full length))	1
Netzgestänge (net support pole (for mosquito net))	1
4 Leinen je 2 m (4 × tent guy rope each 2 metres)	4
4 Zeltpflöcke (4 × tent poles)	
Tropenbrille (tropical goggles (tinted))	1
Tropenwaschschüssel (tropical wash basin (canvas-covered wooden bowl))	1
Rucksack (rucksack)	1
Sonderbekleidung (special clothing)	
Patronentaschen (cartridge pouch)	1
Portepee ((bayonet or sword) knot)	
Meldkartentaschen (map and document case)	
Signalpfeiffe m. Schnur (whistle with cord)	
Labeflasche m. Zubehör (medical canteen (large size) with attachments)	
Neutralitätsabzeichen (Red Cross emblem)	
Armbinde f. Hilfskr. (armband for stretcher bearer)	
Dienstabzeichen (Qualification Service Insignia (specialist trade badges))	
Arbeitschutzanzug ung. (overalls, undyed)	
Hoheitsabz. f. tropenhelm (National insignia for pith helmet)	
Wappen f. tropenhelm ((Tricolour) shield for pith helmet)	
Kf = Überhandschuhe (driver's gauntlets)	
Kf = Schutzbrille (driver's goggles)	
Übermantel m. wollf. (sentry coat with woollen lining)	1
Tropenkoffer (tropical case (lightweight metal))	

The standard Luftwaffe *tropical pith helmet, worn by a Ramcke Brigade paratrooper on right who is talking to a* Feldwebel *in the* Army Feldgendarmerie. *(ECPA)*

Luftwaffe *POWs in Tunis after the general surrender in May 1943. The* Hauptmann *on the right is wearing a Hermann Meyer' cap and the officer cut off by the left edge of the photo has* Luftwaffe *high canvas and leather boots with buckled calf flaps. (Imperial War Museum)*

The short-sleeved Luftwaffe *tropical shirt, worn by a Stuka pilot shot down over El Alamein, July 1942. (NZ National Archives – Alexander Turnbull Library)*

Explanation of colour photographs

Between pages 96 and 97

1. MG34 This machine gun was the standard German Army all-purpose automatic weapon in 1941. It had an air-cooled barrel which could be quickly changed and, to increase further its ability to sustain long bursts of fire, belts of connecting metal links were used for the ammunition. The gun could be used either with a bipod or with a special tripod which effectively converted it into a medium machine gun capable of accurate fire over a greater distance. Standard accessories used with this weapon, and carried by its normal crew of two, included one or more metal ammunition canisters holding 250 rounds and a metal tubular case for one or two spare barrels. When not being fed ammunition from an open belt, a drum magazine, was used. Ammunition was the standard rifle variety of 7.92mm.

2. MG42 This formidable and revolutionary weapon was first used in May 1942 during Rommel's offensive at Gazala. Its high rate of fire at 900–1,200rpm (higher than the MG34's rate of 850–900rpm) gave it a distinctive battlefield sound. Its design was revolutionary in that it used simple-to-manufacture stamped metal as opposed to the expensive machined steel parts of the MG34. Like the MG34 it could be used on a bipod, or on a heavier tripod against ground targets, or it could be employed as an anti-aircraft weapon. Its ammunition was standard 7.92mm.

3. Kar98k The two types of standard rifle infantry weapon used in North Africa were widely issued to German troops both in and out of the line. It used the standard 7.92mm cartridge and was a shortened version of the rifle used by the German Army in World War I. The differences between the two types

shown here were slight: the earlier model, at top, did not have the overlapping buttplate of the later model, or the front sight protective hood. These rifles, despite the prefix 'Kar' denoting carbine (*Karabiner*), were the length of most rifles used in the war. They were bolt action, fired only one shot at a time and required careful sighting to be effective.

4. MP40 Originally designed as a specialist weapon for paratroops, it was in general use with all branches of the *Wehrmacht* during the North African campaigns. It fired a 9mm pistol cartridge, hence its German name *Maschinenpistole*, and proved an effective weapon in close fighting. The magazine held 32 rounds. It had a rate of fire of 450–550rpm, and a supply of spare ammunition had to be carried by those using it – in six spare magazines stored in two canvas web pouches, along with the special tool for loading the magazines. In North Africa it was widely used by Pioneers, tank crews and section NCOs in infantry units.

5. PO8 Commonly referred to as the *Luger* by Allied troops, this pistol was the standard issue sidearm in the German Army until 1942 when its manufacture was stopped because of the cost of making a pistol that had so many precision-made steel parts. In North Africa it was the pistol most commonly issued in 1941 and for most of 1942. It was worn on the waist belt in a hardened leather holster which also carried a spare 8-round magazine and a combination stripping and magazine-loading tool. Its issue was common to machine-gun crews and artillery troops as a close defence weapon, and to NCOs and section leaders in infantry units or to rear area personnel.

6. P38 The replacement for the more expensive PO8 was the simpler designed P38 which first came into service in 1940. Like the PO8 it fired a 9mm round, but the P38 was less prone to stoppages induced by sand (not that this was common, a soldier faced stiff punishment if his weapon was found to be dirty) and had the novel feature in a military service pistol of being fired by a 'double action'. The pistol did not have to be manually cocked to fire, as pulling the trigger cocked the hammer and then tripped it. It too was carried in a hardened leather holster but of a notably different design to that for the PO8. Issue and use was as for the PO8.

7. Flare pistol These were widely used by German troops in North Africa and were carried in all tanks and other armoured vehicles and issued to front-line units down to section level. The style illustrated here is representative of the type known as the *Leuchtpistole*, firing a 27mm calibre cartridge from a smooth-bore barrel. The cartridges contained a load that flared in a variety of colours when fired. The holsters were much larger than the 9mm pistol holsters, and had the added feature of an externally carried cleaning rod. Pistols like this could be modified to fire a grenade, but this modification was not widely used in North Africa.

8. Close combat weapons The stick grenade and the bayonet, as issued for use with the Kar98k, were the accepted means of fighting at short range. The stick grenade (*Steilhandgranate*) had an explosive charge inside the steel-encased head. It was detonated by a friction igniter connected to a string with a porcelain bead on the end which was pulled after the screw cap at the base of the wooden shaft had been removed. Sometimes these grenades had an extra sheaving of steel fitted around the head to increase the fragmentation effect. Other close-range weapons used were an 'egg' grenade, a small cylindrical fragmentation bomb, and an entrenching tool with a steel blade that was used as a club.

9. Shoulder straps – Private rank Top row, from left: Continental green woollen, white piping for infantry, etc.; Continental green woollen with embroidered Gothic 'A' (*Aufklärung*), gold-yellow piping; Continental green woollen with embroidered 'P' and '3' (*Panzerjägerabteilung 3* – 3rd anti-tank unit), pink piping; tropical woollen overcoat, lemon-yellow piping; tropical woollen overcoat, lime-green piping and a silvered Gothic 'D' (denoting Divisional HQ); field manufactured from a heavy hessian-type material and folded edges of white cloth to give white piping. Bottom row, from left: tropical tunic, red piping; faded tropical tunic, black piping; tropical tunic, lime-green piping; tropical tunic, light green piping; tropical tunic, pink piping; tropical tunic, light blue piping; tropical tunic, lemon-yellow piping.

10. Comparison of green pipings From left; grass-green (*wiesengrün*), light green (*hellgrün*), lime-green (*resedagrün*). What was officially 'light' green is, in this range, the darkest of the three greens, indicating that at the time it was termed 'light' green neither of the other two had been introduced.

11. Shoulder straps – NCO rank Top row, from left: Continental green woollen, silver braid, gold-yellow piping; Continental pre-war, no piping and pointed top; black woollen from Panzer uniform, pink piping; field made with *Luftwaffe* tunic material and Army tropical braid, no piping; Continental field-grey woollen, tropical braid,

copper-brown piping; tropical woollen overcoat, red piping; tropical woollen overcoat, black piping. Bottom row, from left: tropical tunic, pink piping; tropical tunic, lemon-yellow piping; tropical tunic, light blue piping; tropical tunic, grass-green piping; tropical tunic, light green piping; tropical tunic, white piping; tropical tunic, cornflower blue piping.

12. Trade specialist patches For specialist trade qualification the insignia was a circular patch with the emblem woven in yellow yarn on to either ribbed cotton (tunic) or brown woollen (overcoat) material. For the lightning flash indicating a specialist signals role in units other than Signals, the *Blitz* was embroidered in the wearer's own *Waffenfarbe* on an oval base made of tunic or overcoat material.

13. Uniform national emblems and collar bars Examples of the breast eagle, the tropical collar bars or tabs, cap eagles, and cockades. They are as worn on tunics and caps and were removed from these items as souvenirs. In the unused form they are as supplied to uniform factories by the manufacturers of this insignia. Note the considerable colour variations of those examples removed from items of uniform caused by wear in the sun and washing.

14. Sleeve rank insignia Examples of tropical chevrons for *Obergefreiter* (Corporal) and *Gefreiter* (Lance Corporal) and the pip for senior private (*Obersoldat*, etc.) on tunic and overcoat backing material. The pip for a senior private was initially embroidered in an olive-grey but this did not show sufficient contrast and blue cotton was used after 1941. Continental chevrons worn in Africa on tropical uniforms included ones with silver braid on dark green or black material, or the later style with mouse-grey braid on a field-grey base.

15. Officer silver bullion insignia The quality and attractive finish of the Continental Army officer uniform insignia is clear in this set of examples belonging to a Field Chaplain (no shoulder straps were worn on a Chaplain's tunic). Many German officers, accustomed to the superior style of insignia worn on their Continental uniforms, were not content to accept the flat coloured tropical insignia common to all tropical issue uniforms, and replaced their woven tropical insignia with parts like the eagles and collar tabs shown in this assortment. However, there were no tropical officer shoulder straps and the standard straps were worn as a matter of course.

16. General rank insignia Examples of the General's ornate collar tabs featuring a design with the *Larisch* motif against the red *Waffenfarbe* for General rank, and the more intricate braided arrangement of the shoulder straps for this rank. The gold breast eagle worn by generals was manufactured either in a cellulose or a gilt wire embroidery. The former was the most popular with generals in Africa because it wore better. The collar tabs embroidered with cellulose coated yarn were also the preferred type.

17. Officer Continental tunic and cap insignia A selection of European theatre uniform insignia that found its way to Africa. Most commonly used were the breast and cap eagles. The combination oakleaf and cockade badges (metal or silver wire) from the *Schirmmütze*, and the old-style officer field cap (woven), did not readily adapt to the tropical field caps and were not used, but the cockade lined with silver wire from the M38 officer field cap was. The silver-coloured eagle worn pinned to the officers' white summer tunic was preferred to the woven tropical eagle because it was easy to remove when tunics were washed.

18. Office shoulder straps and collar tabs Top row, from left: *Leutnant* Panzer in PzRgt8, *Leutnant Panzergrenadiers, Zahlmeister* (Paymaster with rank of *Leutnant*), *Leutnant* Signals.

Middle row, from left: *Sonderführer* (with *Leutnant* rank); *Oberleutnant* Artillery; *Oberleutnant* Supply and *Hauptmann* Transport (same light blue piping and common collar tab); *Hauptmann* Pioneers.

Bottom row, from left: *Hauptmann* Cavalry (or early period Reconnaissance); *Hauptmann* Rifle Regiment (or early period MG Battalion or the Alpine Regiment 756); *Oberleutnant* Medical Services; *Oberst* Infantry Regiment.

19. Metal insignia Top: Army pith helmet shields; edelweiss badge worn on the left side of the cloth field cap by members of GebJägRgt756 and the *Gebirgsjäger* Company in *Sonderverband 288*. Bottom: pair of metal Panzer skulls worn on the tropical tunic lapels by tank crews; traditional (Imperial) eagle worn on field caps and pith helmets by members of Reconnaissance Unit 33 from the former Cavalry Regiment 6.

20. Cufftitles From top to bottom: AFRIKA campaign, instituted 15 January 1943 but not available for issue in Africa until the last weeks of the campaign; AFRIKAKORPS instituted 18 July 1941 and worn by all members of the German Army serving in North Africa who qualified, until late 1942 (no records exist of it being issued to the 5th Panzer Army); *Feldgendarmerie*, worn on tunic and overcoat lower left sleeve by Military Field Police; *Propagandakompanie*, worn on lower left sleeve by men serving in propaganda units; *Feldpost*, worn on lower left sleeve by members of Army Fieldpost units.

21. Unofficial AFRIKAKORPS cufftitles The lower example, presumed to be

for officers, and the upper example, with no silver edging, for other ranks, but evidence exists that where it was used this rank distinction was not followed. This rare cufftitle saw little use and was apparently manufactured by a firm in Tripoli for some units of the DAK in anticipation of the arrival of the official AFRIKAKORPS cufftitle.

22. Luftwaffe cufftitles From top to bottom: KRETA awarded to veterans of the Battle for Crete in May 1941 was instituted 16 October 1942 but was slow to reach the men who qualified for it – it was not common at the time of the fighting in North Africa and only a small number were issued by the time of the campaign in Tunisia; HERMANN GÖRING as worn by officers and NCOs in the Hermann Göring Division; HERMANN GÖRING as worn by other ranks in the Hermann Göring Division: AFRIKA as awarded to all *Luftwaffe* personnel serving in North Africa from early 1942 and available for issue from mid-1942. It was worn on the lower right sleeve.

23. Sonderverband 288 Left: the bronze badge struck in the field early in 1942 and worn pinned on the left breast pocket. Right: the later official woven unit insignia stitched to the sleeve of a tunic from the period of the fighting in Tunisia.

24. Luftwaffe eagles and cockades These tropical versions of the distinctive *Luftwaffe* eagle show the smaller size of the cap eagle, the triangular patch which was worn on the shirt, in contrast to the eagle stitched around the outline which was worn on the tunic, and the reversed direction of the tropical pith helmet eagle. Continental eagles saw more use on *Luftwaffe* tropical uniforms than was the case for the Army. The metal eagle with pin back (lower right) was particularly popular with officers.

25. Luftwaffe shoulder straps and collar tabs Top from left: Hermann Göring Division *Gefreiter* (Continental); Paratrooper *Hauptfeldwebel* (Regimental Sergeant Major) (Continental); *Hauptmann Flakartillerie*; *Oberst* Paratroops; *Generalleutnant* (white *Waffenfarbe* for all branches). Lower, from left: tropical shoulder straps; field-made paratroop private, made from shirt cotton drill and yellow cording for piping; field-made *Unteroffizier* (Lance Sergeant) with cotton twill from tunic and Army NCO braid, no piping, origin unknown; tropical tunic shoulder straps from ribbed cotton twill for paratroop private; shirts belonging to private Flak and *Hauptwachmeister* (Regimental Sergeant Major) Flak; tropical shoulder straps (flat cotton drill) for private Flak; Paratroop *Feldwebel*; Paratroop *Feldwebel* (with silver braid as was used on Continental straps).

26. Army tropical tunic breast eagle on tunic.

27. *Luftwaffe* tropical tunic breast eagle on tunic.

28. Officer tropical field cap with red soutache denoting artillery. A typical example with hand-stitched eagle and machine-stitched cockade and the soutache braid running under the seam joining the headband to the peak or visor. The distinguishing feature of officer caps is the use of silver aluminium-corded piping that was stitched around the circumference of the crown and along the scalloped front part of the lower panel on the sides of the cap. This cording tended to shrink when washed, so well-used officer caps had a gathered appearance along the line where the silver cording was stitched into the seams.

29. Officer tropical field cap with light (medium) green soutache. This example shows the common appearance of a cap in need of a wash. The line of discoloration running around the join of the peak or visor came from perspiration soaking through the material and attracting a layer of fine desert sand and dust. (Caps in photos that show a darker line around this join probably had fresh perspiration soaking through.)

30. Two very typical other ranks caps in that both have been well bleached. The cap on the right has had the soutache removed early in its history as there is no unfaded inverted 'V' showing where the braid would have been originally. On the artillery cap on the left the cotton thread stitched around the eagle and the cockade has faded to a near-white colour. The bright red of this cap's braid shows how resistant some braid was to fading.

31. Other ranks cap with the lime-green of the *Panzergrenadiers*. It shows one feature of many caps that had heavy wear – the soutache braid is starting to disintegrate. The original chocolate-brown of this early-made cap has faded to a soft tan.

32. The two shades of blue used by the German Army in North Africa. The darker cornflower-blue of the medical units is on the left and the light blue of the supply and transport units is on the right. Neither of these caps was ever issued, and both are a smallish size. A lot of the mint and unissued caps that survive today were taken from stores where most of the popular and normal sizes had already been issued, leaving a large number of abnormal size caps. The light blue cap is dated 'Mrz 42' and has a sweatband, as can be seen by the second and higher line of stitching running around the circumference of the headband area. This cap is made of softer, inferior material (earlier caps were made of stiff and closely woven ribbed cotton twill).

33. Other ranks cap that was typical of those issued in the El Alamein position. Its soutache braid has been removed (small tufts of lime-green braid are visible inside the seam joining the peak to the headband). The date of manufacture was 1941.

34. Officer cap manufactured without soutache but with sweatband (on this cap the second line of stitching is lower and does not show). Though having the consistent high quality of officer caps with neatly hand-sewn insignia, this is representative of those made after mid-1942 from the lower grade, softer and thinner, cotton twill. The other ranks cap, contemporary to the officer cap and manufactured in late 1942, shows the inferior standard of machine-stitching on some later made caps. However, this cap is made from a very high quality grade of cotton twill showing that not all manufacturers had run out of stock of the early type of cloth.

35. Officer tropical sidecap with silver piping and pink soutache for Panzer regiments. This style is the rarest of all tropical caps and was manufactured only in small numbers as a special item issued to Panzer officers. The silver cording is as for the peaked variety though the turn-up on the side panel is open and so the base 'tail' of the cording is visible behind the outer layer of cloth.

36. Underside view of two caps illustrating the modification introduced from early 1942 – a sweatband on the lower inside edge. The cap on the left was the pattern made from 1940 until the change in 1942, and had the red cotton lining only.

37. Two examples of other ranks tropical sidecaps showing a light green and a pink soutache, dated 1941 and 1942 respectively. While not as common as the peaked variety, this style was widely issued and used in North Africa, and

the soutache colours are the same as for the peaked caps. Tropical sidecaps were identical to the woollen Continental M38 caps, having only one metal eyelet per side and the side panels not stitched down, the only point of attachment being a double loop stitched above the cockade.

38. Example of tropical sidecap with white soutache. While this cap may have been used in North Africa by an Army anti-aircraft unit, it could have been issued to troops serving in the Balkans or in the southern areas of the Soviet Union, where the infantry colour of the soutache would also have been appropriate in 1942.

39. *Luftwaffe* peaked tropical field cap – the so-called 'Hermann Meyer' cap – showing the large neckflap which was attached by three buttons stitched to the sides and rear points of the headband. The cost of this cap at its time of introduction made it a scarce item and its use appears to have been restricted mainly to officers. This cap is dated 1942 and has the early-style feature of the insignia being hand-stitched around the outer edges rather than the later style of being machine-stitched on to rectangular or triangular patches.

40. An issue other ranks cap with privately acquired silver piping to give it the appearance of an officer field cap. This was done by an officer in an Army anti-aircraft unit in 1941 when a standard issue officer cap in his head size with white soutache was unavailable.

41. Two examples of the standard *Luftwaffe* tropical sidecap used for the duration of the North African campaigns. The cap on the left is made from the standard plain cotton drill material while the one on the right is made from a soft linen material. Both were picked up in Libya during Operation Crusader in November–December 1941.

42. Detail of officer silver cording, here as stitched to the side panel turn-up of a *Luftwaffe* tropical officer sidecap and showing a stores label clipped to the edge.

43. General's field service cap in the 1943 style with gilt eagle and oakleaf surround to the cockade. It belonged to General Gustav von Vaerst when he commanded the 5th Panzer Army and he took it with him to a POW camp in Canada. (The pre-1943 style of this cap for generals had a silver eagle and oakleaf wreath with only the gilt piping and chinstraps to denote general rank.)

44. Officer's field service cap (*Schirmmütze*) with white piping indicating infantry. Though this cap has a white metal eagle and a silver wire embroidered wreath, it was common to see either all-metal insignia, or all-wire embroidered insignia.

45. Officer's woollen M38 field cap, frequently seen in use in North Africa by officers who were either unable to obtain a tropical field cap at a particular time or who preferred this style. This example has the white soutache for infantry and has a simple method of attaching it. This indicates the frequency of inter-unit transfers with the consequent need to change *Waffenfarbe* on all uniform items. In many instances the insignia from these caps was removed and attached to tropical field caps, replacing the less distinctive tropical insignia.

46. An unissued other ranks field cap with the grass-green soutache of the Motorcycle Battalion. The chocolate-brown cotton twill material and the style of embroidered cockade shows that this cap is a very early example. The other ranks field cap with the light (medium) green soutache was used by the Rifle Regiments and members of the MG Battalions in 1941. (This cap was picked up in Tobruk in early May 1941, and

would have belonged to a member of MG Battalion 8.)

47. Black woollen M38 sidecaps issued exclusively to tank crews as part of the special black woollen Panzer uniform. These distinctive caps were widely worn by tank crews in 1941 as a mark of ready identification with their branch of service. However, photos show that this was not as common in 1942 and 1943. The original members of PzRgt5 who arrived in North Africa in February-March 1941 wore their black uniforms as far as Tripoli, but later Panzer crews may not have found it so easy to retain their black woollen caps if issued tropical uniform at bases in Germany. The variation between the two examples illustrated is only in the colour of the eagles, creamy-white and mouse-grey, both of which were current in 1941.

48. Other ranks field cap with the copper-brown soutache of the Reconnaissance units, showing wear and fading fading to the original chocolate-brown material.

49. Field service cap (*Schirmmütze*) of a general in the *Luftwaffe*, with gilt insignia. This was a regular item of headgear worn by *Luftwaffe* generals in North Africa, there being no special general rank cap in tropical style. Another common style of headgear worn by *Luftwaffe* generals in North Africa was the personal tailor-made field caps as worn by Field Marshal Kesselring.

50. Another style of *Luftwaffe* general's field service cap that saw use in Africa was the summer issue *Schirmmütze* with a white linen top as worn in the European summer months. General Ramcke wore such a cap at El Alamein before obtaining a 'Hermann Meyer' cap, which he modified with a raised cockade in place of the woven *Luftwaffe* winged wreath.

51. The standard *Luftwaffenschirmmütze* for officers. This popular and attractive cap saw wide use by paratroop officers, especially in Tunisia when out of the line.

52. Other ranks field cap with the gold-yellow soutache of the first Reconnaissance units to reach Libya in 1941 (the maker's stamp in the lining shows 1940 as the date of manufacture). As was common with caps belonging to troops serving in enclosed vehicles such as tanks and armoured cars, this cap has a deeply ingrained layer of grease impressed into the cloth of the peak or visor.

53. Two examples of the standard *Wehrmacht* helmet as used by the German Army in North Africa. The left one is in its original paint finish (field-green) showing the national colour shield on right side, while the one on the right has had a coating of thick brownish paint. This colour was popular in Tunisia, in contrast to the range of beige/sand/orange-brown/pinkish-yellow colours common in Libya and Egypt.

54. Common camouflage colours during 1941 and 1942. The helmet on the left has had a covering of sand sprinkled over the still wet beige-coloured paint applied evenly over the outer surface of the steel shell. The well-worn helmet on the right shows the remains of two coats of paint, one a pinkish tan and the other a paint of a darker hue.

55. Two further views of helmets showing the great range of paint colours found on steel helmets camouflaged by individuals who used whatever paint was available in desert tones.

56. Two *Luftwaffe* steel helmets. The one on the left has its original blue-grey colour while the right-hand one has been painted a typical orange-tan colour.

57. The standard Army cloth-covered pith helmet with the left side showing the metal shield and Army eagle with wings closed.

58. Tropical pith helmet obtained by the Germans from stores in Holland in 1940 and issued in some quantity to units arriving in North Africa in the first half of 1941. The only modification added the two metal shields to the sides. The example illustrated here is missing the chinstrap and the cloth-covered knob which screwed on to the top.

59. Standard *Luftwaffe* tropical pith helmet, similar in overall design and manufacture to the Army example, but *Luftwaffe* ones had a narrower brim and were covered in a pinkish hued light-tan material.

60. A paratroop helmet taken as a souvenir by an Australian serviceman at El Alamein from a member of the Ramcke Brigade. It has had a light coating of yellowish paint sprayed over the outer surface but not so thick as to obscure the *Luftwaffe* eagle decal on the left side. The darker line of colour in the centre marks the area where the two separate sprays from each side met in the middle.

The interior view of the helmet shows the printed stamps in the lining giving the helmet size (head size for lining and the outer steel shell size) and the manufacturer of the lining. Note the solid rubber packing inserted between the lining and the steel alloy shell. The straps, which crossed over under the lining at the rear of the helmet to hold it more firmly in place on the head, were wider and softer than the straps on the standard *Wehrmacht* helmet.

61. This helmet has a predominantly brownish-tan coloured coating of paint roughly applied with a brush. The helmet was removed from the dead body of an anti-tank gunner at El Alamein, killed by the piece of shrapnel that had pierced the rear of the steel helmet shell.

62. This tropical field tunic of a *Leutnant* in a Rifle Regiment has light green (*hellgrün*) piped shoulder straps and officer silver bullion collar tabs, but has retained the original tropical breast eagle. This tunic, for no known reason, has a modification on the hip pockets: their edges have been stitched down on to the tunic cloth underneath.

63. Tropical NCO tunic, with pleated pockets and pointed pocket flaps. The rank is indicated by the line of gold-coloured braid around the edge of the collar. The shoulder straps are more faded than the tunic, indicating that they may have been worn on an earlier tunic. Piping is lime-green, for *Panzergrenadiers* in late 1942. This item was picked up at El Alamein.

64. Tropical tunic with overcoat shoulder straps piped in lime-green. This is a 1940-dated example and characteristic of the period. It shows fine-quality stitching and is made from thick high-grade cotton twill material.

65. Tropical tunic with a French-made shirt and cotton drill tie. This is an unissued piece as the tunic was removed from a clothing dump behind the El Alamein line. Transport and supply shoulder straps, taken from a separate supply of shoulder straps in an adjacent store, were added by an Australian.

66. Continental woollen tunic in pre-war style with the dark green collar for a *Stabsgefreiter* (senior staff corporal). This style of field tunic was worn by many of the first drafts of the *Afrikakorps* on arrival in February 1941.

67. A later-styled NCO tunic with pleatless pockets, for an *Unteroffizier* in a transport and supply unit. This tunic

has faded from its original olive colour to an off-sand shade.

68. Tropical tunic for an *Oberkannonier* (senior gunner) in an artillery battery, with the AFRIKAKORPS cufftitle in place on the lower right sleeve.

69. *Luftwaffe* tropical tunic, as worn by other ranks in a Flak unit. The usual colour of *Luftwaffe* uniform items, an orange-sandy shade, is clear to see in this unissued tunic of cotton twill.

70. *Luftwaffe* tropical tunic for a *Leutnant* in a paratroop unit shows the neutral faded colour of a tunic that has had considerable wear and washing.

71. Rare paratroop variation of the *Luftwaffe* tropical tunic, with top pockets removed to provide space for two vertical pockets that ran from neck height down to the lower edge. The pockets fastened with press-stud buttons and had loops stitched into the top inner seam to take sections of MG ammunition belts holding 7.92mm rifle ammunition.

72. Army tropical tunic for a tank crewman. The metal skull devices attached to the lapels served to identify the wearer as a tank crewman rather than an anti-tank gunner who shared the same pink *Waffenfarbe*, and was a carry-over from the black Panzer uniform which accorded tank crews the most distinctive uniform in the *Wehrmacht*.

73. Internal view of the Army field tunic, showing the special inside pocket for surgical dressings, the support brace for the equipment hooks, and the manufacturer's markings.

74. Front and rear views of the standard Army tropical overcoat made from a chocolate-brown woollen material. This coat has other rank pink-piped shoulder straps and a tropical sleeve insignia of two chevrons for an *Ober-gefreiter* (corporal).

75. Tropical motorcyclist's, or driving, coat. Made from olive-coloured heavy cotton twill material, this coat was popular in North Africa with others than those qualified to wear it, especially officers, who preferred it for daytime wear in the summer months.

76. Typical example of a German-designed Army tropical shirt, with fibre buttons on the cuffs and front, and metal pebbled buttons on the shoulder seams and pocket flaps.

77. Modified French Army shirt, with the typical three-button front and plastic buttons on the front, cuffs (single buttons), and collar points. This example has the same pockets as the German-designed shirt, indicating the French factory must have been in the process of changing over to the German design when this shirt was being made. The French design had larger, squarish pockets.

78. *Luftwaffe* tropical shirt, short-sleeved style, showing the triangular eagle patch machine-stitched over the right-hand pocket. This shirt has tan-painted dished-out metal buttons, but it was just as common to see plastic buttons. (Brown painted pebbled metal buttons were used for the shoulder straps.)

79. *Luftwaffe* tropical shirt with long sleeves. This shirt has the more common plastic buttons and was, like the short-sleeved style, made in a drill material of a typical *Luftwaffe* orange-tan shade.

80. High leather and canvas tropical boots, with the area of canvas over the instep that was characteristic of this 1940 design.

81. High leather and canvas tropical boot with the smaller area of canvas over the instep and the lower edge of the laces extended towards the leather toecap. This style was introduced towards the end of 1941.

82. High canvas and leather tropical boot with the canvas over the instep eliminated completely. This style was introduced in mid-1942 and was the most common boot issued immediately before and during the Tunisian campaign.

83. Canvas and leather tropical ankle boots, similar in design to the high boot introduced towards the end of 1941. They were made in this style from 1940 until late 1941.

84. *Luftwaffe* leather and canvas tropical ankle boots. These differed from the Army tropical ankle boots in having nine sets of eyelets for the laces rather than the combination of eyelets and hooks as on the Army ones. Like the *Luftwaffe* high boots, and the Army boots introduced in mid-1942, these had the larger leather toecap.

85. *Luftwaffe* high canvas and leather tropical boots, with laces up to ankle height and a flap-over arrangement for the calves with a strap that buckled on the outer side. Canvas used in these boots was a light tan or blue-greyish colour. They were introduced for service in North Africa in mid-1942.

86. Army leather ankle boots with lacing on a combination of eyelets and hooks, a common item of footwear from 1942. They were issued in lieu of the tropical canvas and leather variety when these were in short supply and were also worn by some members of 164th Light Division when they arrived from Crete. These all-leather boots also saw much use in Tunisia. They were worn either with gaiters or just with the trouser ends tied over the ankles.

87. The two styles of rucksack. The larger all-canvas model on the right was the common item of issue, but the smaller 'march' calfskin rucksack was also used widely.

88. The two styles of entrenching tools with their leather carrying frames, rigid (*left*) and folding.

89. Gasmasks/Canisters/Gascape Bags. Shown here are three gas mask canisters, in original field-green paint, and two with desert-colour camouflage paint. The gasmask at the right has two colours of yellowish paint on the metal surfaces, one factory applied and the other painted in the field. The two gascape bags are (left) of heavy drill cotton and (right) of rubberized cloth.

90. *Zeltbahn* (shelter quarters). The left example is in German Army splinter pattern, and the right one is in the mustard colour of the French Army issue items utilized by the Germans in Tunisia.

91. Leather map case and contents: coloured pencils, ruler, measuring device, compass, rubber, chalk, fountain pen, celluloid map case, and map.

92. Rear view of canvas combat Y-straps showing D rings with rolled *Zeltbahn* and mess-tins strapped on. (Obscured is the implements bag, below the *Zeltbahn*.)

93. Canvas and leather Y-straps: comparison of two styles, both of which saw wide service in North Africa in spite of the canvas model being a special item of tropical equipment.

94. Sundry items carried either in breadbag or rolled up inside the *Zeltbahn*: tent pole sections and pegs, rifle cleaning kit, canvas breadbag strap,

plastic lard dish (with screw-top lid), and canvas 'ditty' bag with red marker tag.

95. Pair of MP38/40 magazine pouches. These are early war canvas examples with metal tags on the strap ends.

96. Pioneers' equipment. A special canvas demolition case worn on the Y-strap D rings, a leather holster for wire cutters, a timing device for detonating a fuse, and a bayonet with scabbard painted and covered in sand for camouflage.

97. Two styles of canvas mittens worn with the motorcyclist's, or driving, coat.

98. Officer belts/buckles: top, smooth leather with open claw buckle (Continental issue); bottom, special officer tropical belt with circular buckle.

99. Other ranks belts/buckles: from top to bottom, standard Army canvas and web belt with olive buckle; Continental issue leather belt and silver metal buckle; *Luftwaffe* blue canvas web belt with blue painted steel buckle; and *Luftwaffe* light tan canvas-web belt with silvered alloy buckle (this belt was also issued with a buckle painted a light olive colour).

100. Examples of sand and glare goggles issued in North Africa by the German Army and the *Luftwaffe*. The ones third and fourth from the top are *Luftwaffe* goggles with better optical qualities. The bottom pair are British but were re-issued by the *Luftwaffe* in large numbers from captured stocks.

101. *Luftwaffe* items of equipment: blue linen paratroop ammunition bandolier, gravity knife, bayonet and scabbard in blue web frog, and eating utensil set with *Luftwaffe* eagle stamp.

102. Army waist belt arrangement – leather belt and silver buckle, two black leather ammunition compartments for clips of 7.92 mm ammunition, bayonet and scabbard in web frog attached to a rigid entrenching tool, olive canvas breadbag and water canteen.

103. Four of the most common personal torches, issued for attachment to tunic or overcoat buttons. They were also used for simple signalling, with coloured filters to slide over the bulb.

104. *Dienstglas*, the standard issue Army 6 × 30 prismatic binoculars, usually with a grid in radians over one eyeglass. The small leather loop around the frame was attached to a button on a tunic or coat to stop sideways movement. The carrying case here is made of a black moulded Bakelite and could be carried either on a shoulder strap or looped through a waist belt. Black leatherette, as shown here, was standard for the period of the North Africa campaigns, though many troops camouflaged the metal and leatherette surfaces with a light-coloured paint.

105. Water canteens: from left, a large-capacity canteen as used by medical personnel (or officers who had no attachments for the normal canteen's belt clip); a large-capacity, specifically tropical type, with small Bakelite drinking cup; a smaller-capacity canteen, with plastic impregnated wood fibre covering. It was introduced first in 1941, when it was wrongly identified by Allied Intelligence as a tropical item of equipment, which it was not as it was more widely used in Europe; a smaller-capacity canteen with large black-painted aluminium cup; and a smaller-capacity canteen with small aluminium cup that has been painted with a beige-coloured paint.

106. Cover of the Army paybook.

107. Cover of the *Luftwaffe* paybook.

108. Stiff cardboard covers purchased privately for the Army and *Luftwaffe* paybooks.

109. Cover of the *Wehrpass* (Service Record).

110. Cover of 'The Soldier in Libya'.

111. Colour fold-out from 'The Soldier in Libya' showing guide to British Army uniforms.

112. Colour page from 'The Soldier in Libya' showing French Army formations stationed in Tunisia.

113. Colour fold-out from 'The Soldier in Libya' showing different formations, and Allied armies.

114. Covers of the 1942 and 1943 pocket diaries issued to all German troops in North Africa in late 1941 and late 1942.

115. Cover of the *Luftwaffe* magazine *Adler von Hellas* for the issue of 17 October 1942.

116. Front page of the British Army propaganda paper 'African Campaigner' (*Afrikakämpfer*) air-dropped over German lines in Libya at the end of 1941.

117. Typical page from a colourful propaganda magazine clearly showing the strategic advantages enjoyed by the Axis in the Mediterranean. Such magazines were plentiful and the propaganda was always vividly and logically presented.

118. German propaganda leaflet in Arabic prepared for distribution in the Nile Delta during the summer of 1942.

119. Certificate of proficiency in first aid and qualification to act as a stretcher bearer, carried in the paybook.

120. Postcards and letters received by German troops in Africa.

121. Pocket books taken from German POWs: an Italian language primer for Germans, a Post Office Savings passbook, a 1942 diary, a photograph folder, and playing cards.

122. Items taken from German POWs: a souvenir postcard folder of Nuremberg, a songbook published by Radio Germany, a pocket atlas, a special military atlas, and more playing cards.

123. One of the pages from scientific and popular magazines that had been propped up against the walls of a German dugout at El Alamein as a homely decoration. The other full-page illustrations used in this manner included photos of details of the interiors of mediaeval churches, and woodcut prints of old German cities like Nuremberg. In this collection of photos and paintings can be detected a homesickness and a longing for the greenness and the architecture of a landscape so different from the featureless desert.

124. Contents removed from tunics worn by POWs. Top row, from left: paybook, private letter, wedding photo, Feldpost card, leather wallet with pith helmet shield attached, silver medallion, paper money, fountain pen and pencils. Middle row: packet 9mm pistol ammunition, pack of 'Skat' cards, notebook (this example a Christmas gift from a Nazi Party branch), cigarette packet and matches, small privately purchased diary, Post Office Savings passbook, packet of camera film, metal can used for holding personal knick-knacks, and pocket-size photo album. Bottom row: eating utensils and safety razor blades laid out on a folded olive-coloured issue cotton handkerchief, toothbrush and cut-throat razor, toothpowder block in cardboard carton

and cake of Army issue soap (this normally carried in a cellophane wrapper), metal comb (type sold in Army canteens and known popularly as a 'horse comb') and a black plastic comb (privately purchased), sealed wound-dressing pack and container for gas contaminant solution, alarm clock in leather case, disposable dust goggles which folded flat, sewing kit containing needles, thread and spare buttons, and a gauze face mask used as a protection against flies.

125. Dressings for wounds, carried either in the special pocket inside the front flap of the tunic or tied under the leather lining in the steel helmet.

126. Field art: a pen-decorated wallet showing the DAK tactical symbol in coloured ink, an embroidered DAK symbol on a piece of material which had been stitched to the flap of a breadbag, a Perspex *Luftwaffe* eagle cut from the windshield canopy of a shot-down aircraft, and a *Luftwaffe* unit symbol showing a pyramid with a superimposed eagle flying against a yellow sun.

127. Field art: a flattened section of brass shell case showing the DAK symbol and pyramids. The detail has been etched out with sharp edges of shrapnel fragments. This plate, and the Perspex *Luftwaffe* eagle shown in No. 126, were made by POWs inside the large POW compound in Tobruk in December 1941 to exchange for cigarettes and fruit with passing Allied troops.

128. Mess-tins decorated by German troops with their name and North African motifs.

129. Colour photo of Rommel taken by an Army photographer in Libya shortly after the first offensive had reached the Egyptian border in April 1941.

130. Adhesive stamp printed by the DAK field newspaper *Die Oase* and dis-

tributed among German troops to stick on items of mail posted back to Germany. It had no monetary value.

131. Two examples of the stencilled DAK tactical symbol: the left one is sprayed in white paint on a section of a motorcycle sidecar mudguard against a background of sandy-coloured camouflage paint. The one on the right is in ochre on a section of rubberized canvas.

132. Pennants from North African battlefields. Top left: a Panzer Divisional Commander's pennant removed from a Panzer IV Special tank which was disabled and abandoned at Medinine in southern Tunisia on 6 March 1943 (it probably carried the CO of 10PzDiv). Lower left: two pennants removed from motorcycle combinations knocked out near Tobruk in early December 1941. These were non-regulation and may have originally been political pennants. Top right: examples of the small skull and crossbones pennants which were put on metal stakes stuck into the ground to warn of the existence of a minefield. Centre: square flag denoting the staff command post of a signals unit. It was removed from a half-tracked vehicle when the DAK HQ was overrun at Bir el Chleta on 23 November 1941. Right centre: a number of non-regulation double-sided pennants featuring the Italian flag on one side and the German Nazi flag on the other.

133. A representative range of medals and combat awards worn on uniforms in North Africa. Top: Knights Cross of the Iron Cross, worn on a ribbon around the neck; Iron Cross, 1st Class, with the 1939 bar below; Iron Cross, 2nd Class, with the 1939 bar. Both the latter were worn on the tunic as a ribbon, through a buttonhole only. Centre: German Cross in gold and German Cross in silver. Bottom: Infantry Assault in silver; Infantry Assault in bronze; Tank

Assault in silver; Tank Assault in bronze; and General Assault in silver.

134. Personal stamp of the Commander of the 15th Panzer Division, General Walter Neumann-Silkow. This stamp, together with the General's *Soldbuch* and driving licence, were found in a knocked-out staff car on the Trigh Capuzzo west of Bardia by NZ troops on 2 December 1941.

135. Canvas breech cover issued in North Africa for use with the Kar98k, consisting of a canvas square reinforced on the inner side with patches of leather where the cover rested against the bolt handle, safety catch, and rear sight. Four web tapes were stitched in place on each side for tying the cover on.

136. A representative range of badges worn on uniforms in North Africa. Top row: Army parachutist badge, for those *Luftwaffe* troops who had qualified in the original Army Paratroop Battalion; *Luftwaffe* parachutist badge; *Luftwaffe* ground assault badge; *Luftwaffe* Flak badge and Army Flak badge. Second row: vehicle driver's badge of merit in three grades of gilt, silver and bronze. These only appeared in early 1943 but many DAK drivers qualified for the awards after long periods of driving in the desert. Third row: three grades of Wound Badge in gilt, silver and black. On the right is the Krim Shield for those veterans of the Crimea campaign in 1942. Many members of the divisions who arrived in Tunisia late in 1942 and early in 1943 wore this shield. Fourth row: State Sports Badge (pre-Nazi period) in bronze; State Sports Badge in silver (Nazi period issue); the S. A. Sports Badge in bronze and silver

grades; and the Horse Driver's Badge in silver. Bottom row: three examples of ribbon bar. The centre example shows the effects of desert wear and the one on the right, belonging to Paul Erich Schläfer, bears the ribbons for the Iron Cross, 2nd Class, and the Italian–German Campaign Medal.

137. Obverse and reverse views of the Italian-German Medal. The ribbon included the national colours of Germany and Italy. The obverse side depicted the *Arco dei Felini*, a massive monument erected on the coastal road at the boundary between the provinces of Tripolitania and Cyrenaica, flanked with the symbols of the Italian Fascist and German Nazi States. The reverse side showed a crocodile, symbolizing the British Empire, its jaws representing the Suez Canal, with two armour-clad figures, standing for the Italian and German Armies, clamping the jaws closed. This was widely issued to members of the German Armed Forces in Africa from early 1942 until the closing stages of the Tunisian campaign.

138. Condom as issued to German troops in Africa. The legend on the packet identifies it as being a 'tropical type' (*tropenfest*).

139. Two examples of the *Afrikakorps* ring: on the left is the original style with gold inlay for the central motif; the other is all silver and shows the detail crudely etched on.

140. Manufacturer's plate removed from a Messerschmitt Bf109F4-TROP which was shot down south of Tobruk during Operation Crusader in November 1941.

141. Camouflage colour on a 20mm automatic cannon magazine canister, (with magazine), taken from a disabled armoured car.

142. Contents of the standard first-aid chest carried in all vehicles in North Africa. The contents are listed on the sheet attached to the underside of the lid. They included sealed gauze dressing packs, bandages, slings, sealed cans with special bandage dressings for burns, tourniquets, safety pins, tweezers, heavy-duty scissors for cutting away uniform clothing and boots from wounds, and phials of antiseptic solution, etc. The case was painted either in field-green (for Army) or in blue-grey (for *Luftwaffe*) with a red cross in a white circle and the legend *Verbandkasten* stencilled in white on the lid.

143. A piece of German shrapnel dug out of a trench wall at El Alamein beside a 7.92mm rifle cartridge and a 9mm pistol round. The exploding shell fragmented on detonation into hundreds of red-hot pieces of jagged metal that exploded outwards, cutting down anyone in range. Of all the deaths in the North African fighting, artillery fire was by far the greatest single killer.

144. The famous 'Jerrycan'. On the right is the first model with a simple cross reinforcing channel on the side panel. On the left is the later model with extra grooving. The North African campaign could not have been fought without this canister. It carried the fuel and water of the *Afrikakorps* – and of the 8th Army which used as many captured cans as it could get until the can could be copied and made in British and American factories.

Bibliography

Agar-Hamilton J. A. I. and Turner L. C. F., *The Sidi Rezegh Battles of 1941*, Capetown, Oxford University Press 1957

Altman Karl, *Ritterkreuzträger des Afrikakorps*, Rastatt, Erich Pabel Verlag 1968

Barker A. J., *Afrikakorps*, London, AP Publishing 1978

Barnett Corelli, *The Desert Generals*, London, William Kimber 1960

Bender R. J. and Petersen G. A., *Hermann Goering – From Regiment to Fallschirmpanzerkorps*, San Jose, R. J. Bender Publishing 1975

Bender R. J. and Law R. D., *Afrikakorps – Uniforms, Organisation and History*, Mountain View, R. J. Bender Publishing 1973

Carell Paul, *The Foxes of the Desert*, London, Macdonald & Co. 1960

Cave Brown Anthony, *Bodyguard of Lies*, London, W. H. Allen & Co. Ltd 1976

Chamberlain Peter and Ellis Chris, *Afrikakorps*, London, Almark 1971

Clifford Alexander, *Three Against Rommel*, London, George G. Harrap 1943

Cody J. F., *21 Battalion*, Wellington, Department of Internal Affairs 1953

Collier Richard, *The War in the Desert*, USA and Canada, Time-Life Books Inc. 1977

Culver Bruce, *Afrikakorps in Action*, Warren, Michigan, Squadron/Signal Inc. 1979

Davis Brian L., *German Army Uniforms and Insignia 1933–1945*, London, Arms and Armour Press 1971

Davis Brian L., *German Parachute Forces 1935–1945*, London, Arms and Armour Press 1974

Forty George, *Afrikakorps at War Volume One*, USA and Canada, Charles Scribner's Sons 1978

Forty George, *Afrikakorps at War Volume Two*, Shepperton, Surrey, Ian Allan Ltd 1978

Hall Timothy, *Tobruk 1941 – The Desert Siege*, North Ryde, NSW, Methuen Australia Ltd 1984

Haupt Werner and Bingham J. K. W., *Der Afrika Feldzug 1941–1943*, London, Macdonald & Co. 1968

Heckmann Wolf, *Rommel's War in Africa*, New York, Doubleday & Co. Inc. 1981

Held Werner and Obermaier Ernst, *Die deutsche Luftwaffe im Afrika-Feldzug*, Stuttgart, Motorbuch Verlag 1981

Holmes Richard, *Bir Hacheim: Desert Citadel*, London, Ballantine Books Inc. 1971

Irving David, *The Trail of the Fox – The Life of Field Marshal Erwin Rommel*, London, Weidenfeld and Nicolson 1977

Irving David, *Hitler's War*, London, Hodder and Stoughton Ltd 1977

Jarrett G. B., *West of Alamein*, Northridge, California, Century Books 1971

Jones Kenneth M., *Focus on Armour, Camouflage and Markings – Germany/North Africa*, New Malden, Surrey, Almark 1977

Jones R. V., *Most Secret War*, London, Hamish Hamilton Ltd 1978

Kennedy Shaw W. B., *Long Range Desert Group*, London, Collins 1945

Kühn Volkmar, *Mit Rommel in der Wüste*, Stuttgart, Motorbuch Verlag 1977

Kurowski Franz, *Endkampf in Afrika* (Der Opfergang der Heeresgruppe Rommel in Tunisien 1942/3), Leoni Am Starnberger See, Druffel – Verlag 1983

Law R. D. and Luther C. W. H., *Rommel*, San Jose, R. J. Bender Publishing 1980

Lewin R., *The Life and Death of the Afrikakorps*, London, Transworld Publishers Ltd 1977

Llewellyn Peter, *Journey Towards Christmas* (Official History of the 1st Ammunition Company NZ Expeditionary Force 1939–45), Wellington, Department of Internal Affairs 1949

Long Gavin, *To Benghazi*, Canberra, Australian War Memorial 1966

Lucas James, *Panzer Army Afrika*, London and San Rafael, Macdonald and Jane's 1977

McKinney J. B., *Medical Units of 2NZEF in Middle East and Italy*, Wellington, Department of Internal Affairs 1952

Macksey K. J., *Afrikakorps*, London, Macdonald & Co. 1968

Macksey K. J., *Rommel – Battles and Campaigns*, London, Arms and Armour Press 1979

Maughan Barton, *Tobruk and Alamein*, Canberra, Australian War Memorial 1966

Mellenthin von F. W., *Panzer Battles*, London, Cassell & Co. 1955

Messenger Charles, *The Unknown Alamein*, Shepperton, Surrey, Ian Allan Ltd 1982

Mollo Andrew, *German Uniforms of World War 2*, London, Macdonald and Jane's 1976

Moorehead Alan, *African Trilogy*, London, Hamish Hamilton Ltd 1944

Münnich Ralf, *Panzer in Nord-Afrika 1941–1943*, Friedberg Podzun-Pallas Verlag 1977

Murphy W. E., *2nd New Zealand Divisional Artillery*, Wellington, Department of Internal Affairs 1966

Murphy W. E., *The Relief of Tobruk*, Wellington, Department of Internal Affairs 1961

Pitt Barrie, *The Crucible of War – Western Desert 1941*, London, Jonathan Cape Ltd 1980

Quarrie Bruce, *Panzers in the Desert*, Cambridge, Patrick Stephens Ltd 1978

Quarrie Bruce, *German Paratroops in the Med*, Cambridge, Patrick Stephens Ltd 1979

Rommel Field Marshal Erwin, *The Rommel Papers* (Edited by B.H. Liddell Hart), London, Collins 1953

Rutherford Ward, *Kasserine: Baptism of Fire*, London, Macdonald & Co. Ltd 1970

Ryder Rowland, *Ravenstein – Portrait of a German General*, London, Hamish Hamilton 1978

Schmidt Heinz Werner, *With Rommel in the Desert*, London, George G. Harrap Ltd 1951

Scoullar J. L., *Battle for Egypt, The Summer of 1942*, Wellington, Department of Internal Affairs 1955

Von Thaysen, Adalbert, *Tobruk 1941: Der Kampf in Nordafrika*, Freiburg, Rombach Verlag 1976

Windrow Martin, *Rommel's Desert Army*, New York, Hippocrene Books Inc. 1976

Young Desmond, *Rommel*, London, Collins 1950

Periodicals:
Die Oase, Journal of the association of former Members of the German Afrikakorps, published by Heinrich Pöppinghaus, Bochum-Langendreer, volumes 9 (1959) to 35 (1985).

Review, Journal of the New Zealand Returned Services Association (Inc.), published by the NZRSA, Wellington, volumes LIV (1977) to LXI (1984).

Wartime German Publications:
Afrikakorps, Propaganda Ministerium – Volkshilfwerk der Arbeitsgemeinschaft der Optanten für Deutschland, Berlin 1942

Balkenkreutz über Wüstensand (Farbbilderwerk des Deutschen Afrikakorps), Oldenburg, Gerhard Stalling Verlag 1943

Der Soldat in Libyen, Oberkommando des Heeres, Berlin 1941

Gegen England in Nordafrika, Zentralverlag der NSDAP, Franz Eher Nachf. GmbH., Deutscher Verlag, Berlin 1942

Generalfeldmarschall Rommel und der Feldzug in Nordafrika, Erasmusdruck Verlag, Berlin 1943

Helden der Wüste, von Esebeck, Hans Gert Frhr, Verlag der Heimbücherei, Berlin 1942

Marsch und Kampf des Deutschen Afrikakorps, Band 1 1941, Carl Rohrig Verlag, München 1943

Militärgeographische Beschreibung von Nordost-Afrika, Generalstab des Heeres, Berlin 1940

Mit Rommel in der Wüste, Wilhelm Wessel, Bildgut Verlag, Essen 1943

Signal, Various issues 1941–1943, Deutscher Verlag, Berlin

Die Wehrmacht, 1941–1943, Verlag 'Die Wehrmacht', Berlin

Unpublished Diaries and Memoranda originating from the German Army in North Africa 1941–1943 in the author's possession.

Unpublished German military documents pertaining to the Afrikakorps in the Charles J. Hinz collection.

Official collections:
Extracts from files in the Bundesarchiv-Militärchiv, Freiburg, referring to tropical uniform and *Waffenfarben* in the period 1941–1943

Original and Microfilm copies in the New Zealand National Archives relating to the various German Army commands in North Africa 1941–1943 (War History Collection, Wellington)

German Army documents held in the Library of the Auckland War Memorial Museum and Institute

Archives of the 21 NZ Infantry Battalion Association held in the Association's Clubrooms, Fearon Park, Auckland

Index